TWO MILES AN HOUR

TWO MILES AN HOUR

A TRIP

ROBERT BUCKLEY

Original sketches by Michael J. Buckley
Cover design by Gary Anderson

Text set in Georgia

Manufactured in the United States of America

3 5 7 9 10 8 6 4

Library of Congress Control Number
ISBN: 978-0615853840

Other works by Robert Buckley

The Slave Tag

Ophelia's Brooch

CONTENTS

PREFACE

It was late in life before I began taking long walks. Long walks for long distances. How and why I got started I have no clear idea, but shortly before I retired from work, I took off.

I've always bicycled. When I was in my forties I damaged my right knee and had the cartilage removed. My doctor recommended I take up bicycling to strengthen it. I did and found I enjoyed it a great deal. I later became a frequent participant of RAGBRAI; an acronym for the Register's Annual Great Bike Ride Across Iowa. The Des Moines Register is Iowa's largest newspaper.

RAGBRAI was (and still is) a wonderful event which every July attracts thousands of bikers from across the country, and indeed, from around the world. It's been described as a week–long, 500–mile party on wheels.

Well, I don't know about the 'party' part. Going to bed at 9:00 p.m. and rising at 5:30 a.m. does not really lend itself to much partying. However, peddling at your own pace through the sun-kissed, rolling Iowa countryside and munching your way through dozens of small, friendly communities spread along the route was something to brag about and enjoy.

The starting place is always the banks of the Missouri River and it always finishes on the banks of the Mississippi River. The actual route changes every year.

I rode RAGBRAI for ten years and then I was ready for something else. I was ready for a new experience, a different challenge. I was still in good health and my legs and feet were still in good shape so I took up walking.

Two Miles An Hour is a compilation of the five walking trips I've taken over a period of ten years. The title comes from statistics I've kept from my logs during these walks.

Everyone walks at a different pace. For me, two miles an hour is what I averaged over the long haul. It's not just walking time. It includes time to stop and visit with locals along the way. Time to sightsee and take photos. Time to stop and buy some cheese and apples. Time just to sit along a high ridge somewhere and look down on a small village. Time to get lost, and found again.

I knew from experience that if I left my campsite, or B&B, or hostel, or country inn at 8:00 in the morning, I could count on ending up sixteen miles down the road by 4:00 p.m. that afternoon. It didn't seem to make much difference whether the terrain was flat or hilly. Sunshiny or rainy. Slippery or dry. Sixteen miles. Eight hours. Two miles an hour.

My stories are not meant to be a 'How To Guide.' I think you'll find in many cases they may be better suited as a 'How *Not* To Guide.' A good example is my maiden hike on the world famous Appalachian Trail. It was a fiasco from the very beginning.

As you will soon read, I was totally ill–prepared for such an endeavor and made every mistake you could possibly imagine. If you've read Bill Bryson's wonderful book, A *Walk In The Woods*, you'll have a good idea of my adventure. There are uncanny similarities.

I was at the brink of retirement when I took that first long walk. Although I never had any intention of tackling the entire trail, there are many who take the time to do just that. I admire them greatly. Thank goodness I didn't try. I'd still be wandering around lost somewhere in the Berkshire Mountains.

On the flip side, I managed to survive and it was a great learning experience. For all the dumb mistakes I made, I still had a marvelous time. Most importantly it gave me confidence to try again. And I did.

I hope you enjoy reading my adventures for what they are. Better yet, if they inspire you to take a crack at some long distance walking yourself, it would please me very much and I hope you would let me know how you did.

You'll find my writing style for each of the five walks to be a little different. Keep in mind the stories are developed from my original trip logs and I decided to follow them as closely as possible – so don't get confused. It's just the way my note taking changed from year to year.

All set? Here we go.

UNITED STATES

The Appalachian Trail

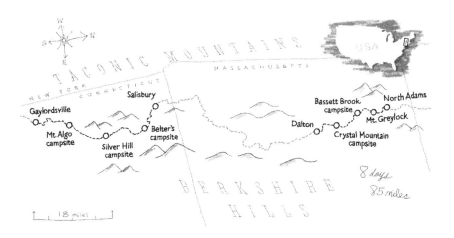

THE BEST LAID PLANS

Somewhere along the way I convinced myself it would be a
wonderful thing to walk the Appalachian Trail (or at least a bite–
sized chunk of it).

As I think back upon it, I can't for the life of me recall where I
ever got that idea. Yet, for a long time I enjoyed visual snatches
of myself effortlessly hiking along cloudy pine ridges, hiking staff
firmly in hand, my tanned, rugged face smiling and my lungs
bursting with surplus oxygen.

I pictured myself looking down upon distant villages and
seeing tiny, silver ribbons of rivers glinting up at me. I imagined

hearing the lowing of cattle on hillsides, and the faint barking of a dog from some distant farm. I snickered at the thought of the houses filled with the common people — most of whom would pale at the thought of leaving their comfortable, warm beds, their television sets and microwaves and march with me through the mountains. Wimps all.

The seed for my adventure may have been planted from a television special I'd seen featuring a blind man and his dog who walked the entire length of the Appalachian Trail – all 2,200 miles of it. Just the two of them. His name was Bill Irwin and he was 50 years old and he completed the walk in eight months.

The ATC (Appalachian Trail Conference) discourages hiking alone. Irwin's companion for the journey was a German Shepherd guide dog named Orient. Bill may have been blind – but he had Orient and a ski pole and made it look rather easy. So really, how hard could it be?

I would also be walking alone but I didn't have Orient to ask questions of. I did have a hiking staff to assist me with the ups and downs although everyone knows the Appalachians are not serious mountains anyway — but pitiful, ancient, worn down remains. More like foothills than mountains. Let's be clear, folks — we're not talking the Rockies here.

Two months earlier, at age 57, I had just finished RAGBRAI XX, a 500–mile bike ride across my home state of Iowa. My legs were like pistons — my lungs like bellows. If I was going to walk the Appalachian Trail, now was the time.

Of course, I realized I couldn't walk the entire trail. That would take more time and commitment than I had to offer. On a normal thru hike, which is a non–stop journey from one end to the other, hikers start out in early spring at Springer Mountain, Georgia and work their way north to Mount Katahdin in Maine. The goal was to finish the walk before the weather turned nasty; normally a six–month trek.

But since I had only a two-week vacation I could only do part of it. I selected a section that began at the New York/Connecticut border, continued through Massachusetts and on to Vermont. I wasn't sure how far I'd get but there was no need to hurry.

I thought when I was ready to take a trail break, I could go and spend a few days relaxing with my niece, Kathy, and her family in Amherst where she and her husband worked at the University of Massachusetts.

I looked forward to some snappy New England cocktail party chatter about my adventure.

I decided to begin the walk in September. I believed the weather that time of year would be ideal and the changing autumn leaves gorgeous. I also decided to walk from south to north, although in the fall of the year, people usually hiked the opposite direction to keep ahead of the winter weather. But I was only going for a couple of weeks and knew this wouldn't be a problem.

With all the major decisions out of the way, I could now get my stuff together and ... walk!

From studying maps, I knew the trail exited New York State and entered Connecticut near Gaylordsville, a small town in southwestern Connecticut. The closest town to Gaylordsville was Danbury. I checked airline schedules and learned I could fly into Hartford, catch a bus to Danbury and stay the night. Next day I would get an early morning start, hitting the trail fresh and ready.

Problem was, I couldn't figure out how to get from my Danbury motel to the trailhead. It never occurred to me to walk.

The solution presented itself in a last minute piece of correspondence with Nancy Mortimer, an excellent employee of the Housatonic Valley Convention and Visitors Bureau. Nancy answered one of my inquiries and said she would be more than happy to come and pick me up at the motel and drive me to wherever the trail began.

"I will do it for Connecticut," she wrote. Wonderful, I thought — problem solved.

Had I mentioned I'd never really backpacked before?

Oh sure, I'd been in the Army and done my share of marching — but that was years earlier. Of course I used to take my three boys camping when they were small, but that was also a long time ago. The truth of the matter was I had never actually *backpacked*.

I dug out an old Boy Scout pack in the basement – a relic from long ago outings to Walnut Woods State Park in Des Moines where we lived at the time. I also had a temperamental cook stove that I could never keep burning for very long. And I had a patchy old, flannel sleeping bag. That was about it.

Oh, almost forgot. I had a tent, too. You need a tent. It was a family–size cabin tent, large enough for five people. Perfect, I thought at the time. Plenty of room to stretch out. (What was I thinking ... a five person tent?)

I knew from reading the sage advice of experienced hikers that boots were of paramount importance — so I went out and bought a pair of lightweight, Gore-Tex Vasques and wore them around the block a few times to break them in. I also ordered a modest supply of freeze–dried food from an outdoor catalog. When I packed all this – plus some shorts and shirts and candles and knives and other stuff and weighed it, it came to 36 pounds. That seemed about right.

Who was I kidding? I was rationalizing, of course. Thirty–six pounds was a lot. I was originally shooting for 25 pounds – tops. I'd read that for *experienced* hikers, carrying 20% of one's weight for prolonged distances was as heavy as you'd want to go. I weighed 145 pounds so, at 36 pounds, I was just a smidgen over 25%. What's an extra 5% ... certainly not enough to worry about.

"Eleven pounds is nothing," I pointed out to my family. "A lot of the weight is food which I'll eat up in a few days."

My ever sensible wife suggested I might practice walking with the loaded pack before I left home — you know, to get the feel of it. I took her advice and immediately experienced a bit of a problem. I found I could neither stand erect nor walk in a straight line.

"That could present a bit of a problem as you march along your cloudy pine ridges," she pointed out. All right, big deal, so I needed more practice. The trip was still ten days away. There was plenty of time for fine–tuning.

I took my first real outside practice walk around the neighborhood early one evening at twilight. A big mistake. People stared at me. They didn't say much, they just stared — and called in their kids. Perhaps if I hadn't wobbled so much ...

What's the matter with them, I thought? Haven't they ever seen a backpacker before? Don't they subscribe to National Geographic? I managed to walk three miles before I staggered back home — exhausted. Back to the fine–tuning.

During the next several days I improved and regained a bit of lost confidence. I restricted my practice hikes until after dark and got so I could walk straight enough to generally stay on the sidewalk. I had acquired a hiking staff by this time — carved by my middle son, Michael. It was professionally equipped with a rawhide hand strap. It was long and strong ... and heavy. Just the thing, I thought, if I should run into any bears.

The freeze–dried food had arrived by this time, and it was added to the pack along with a rain jacket plus a few more odds and ends and finally it was time to go. I was ready!

When I checked my stuff in at the airport, the wretched backpack now registered 47 pounds!

"No problem," I exclaimed to my now extremely nervous wife. "I will quickly eat up the excess 22 pounds!"

I was desperate. It was too late to turn back.

My trip to Danbury was long and uneventful. I did, however, receive a quick lesson on airline rules and regulations regarding hiking staffs.

It seems that anything that is — or resembles — or could be used for a weapon cannot be carried on a plane as luggage. This would include rifles, swords, hockey sticks and baseball bats. The flight attendants just weren't sure about hiking staffs. It made them a bit nervous — but they finally caved in.

Storing it above, or below the seat was another matter. Somehow I managed this on both airplanes and buses, but it took a little imagination and good–natured, fellow passengers.

I didn't get to see much of either Hartford or Danbury – but I did get to see all there was to see of the bus terminals in between. Bus stations always seem to be buried in the middle of the inner city and attract the fringe elements of society, such as myself. Being extra cautious, I never let my backpack out of my sight although I couldn't imagine anyone grabbing and running off with it. After all, it weighed 47 pounds!

Danbury was dark by the time I arrived — and dreary. I checked into a cheap motel and called Nancy Mortimer, my Housatonic Valley Convention and Visitors Bureau guardian angel. Yes, she chirped, she was still planning to come and pick me up in the morning and how did 7:00 sound?

It sounded early, but I told her fine. I still couldn't get over my good luck in running into her and didn't want to mess things up by trying to change *her* itinerary.

That evening I walked up the highway to a roadhouse called *Nick's* for dinner. The Iowa–Miami football game had just started so I had a couple of beers, ate a steak sandwich and watched the game until it turned into a disaster for Iowa. I needed some sleep anyway and returned to the motel.

TOO LATE TO TURN BACK NOW

Nancy Mortimer *was* a jewel! A one–of–a–kind grandmother type you read about in children's books. She arrived at the motel at 7:00 sharp, all smiles and full of life. We drove toward Gaylordsville, about 25 miles away, and stopped for breakfast and exchanged addresses and a little background about each other.

Nancy was an ex–teacher who married late in life. Her husband had died several years earlier. Now, in her late 70s, she was keeping busy and stretching her income with a job at the local Chamber of Commerce and loved her work. She considered all this a wonderful adventure and seemed as excited as I was about my trip.

Driving slowly down the highway we found the trailhead by 9:00. I barely spotted the white blaze mark through the break in the trees. We pulled over to the side of the road and I hoisted on my backpack. I may have appeared a little unsteady — at least Nancy started to rush to my aid before I waved her off with a brave smile. I thanked her for her help again, said goodbye and wobbled up the trail like I knew what I was doing.

Setting an early tone for my trek, within the first ten feet I came upon a man sprawled out in the middle of the path. He looked rather dead; an omen I should have taken note of. As I cautiously approached him, he stirred (thank goodness) and said he was waiting for his friend to catch up. He was fine, he assured me, just resting.

Sure enough, I met his friend puffing along in the next ten minutes and I waved him down and reported that his friend was dead ahead (a little levity).

This is going to be fun, I thought. Lots of interesting people to talk to along the way.

The trail itself was not that hard to follow which was a relief. Not as wide as expected, probably two feet at most, but well–marked with white blaze marks on trees or rocks about every 100 feet. The trick was to keep an eye out for the markers as you went along. Hikers are warned that if they couldn't spot a marker from where they were standing at the moment, to go back to the last trail marker and look around until they did.

My day's plan was to have lunch in the town of Dogtail Corners (I'm not making that name up) — and continue on to the Mt. Algo campsite in plenty of time to meet any trail comrades, set up my tent, prepare a nutritious dinner, etc.

I began whistling as I marched along.

My honeymoon with nature ended within the first hour. I was still wearing my Levis and a heavy, long–sleeved denim shirt, both of which quickly got soaked with perspiration. The trail was much harder than I thought it would be, very rocky and unusually steep in parts. Not at all like walking around the solid, flat sidewalks of my neighborhood at home.

I plodded on, up and down Ten Mile Hill and arrived exhausted in Dogtail Corners around noon. To my dismay there was not a restaurant or even a store open in which I could kick back and spin yarns with the locals. I kept going – munching on peanut butter and crackers and a Powerbar. So far I had walked a little over four miles in three hours. Slow. It seemed like forty.

The scenery *was* lovely, however. I was at least right about that. I was passing through the historic Schaghticoke and Algo Mountain ranges loaded with trees, cascading creeks and birds galore. But who was looking? I started to die at about eight miles. My legs turned wobbly and my breathing came harder and harder. I ordered a major rest stop for myself and stretched out on the rocks near a place called Rattlesnake Den. Rattlesnakes were the least of my worries. I was dying.

It must have been the steak sandwich and beer at Nick's the night before I told myself. Tomorrow will be better.

I finally dragged into the Mt. Algo campsite around 4:00. I was bushed. I was whipped. There were several people already there which lifted my spirits somewhat. Unfortunately one couple, along with their four kids, had already moved into the camp's only lean–to. No problem, I was proud to have finished twelve miles still alive and recovered quickly.

I found a spot to pitch my tent. It was a lovely camp area with a clear cold creek running through it – and very woody and shaded. I was told it really got dark early in the hills early so I hastened to set things up.

I was surprised to find I really wasn't very hungry. I fixed some soup and ate some more peanut butter and crackers and drank some tea. Afterwards, I went down and visited with my new trail mates. They were both teachers who were ending their Memorial Day vacation the next day. They had two teenage girls and two younger boys were with them.

They told me they had recently visited Mt. Katahdin – the end of the trail in Maine – where they saw a woman finish her thru hike. They were very impressed and thought it was quite exciting. They asked how far I was going. I gave them a vague answer.

We chatted for a while but I was having trouble keeping my eyes open so I bid them good night and returned to my tent. It was only 7:00 but pitch–dark by that time. I slipped into my cozy sleeping bag and wrote my daily journal by the light of my fat, five–hour candle. I had brought along two of them and figured that if I restricted my use to an hour a night they should last the entire trip.

I still couldn't believe how hard this first day had been and how I had perspired so much. My shirt and pants were hanging up outside to dry. I supposed I had overdone it. But I needed to pick up the pace.

I woke at 7:00 in the morning to the sound of a light rain falling outside ... on my clothes. I couldn't remember where I was for a moment. I had been asleep for almost 12 hours! I lay back until 8:00 and finally forced myself up and discovered I had fallen asleep with my five-hour candle still burning. It was now completely used up. What a stupid thing to do! Lucky it didn't set the tent on fire. I had one more candle left to last me the rest of the trip. There was no way it would last.

Amazingly, I wasn't very sore, but I still felt tired which I knew was a bad sign. I forced myself up and started to heat some water for coffee when I noticed that during the night, a new tent had been set up around 20 feet away. The camper, a twenty-something young man was fussing with some type of large contraption that looked strangely like a blender. Soon a loud whirring sound told me it *was* a blender. What in the world?

I walked over and found this guy feeding celery and grapes and nuts and yoghurt and who knows what other yucky things into a battery-powered blender. The battery alone must have weighed ten pounds! He tried to defend this bizarre behavior with some nonsense about how important it was to consume the proper blend of calories and electrolytes, yada, yada.

The hills were alive with yuppies. On the other hand, he had remembered breakfast. I had nothing.

I broke camp around 9:00, put on my wet clothes, packed away my wet tent and headed down the wet mountain. I stumbled out of the woods onto Hwy. 341 and instead of crossing the road and back into the woods, I continued down toward Kent, Connecticut. It was about a mile down to the Housatonic River bridge and the town was just on the other side. I arrived at a church yard where I noticed an elderly woman standing watching me. I was searching for a restaurant and went over to ask her if she knew of one.

"My poor dear, you look so exhausted," she said in a concerned, motherly voice. "And your clothes are all wet. Perhaps I should drive you."

I was a bit miffed and told her I always looked that way and please, where was the restaurant? She never took her worried eyes off me but gestured up the road and said, "Not far. Sure I can't drive you?"

I left the pack sitting by the side of a small church and walked another half mile to a wonderful little bakery that turned out to be one of the few stores open in town. I had forgotten it was Memorial Day. I bought some juice, coffee, milk, an apple turnover and a date bar. They tasted great. If fact I bought an extra date bar to take along with me. I think I had all the basic food groups covered but not sure about the electrolytes ...

On the way out of town I stopped at a small grocery store to buy a toothbrush, which I had forgotten, a can of spaghetti and an apple. (A can of spaghetti ... what was I thinking?) I also called my wife, Lois, to tell her I was still alive.

She informed me a Nancy Mortimer had called her to check on my progress? She wasn't too clear who Nancy Mortimer was so I explained the best I could. It didn't help that Nancy had told her we had breakfasted together.

ALONE IN THE WOODS ... YIKES!

I retrieved my pack and quickly left Kent behind. Rather than walk back up the highway to where the trail entered the woods, I walked along the river to intercept the trail about a mile farther down. It was a smart move as the hiking was relatively flat and scenic along the river. I did not realize it until later, but I also avoided a very steep and dangerous descent called St. John's Ledges.

I followed the river for several miles managing to dry off as I went along. This stretch is one of the longest river walks on the entire trail. It led through a red pine stand of trees that was one of the most photographed sections of the trail. Unfortunately, most of the trees remaining are dying from a blight and not expected to survive much longer.

I made very good time and stopped around noon to eat my apple and faithful peanut butter and crackers. As I strolled along I saw several people fly fishing — and met a few day hikers. The river appeared to be full of black bass and it seemed one was hooked on about every other cast. Soon I saw a canoe coming down stream and I stood there quietly watching — only to be stung on my exposed leg by a couple of hornets. YOW! That got me moving again!

Soon the trail left the road and headed back into the woods and up a very steep hill to my night's second planned stop, Silver Hill campsite. By the time I got there I was sweating like a boxer again — soaked clear through. This sweating thing was a new experience for me and bothered me quite a bit. I've ridden bikes for hundreds of miles and never perspired like this.

It had sprinkled earlier in the day and it was still overcast and misty when I arrived. It was late afternoon and the campsite was deserted. That's spooky, I thought to myself. I'd be up here all by myself? All night? Yikes!

It was one of the few campsites located at the top of the ridge — rather than the bottom. Most camp sites were at lower elevations because running water was usually not available higher up. However, this site was supposed to have a pump — but it was broken according to a hiker I had passed along the way. My canteen was only half full. It would have to last the night.

Silver Hill camp is in a clearing overlooking a deep valley. Someone had built a little deck and table where I sat and ate my dinner. I checked my feet carefully as they were beginning to hurt a bit. My right toe had started to bleed a little from being pinched – but nothing serious that I could see — and no blisters! I changed socks and hung up everything that was damp to dry out. That would be just about everything I was wearing.

It was my second night on the trail. I was alone and had too much time to think about myself and I must admit I was a bit worried. After only two full days of hiking, my feet were tender and my hips were bruised where the ill–fitting waist strap of the wretched Boy Scout backpack bit into them. I was already out of dry clothes and I was concerned about making it to my next stop tomorrow – Belter's Camp – a 13–mile haul. The map looked like the trail was going to be up and down all day. I needed to find a way to lighten my pack.

I remember reading about a recent hiker who had covered the whole trail in 59 days. And don't forget my blind hero, Bill Irwin, doing it alone with his dog, Orient. Maybe the point of all this was regardless of how far I get I will have a much better appreciation for people who do make it the whole way. Or even try, for that matter.

Was I setting myself up for failure?

Most campsites on the Appalachian Trail have log registers where people wrote down their thoughts as they passed through. There was a well–used log here and I read parts of it. Here are a few choice selections from earlier in the year:

March 9 – I guess it's warm today (50 degrees). Rain tomorrow and then back to winter again the rest of the week. Ooops – just picked a tick off me. Gotta watch out for those critters.

April 26 – We pass through this beautiful place as we come to challenge ourselves, commune with nature and listen to God. Yours in Scouting – The James Gang, Nassau County Council.

July 25 – What a great day. Low mileage, lunch by the river, and this beautiful campsite. Our journey is coming to an end and I'm sure Dylan will agree that these have been the best four months of our lives. I hope everyone appreciates this beautiful experience the trail enables us to have. – Grumpy, Smurf, Credence Spelledrang.

August 28 – Attn. northbound hikers: While Sher's Pine Tree Inn welcomes hikers, please don't abuse their kindness.

August 30 – Good Morning – Jonathan – AMC Guide

September 6 – Richard and son, Josh, here to beat the Butler, Alabama, heat. Great to get outside in the Northeast again. I'm gonna kill all of these damn little bugs.

By 5:00 p.m. no one else had arrived. I pitched my tent, ate the whole can of spaghetti, drank about half my remaining water and devoured the rest of the date bar. By 6:00 I'd done all I could do.

Unfortunately you weren't permitted a campfire along the trail in Connecticut and I really missed that. It had something to do with the trail being on such a narrow right–of–way. It sounded a little silly to me, but rules are rules. I was a bit uncomfortable to be there all alone so I took my heavy-duty staff in the tent with me and went to bed. (You never know.)

Another wild and carefree night in the woods.

INTO CORNWALL BRIDGE. WHERE'S GEORGE?

I had a restless night's sleep with mysterious sounds of sniffing, snorting and pawing going on outside the tent all night long. The cries of tree frogs, in particular, almost drove me nuts. They kept at it until some mysterious 'off' switch was thrown around 4:00 a.m. and then, absolute silence! That was just as bad and the sudden absence of any noise woke me back up.

I finally gave in and got up at 6:00. I used what little water I had left and fixed some coffee. It tasted great on such a damp, foggy morning. Wet, cold clouds drifted by me and across the crest. I couldn't see anything at all below except the tips of pine trees. There was scarcely a breeze but plenty of gnats.

I headed down around 8:00 and came to a highway leading to town. Again, I chose to go in for breakfast before crossing the road and continuing back up into the woods.

It was a mile down to the historic village of Cornwall Bridge. I left my pack by the side of a rustic florist shop on the edge of the village and walked in to mail some postcards. It was a gorgeous little New England town and apparently a favorite overnight stop for George Washington. Unfortunately he was long gone.

It was still very quiet when I arrived at a quaint little general store. I bought some chocolate milk and a fried egg and cheese sandwich and sat outside eating and watching the locals come in for coffee and their morning papers. I filled my water bottle. No one paid much attention to me as I sat and rested. Of course by this time I was beginning to look a little 'earthy.'

I walked back to the florist shop and swung on the pack. I had this process down to a science by this time — knowing just how to lean and twist to set it properly on my back. About a mile north the map showed a county park with trails that led back up to the 'real trail' and I elected to go that way rather than backtrack up the highway.

The trail was very steep and slippery. The exposed rocks were sharp and plentiful and required constant monitoring to avoid tripping. I found I could climb about 100 yards and then had to stop and catch my breath until my heartbeat came back down to a manageable 150. The trail continued upwards all the time —

and the forest seemed to become denser and denser. Thank heavens for my hiking staff.

I remembered reading that all the mountains in this area were completely devoid of trees just a century earlier. It was all farm land then. Even now you can see stone fences running off through the trees.

Occasionally I was startled by an explosion of Hungarian Partridge. I never did see them – just a blur – but I could hear them take flight and rush madly through the trees. I'm amazed they can find the room to fly as thick as the trees were. I've heard that successful hunters often turn and shoot at the sound.

I continued on throughout the day — and never once met any other hikers. It was hard going and I was quickly consuming my water. By 2:30 I arrived at Pine Swamp Brook campsite and stopped for lunch. I finished off what little water I had left and boiled some more to take with me to last the rest of the day. The streams in the area appeared clean and clear but I didn't want to take any chances on picking up any nasties.

Of course my shirt was drenched by this time and I took it off and spread it out on a large bush for the wind to dry. I rested for around 30 minutes and even toyed with the idea of stopping there for the day. There was a comfortable looking lean–to nearby and a convenient nearby creek. But I couldn't imagine what on earth I would do for the rest of the afternoon. With six more miles to go, I went on. I think I was beginning to feel a little stronger.

I soon came to Sharon Mountain campsite — but still I didn't stop. In another mile I came to Hang Glider View — and it's obvious why it's called that. There was a large opening in the trees where a wooden runway had been built that ran off into space. This is where locals climbed, packing all their hang–gliding gear with them and zoomed out over a beautiful valley leading down to Falls Village, Connecticut. What a gorgeous view — I wish it had been sunny.

The last three miles about killed me. I was totally exhausted and pestered by bumble bees most of the way. Finally I arrived at Belters Campsite. I had gone twelve and a half miles. A long day! I arrived a little after six and it was almost dark so I hustled to set up camp.

It was really dumb to have gone so far and risk the chance of missing the campsite in the dark. That would have been a disaster. I would have to sleep on the trail, itself.

All campsites were off the main trail, some as far as a half mile, and you really had to pay attention to see where they split off. The blaze marks changed from white to blue and were harder to see. I couldn't imagine sleeping on the trail which was rocky and rough and not even wide enough to accommodate two hikers walking abreast.

Belter's Campsite was about as boring as you could get. There was no view at all. It was deep in the woods with no picnic tables. I put up a line to hang food and my shirt on and quickly boiled some water for tea and soup. I took a sponge bath before setting up the tent.

I spread out the maps and reevaluated my plans. Earlier in the day I was in good spirits and feeling strong. Now I was not so sure. I think I overdid it again and was considering staying in Falls Village tomorrow night. It was only four miles followed by another eight to Salisbury. I was really feeling bushed and surprised how hard and dangerous the trail really was. And to think I hadn't seen another soul all day long really bothered me. I decided to sleep on it and see how things looked in the morning.

The night was filled with more mysterious bumps and noises. Something woke me up a couple of times sniffing and scratching at the tent. I tried to see what it was with my flashlight — but never did. Probably a porcupine or raccoon ... or Freddie Krueger. However, this was also bear country.

I hated camping alone!

FINDING SALISBURY – AND A REAL BED

I woke at 7:30 feeling semi–rested. I fixed some coffee and ate a complete package of one of the freeze–dried cereals of granola, milk and blueberries. It was designed to feed two people but I ate the whole thing. Afterwards I packed and went to look for a privy. I thought I knew where it was.

I never did find it — but did stumble upon the shell of a 1959 Ford Galaxie! Not to be confused with the newer Ford Galaxy (different spelling, different car) ... this one was a real collector's item. How in the world did it get there, I wondered? It was sitting deep in the woods, pointing uphill, perhaps abandoned by some mad moonshiner who had tried to cut cross country to escape the law. As far as I could see there were no roads anywhere nearby.

I kept on moving and looking for the privy when I suddenly stumbled on someone's campsite. I stopped and shouted out "hello" not wanting to startle whoever was camping there. When no one responded I moved forward cautiously only to discover it was *my* campsite! Somehow I had managed to walk in a complete circle! So much for my Boy Scout training.

I loaded up my gear and walked down to the trailhead. There, for the first time in days, I met a live person; an older gentleman standing and reading his trail map. He told me he was staying in Falls Village for a couple of days to rest. He had started in Maine and was headed south. He must have been around 70 and appeared to be in excellent shape. He said his son had been mailing supplies to him all along the trail and he was sleeping in motels so other than snacks and water he didn't have to carry much. Smart idea!

We chatted for a while and I continued down a steep part of the trail and hadn't gone very far when I had a sudden dizzy spell. I stopped and leaned back against a tree for a minute before starting up again. I still felt wobbly and a little rubber-legged. I slowed way down after that but didn't want to stop. I didn't think I was having a heart attack — but I didn't want to be *off trail* if I were. I felt really out of sorts all the way down the mountain and took it very slow and easy.

After a couple of miles I came to a road, took off the pack and sat against a fence post to rest. It was time for a decision. Should I walk into Falls Village and stay the night? Or should I continue on to Salisbury?

I looked down the road and saw a sign pointing to Salisbury — eight miles away. It was too early in the day to quit. I could surely make it to Salisbury. I looked at the trail map and saw Salisbury was seven miles — all up and down. Hmm ... eight miles by road, seven miles by trail. I didn't want to stop, but I didn't feel up to seven miles of up and down. I'd walk the highway even if it was an extra mile.

It was a pleasant walk. Quiet and peaceful. However, I should have been paying better attention because I missed the trail blaze and went three miles out of my way. Argg! If there's one thing hikers hate to do, it would be missing a trail marker and going out of the way. I'd just doubled my distance!

I passed some really ancient looking farm houses and finally turned down a rough lane to get back on the right road. I ran out of water late in the morning and stopped at a vacant-looking farm house to get some out of the outside tap. It was rusty and warm but I didn't care. I was afraid I was dehydrating.

By early afternoon I arrived at Salisbury and immediately fell in love with the looks of the place. Close to the Massachusetts border, it is the essence of rural New England Americana. I walked down its main street and stopped at a marker to read how this town produced most of the steel for the cannons used during the Revolutionary War.

I passed a gorgeous old library that dated back to the late 1700s and was still going strong. It was the first lending library in the country.

The White Hart Inn was easy to find. I had read about it in some of the information the state tourism people had sent me and I had decided to stay there. The inn was built in 1790 and was very old–world elegant, three stories high and surrounded by a huge porch filled with white wicker furniture.

A large, hand–painted sign of a white hart, or stag, bordered by the Connecticut and American flag was featured over the front entrance. The price of a room was more than I expected to pay — but at this point, I didn't care. I asked for a single room facing the village green. I'm afraid I looked (and probably smelled) like a homeless vagrant and wouldn't have been surprised if they had thrown me out on the street. But they smiled and said how pleased they were to have a 'walker' staying with them. That made me feel good.

I took a long, long shower and lay down and rested for an hour. I was a bit shocked by the bruises the pack had caused on my hips and after checking the mirror I really did look beat. Today's twelve mile walk had turned into fifteen and taken its toll.

I decided it was time to take a short break and visit Kathy and Rich in Amherst. I could rest at their place for a couple of days and head on from there. I called Kathy and she told me they had been expecting to hear from me and to come on over. She said she would meet me at the bus station when I got to town. Great – I was temporarily rescued. I felt better already.

It didn't take long to visit all of Salisbury. The town was only five or six square blocks. I bought an ice cream cone, a paperback book, more postcards and visited the library. Then I bought a can of beer and took it back to the inn and sat sipping it in a wicker chair on the huge porch. The late afternoon sun was just disappearing below the mountain ridge casting a golden glow across the village green. It was quite lovely.

At twilight I went up to my room, dug out the last clean clothes I could find, and went down to dinner feeling rather civilized. The main dining room was out of the question. Very formal and very expensive. The woman taking reservations recommended The Pub which was part of the inn but a part I had not noticed before. It was perfect; dark and woody and full of antiques. I ordered a beer and the roast beef special. It was marvelous and almost more food than I could eat — and I was hungry! I think the waitress took pity on me and told them to *load up* my plate.

After dinner I crossed the village green and walked the few blocks through town again. It was a beautiful night, clear, cool and quiet. Salisbury is surrounded by black and silent mountains called the Wetauwanchus, and sliced in two by Wachacastinook Brook. I wondered what it must have been like back in the 1700s. White settlers, the **Schaghticoke and Paugussetts** Indians,

English troops, clay pipes and cannons. I strolled slowly back to the inn and took another long, hot shower and collapsed into bed. It was almost 9:00 and I was soon out like a light. I was just not used to all this excitement.

Next morning I woke feeling great. I showered and walked back downtown and bought orange juice, yogurt and coffee and sat eating on one of the benches lining main street. I was planning to hitchhike to Caanan and from there catch the bus to Amherst. I checked out the traffic. It was sparse.

I went back, repacked and checked out at 10:00. A bus was scheduled to leave Caanan at 11:45 so I wanted to allow plenty of time. I figured I'll try to catch a ride for 30 minutes and if I didn't have any luck I'd call a cab to take me the eight miles.

I caught a ride within 15 minutes. He was an ex–hiker so he was sympathetic with my plans. He took me right to the bus station in town — which was just a tiny shelter. The tickets were sold in the drugstore across the street. There was also a teenager waiting there. He told me he attended some fancy prep school near Salisbury and was returning home to Boston. We talked a little about my hike but he didn't seem very interested.

As it turned out, the bus did not go straight to Amherst. It went to Lee, Connecticut, where one changed to the Peter Pan Line. (I kept my eyes peeled for Tinker Bell.) Lee was much larger than Salisbury but still not large enough for a bus station. In Lee one bought their ticket in a restaurant right on the main street across from the Town Hall. We arrived there at 12:30 and had ninety minutes to kill. I walked to a nearby Pizza Hut for a personal pan and Pepsi. It tasted great as I sat there in the town square soaking in the history of the surroundings.

DECADENT CIVILIZATION ONCE AGAIN

Kathy and her daughter, Elizabeth, met me as I got off the bus. It was great to see a friendly face again. We drove to their home and talked for a long time. I told her about the trip and how things were going back in Iowa. Rich was working late that night so she fixed us a great dinner of grilled halibut and caesar salad and ice cream and cookies for dessert. Not quite the same as freeze–dried – but I forced it down.

Kathy is the eldest of six children of my sister, Mary. She is also my goddaughter. Their son, Aaron, was a bit under the weather, but up and about. He'd been suffering from strep throat but they believed he was past the contagious stage (I hoped so.)

I called Lois and filled her in on my progress. She told me she'd received another phone call from Nancy Mortimer who hadn't heard from me and was very concerned about my progress. "Tell me again about Nancy Mortimer," she said.

Rich came home around 8:30 and there was talk of a Rhode Island surf fishing expedition that weekend and I was invited to go. It sounded tempting. They were leaving Saturday morning and returning Sunday evening. However, since Aaron was questionable I had a day to think about it until they decided for sure whether they'd go or not.

I went to my room and read for a while and got sleepy. It was raining steadily and hard out and I slowly faded away thinking how great it was to be inside in a comfortable, warm, dry bed. I slept like a log.

I woke Friday feeling drugged. I think this was the first really sound rest I had in days. I cleaned up and Kathy and I took the kids to school. She had to be at work at 10:00 so I had the day to wander around and relax by myself.

I walked around campus, visited the shops and took a long bus ride around the area. Afterwards I studied my trail maps trying to figure out where to get back on the trail. Dalton appeared to be the closest town to the trail head.

Kathy and Rich both came home early in the afternoon. The Rhode Island fishing trip was officially on and I had decided to go with them. It sounded like a lot of fun. And I had never been to Rhode Island before. This was becoming a trip of firsts.

Saturday morning found everyone rushing around, as my mother used to say, like chickens with their heads cut off. A flurry of packing, and we're on our way by 9:30. The eastern seaboard being like it is, Rhode Island was less than a three-hour drive from Amherst. The kids were excited. I was excited. Rich carefully packed his new surf fishing rod on top of the car. Only the dog, who stayed behind with a sitter, was unhappy.

We passed through quintessential New England countryside. Delightful small villages and lovely stone houses and buildings all along the way. By noon we arrived at Watch Hill.

Watch Hill sits at the most-southwestern point of Rhode Island. According to *The New York Times*, it was historically home to "a select group of wealthy families," whose lives revolved around golf and tennis at the Misquamicut Club, bathing and yachting at the Watch Hill Yacht Club and tea and cocktails at Ocean House and Watch Hill's other grand hotels.

Included among it's past and present residents one could possibly see the likes of Clark Gable, Taylor Swift, Henry Ford and Conan O'Brien hanging around.

But we weren't there to mix it up with the jet set. We were there to relax and go fishing. We stopped at a deli and bought pop, chips and sandwiches, checked into a motel and headed straight for the beach.

It was a great beach — around three miles long from jetty to jetty. We walked its length and generally took it easy. Around five in the afternoon we went to visit a fishing buddy of Rich's. The surf fishing expedition begins at 5:30 in the morning.

"You should have been here an hour ago," seemed to be the common phrase in Watch Hill as well as back home when we arrived at the beach early the next morning. We worked mightily at it but caught nothing. It was still fun and exciting and different. We stayed until it got light — and headed back to the motel to shower and change.

We soon returned to the beach to spend the day. It had warmed up considerably by this time and the kids were ready to go. We spent the whole day lounging, walking and fishing. The weather was perfect and the scenery beautiful. There was one great moment of excitement when Rich finally hooked a Bonita – only to lose it before landing it. But in surf fishing, that's okay. It initiated the ritualistic questions of technique and lure selection and weight estimate that really seemed to me to be the essence of the sport.

We remained as long as we could — but finally packed up and headed back to Amherst pulling into their driveway by seven. Our weekend adventure was over.

It had been another great day — but the fresh air and salt water had taken its toll and I was falling asleep in my chair.

I woke early Monday and said goodbye to Rich and Aaron. Kathy offered to drive me over to Dalton, where I planned to pick up the trail again. By jumping ahead to Dalton, I missed out on a long but relatively flat stretch of trail. Unfortunately there was no other good place to intercept it near a convenient highway. Dalton is around 40 miles from Amherst and we planned to leave late morning.

The evening before I had taken the time to repack and pick out a few things to leave behind for her to ship home for me. I managed to lighten my load around 10 pounds. Should make a huge difference.

Kathy came home from her job around 11:30 and we picked up Elizabeth from her day school and took off. They dropped me off on the edge of Dalton, we said our goodbyes and I was back on the trail by 2:00.

Staying with them had been a great break in my trip and I really enjoyed seeing them. I left feeling very rested, healthy — and the lightened pack was a dandy plus.

I headed up the trail feeling strong and rested. Of course, at this point I was running out of time.

SHARING A COZY CAMPFIRE

It was a steady but gentle climb to Crystal Mountain campsite going from 1,000 feet to 2,000 feet. Along the way, I actually passed another backpacker! Can you believe it? It must have been the ten pounds I shipped home. I arrived around 4:00 and set up camp right away. I was excited. In Massachusetts you are allowed campfires so I gathered a load of wood while it was still light and sat back and read.

The backpacker I'd passed earlier showed up around 5:00. His name was Ted and he told me he was a thirty-year-old street lawyer — on vacation from the Bronx in New York where his job was prosecuting drug dealers who buy and set up drug houses in different neighborhoods. Lovely. His girlfriend dropped him off somewhere along the route and he was spending a few days alone to unwind. Now that I could understand.

I couldn't help but notice he had no tent — just a light weight sleeping bag, a ground cloth, a canteen and a little food. Yikes!

I got the fire going and Ted joined me and we sat and talked about how things had changed since I was a kid living in New York. Soon, another backpacker, North Wind, showed up. North Wind was probably 10 years younger than Ted and had been on the trail for two months heading south. He'd hurt his leg and had been resting in a small town for the last couple of days. He had been traveling with two friends who had gone on without him — but he figures the last ride he caught put him ahead of them. He was going to wait for a day or so until they caught up. Unlike Ted, this fellow was carrying a huge pack and really seemed to know what he was doing.

I fixed myself some freeze-dried beef stew and apple cobbler. It was excellent. The three of us sat and traded lies until around 8.00 when I finally headed to bed. It makes quite a difference having others sharing the campsite with you — and a warm, cozy fire made it much more like the kind of camping I was used to.

I slept very well and got up around 7:30. Ted had already left. I never saw him again. North Wind was still sound asleep — and snoring loudly. I fixed hot cereal and coffee and hit the trail by 8:30. Within a mile I reached Gore Pond – a large, upland, beaver pond — wild and scenic. I took off the pack and sat awhile to read the camp register:

May 20 – Very buggy. I want a steak. – Jim Weaver

August 26 – Bear signs up here. Surprised to see such a big pond. Been here for a couple of months doing survey work for the AT – Joe & Melanie, Lake Lucerne, NY.

September 3 – May the four winds blow you home safely again. – GA – Strolling Bones – ME

As I read the first comment it occurred to me there were really very few bugs. Other than some hornets and bumble bees, I can't say I'd been bothered much by mosquitoes or flies or ants – or anything else. Gnats from time to time. Must have been the right time of year.

I continued on to a place called The Cobbles where there were some outstanding views looking down on Cheshire, Massachusetts, a couple of miles away. I was toying with the idea of taking it real easy and staying in Cheshire for the night and decided to wait and see how I felt when I got closer.

Just as I was starting down, I came upon a couple of younger hikers panting their way to the top. I remembered North Wind told me one of his friends had the trail name of "Harley" and I surprised them when I asked if one of them was called Harley. Of course, one was, so I filled them in on what I knew about their friend and they were delighted to learn he was just a few miles ahead. They'd thought he had quit and gone home with his bad leg. They were determined to finish the walk at Springer Mountain, Georgia, before winter set in. I wished them luck.

Cheshire turned out to be a disappointment as far as quaint New England towns go. Very small with not much in the way of accommodations. Why would I want to stay there, I thought? Besides, it was early and I was feeling strong. I stopped at a general store and bought some juice and chocolate milk and filled up my canteen with fresh water and headed back up into the hills.

The next campsite, Bassett Brook, was five more miles and 2,000 steep feet up. I knew it would be a tough climb, but on the plus side it would leave an easy hike up to Bascom Lodge the following day.

I arrived at the campsite around 4:00 — really whipped. Again, other than Harley and his friend, I hadn't seen anyone all day and I had the campsite to myself. I wasn't too keen about another lonely campsite – but it had a brand new lean to and I hadn't slept in one yet. I wouldn't even have to pitch my tent.

I stretched out to test one of the pine bunk beds when Carolina John, a local trail volunteer stopped by unannounced and scared me half to death. He was on a day hike checking the trail for any problems. He was a very likable young man who told me he helped build the shelter back in April. We talked for a few minutes before he was up and gone.

By 6 p.m. I had a fire going and finished off what was left of the freeze–dried beef stew and apple crisp and fixed a couple of cups of hot tea. It had been a sunny and cool day and steep as the climb was, I found it quite manageable, probably for a number of reasons. One, my pack was around 10 pounds lighter. Two, I was finally getting in shape — they say to allow at least six days for your body to get used to the routine. In addition, I was managing my expectations better. Wouldn't you know it, the trip was almost over.

Tomorrow I planned to sleep in late and stroll into Bascom Lodge around noon, clean up and have lunch and relax. I was a day ahead of schedule now so I needed to decide whether I would stay there a couple of days or continue on the trail toward Vermont.

I finished reading my paperback, *River of Emeralds,* and checked what the local camp log had to offer:

November 2 – I seem to be the only one out today. Unusual peace and tranquillity found on this sodden, foggy day. A lone woodpecker is hammering away out there somewhere. Just out doing the Jones Nose Triangle. A true Greylock day. – Kristin

May 27, or 28 (Not sure) – When does it get warm? – Peace

July 17 – Stopped by to wash my hair. To whomever left the shampoo, thanks. After four and a half months on the trail, dish soap gets a little tiresome. I meet my husband at Rte. 2 tomorrow morning. I'll take a few days at home and then hit the trail again. On to Katahdin! – Shortcakes

And finally, Number 13 under the "Please list your comments on the JFK murder" – *It was a trick all done with mirrors. Now he, Elvis and Marilyn Monroe are all living happily ever after on the Appalachian Trail! — Wacky John*

I had a terrible night's sleep. The moon was FULL and absolutely brilliant all night. I had to cover my head with my shirt to get what little sleep I did get.

I caught a chipmunk (called *chipmonsters* in this part of the world) dining on my freeze dried cereal in the middle of the night. How could so small a creature make so much noise? It was so bright out, you didn't even need a flashlight to see him sitting there on the edge of my pack chumping away. We made eye contact and I swear it smiled at me! Gutsy little critter. I let it be.

I tossed and turned all night long. I think it might have had something to do with the fact I was sleeping without a tent. A little different feeling, for sure.

MT. GREYLOCK IN MY SIGHTS

I got up at 7:15 feeling quite discombobulated (I love that word). I was woozy and dizzy and groggy as if I hadn't been asleep at all. I fixed some coffee and cereal (what my midnight visitor had left uneaten) and hit the road by 8:45.

It was less than five miles to the top of Mt. Greylock – 3,500 feet – where Bascom Lodge was located right in the middle of the Berkshire Mountains — and it was a tough climb. Occasionally I could spot the lodge through openings in the trees but it didn't seem to be getting any closer.

I finally arrived around noon — and was quite pleased with myself. It had been a hot and very hazy day when I walked into the lodge like a seasoned trooper. Since I qualified as a thru hiker as opposed to a day hiker, I was asked if I wanted to work for part of my room and board. Sounded fun. I'd save a little money and it would give me something to do.

"Sure," I said. "Be happy to help."

Bascom Lodge is huge. Of rustic stone and wood construction, it was built by the Civilian Conservation Corps in the 1930s to provide accommodations for hikers, vacationers, and nature enthusiasts. One end of the first floor is a large kitchen and dining room. There is a reception room in the middle and rooms for the permanent help on the other end. There's also an enclosed porch that runs the length of the building filled with stuffed animals and various nature displays.

Upstairs there were a series of bunk rooms, each with several double–decker beds. A large bathroom and shower is on each end of the upstairs hall. I was assigned to bunk room four. It was a large room with four bunk beds – but there were only two other people there. I unpacked and went back to the dining hall, ate a hamburger and fries and then went back to the room to take a long, hot shower and lay down and puttered around until it was time to go and work in the dining room.

My job was to mop the floor and set the tables. (I knew my Army training would come in handy someday.) They were only expecting twelve people for dinner so I finished quickly. The cook, Sean, was an interesting character; a bushy bearded, red headed giant who piped Irish music into the dining room all evening long. He liked me because I was the only one who really seemed to appreciate it.

When dinner was served I sat and ate with the rest of the guests. I met a middle—aged couple from Pittsfield, Massachusetts. The husband sold meat specialities and has been to Rath Packing in Waterloo, close to my home. He sold through specialty counters in stores and was familiar with HyVee Foods, our local grocery chain.

There was another couple from Springfield, Massachusetts and a few scattered others. Most of the guests had driven up to the lodge and day hiked on the many trails in the area. We chatted during an excellent dinner beginning with borsch, baked beans, kielbasa and sauerkraut, homemade bread and all kinds of liquids and vanilla ice cream for dessert. Plenty of good food.

After dinner, I put all the chairs back on top of the tables, swept and mopped the hardwood floor and was through by 7:15. Easy job. After I finished I took a walk outside the lodge. The mountain top was dark and mysterious. Weather wise it had turned a little windy and misty. I could look down upon the blurred lights of Williamstown and North Adams far below ... a very lovely scene, indeed.

I went back to my room and thought about what my plans would be from there on. I had two days left before my flight home and I needed one of those days to get back to Albany. I wasn't sure if I wanted to continue hiking another day or not. I decided to sleep on it and see how things looked in the morning. I had to be at work at 7:30 a.m.

It felt good to be between clean sheets again.

The following morning I went down to the kitchen early. I had a huge breakfast and worked until 9:00. I settled my bill for the first day and they charged me a total of $5 for room and board. I'm not sure how they came up with that amount, but I didn't argue.

I was offered a ride into town if I wanted to go so I made the decision to stay at the lodge another night and head back in the morning. I decided I really wouldn't see much more by continuing north and would just be that much further away from North Adams where I had to catch my bus.

It was a crisp, clear fall day and I wanted to see Willamstown anyway and this seemed like a good opportunity. I rode in the supply truck and got dropped off at the art museum. They said they'd be back to pick me up at the post office later in the afternoon.

The Singer Museum (previously owned by the Singer sewing machine family) was very interesting. A special Toulouse Lautrec exhibit was there and I bought my Number Two son, Michael, a commemorative tee shirt. I spent around an hour browsing around and headed toward town.

On the way I passed by the Williamstown Play House and I remembered visiting it many years earlier with John Youker and Harold Krebs, a couple of fraternity brothers of mine from Iowa State. They were paid delegates to a convention and I went along with them for the ride. It must have been in 1958 or 1959. (My Lord – it seemed like a lifetime ago.)

One evening the three of us went to the local Playhouse to see *Our Town*. As fate would have it, Thornton Wilder, the author, was reading the role of the narrator. What a treat that was!

I stopped at the Playhouse to make sure my memory was correct and sure enough, it was. The director was there and I told her about it. She had also been working there at the time, just out of school, and she went through some files and found one of the original playbills.

Williamstown is a small, New England town near the corners of Vermont, New York and Massachusetts. It's home to Williams College, recently named the number one liberal arts college in the country. I wandered around campus enjoying all the traditional Ivy League architecture and the changing color of the leaves.

After lunch I bought a Christmas present for my daughter–in–law, Ann, and walked to the small downtown section and barely got settled on the steps of the post office when the supply truck pulled up – 30 minutes early.

We headed back up the mountain to the lodge and found a couple of new thru hikers have arrived — rushing to get to Katahdin before the snow flies. I doubt they make it. One had decided to keep on going and one decided to stay at the lodge for the night, to shower and rest and catch up with his friend in a few days.

These guys were *real* thru walkers and had been on the trail for months. They had that special "look" about them ... haunted is the best way I can describe it. Driven, perhaps. And probably borderline insane with worry, knowing their number of days were limited before the weather turned on them.

HEADING HOME – BACK TO THE PRAIRIE

My last meal at Bascom Lodge was equally memorable; a bowl of lentil soup, turnips, rice pilaf, egg plant parmesan, tomato herb bread and apple pie with ice cream. Sean, my Irish cook buddy, was a genius. After dinner I cleaned up and went out and walked around the mountain top for the last time. Again it was windy, overcast and very cool. I stood there silently in the shadows as three deer came up out of the woods and passed slowly by.

Back inside I called Kathy and Rich to thank them again for their hospitality and let them know I was heading home in the morning. I also called my wife who asked me if had called Nancy Mortimer yet. No - but I had sent her a postcard.

Afterwards, I sat and chatted with Eddie, the remaining thru hiker. He told me he had started off in Georgia on May 1st and managed to come 1580 miles in 4 1/2 months but still had over 500 miles to go. I wished him luck — the weather was already starting to turn in the short time I'd be on the trail and he had the toughest part ahead of him!

I got up early Friday and headed to work in the kitchen only to find Eddie had been given my job — I'd been replaced! No problem, he deserved it more than I did anyway. I ate breakfast and settled my bill. Only $8. They'll never get rich at that rate. A great deal and a great place for thru hikers to rest and eat well.

I packed up, said good-bye to Sean, the cook, and headed down Mt. Greylock toward North Adams, around six miles away, mostly downhill. I figured two and a half hours would give me plenty of time to get there. I'd earlier made some inquiries and learned the bus left for Pittsfield at 11:00. There I had to switch to another bus for Albany.

It was a long, slippery and very steep hike down the mountain and I slipped and fell a couple of times. At one point I surprised a wild turkey drinking from a mountain steam. It seemed to take me forever to get down. Finally, I reached the bottom, broke out in the open and headed down a gravel road toward town. I looked back and was surprised to see how steep and wild the mountain looked once I was out of the woods.

I arrived at North Adams later than planned and had to hurry to find the bus stop. I got there just as the bus came around the corner. Talk about timing. I was only a mile or two from the Vermont border at this point and if I'd had enough time I would have walked there just to say that I did. Maybe another time.

The ride to Pittsfield took another hour. On the way we passed through Cheshire, a town I had walked through just a few days earlier. (Gee, that didn't take long.) The route followed the Hoosic River and I could look up and see the ridges I had hiked. My hips were really tender from the walk down from the lodge. It must have been due to all the jerky ups and downs as I went downhill. It felt good just to sit back and relax.

I arrived at the Pittsfield bus terminal with another hour to wait before the bus to Albany arrived. I bought my ticket and walked up to Jimmy's Italian Restaurant and ordered a Bass ale just to kill a little time.

Back at the terminal I found a copy of John Grisham's *A Time To Kill* left behind on one of the benches. I picked it up and started reading it — and kept it with me for the rest of the trip. I ended up liking it the best of his three books I'd read so far.

I met an elderly woman in the station. She came up to me and wanted to know if the Albany bus had arrived yet. She had a look of panic about her until I assured her I was waiting for the same bus.

Although it was rather warm that day, she was dressed in a large black hat and veil, white gloves, long black wool overcoat, and was carrying an umbrella and a heavy cloth bag that looked like what I imagined a carpet bag would look like. She could have been Mary Poppins' older sister.

She was a grand person with a sharp, lively sense of humor, very well-read and interested in everything. We sat in the station and passed the time talking about all types of things — Frank Lloyd Wright, Aaron Copland, advertising, automobiles, the Midwest, etc.

I suspected her of being a nun or ex-school teacher and she laughed out loud when I told her so. No, she assured me, she was just a small town widow trying to get by. She said she was going to Albany to stay with a sick friend that she hadn't seen in a long time. She asked me to sit by her on the bus and visit. She admitted she hadn't traveled that far from home in ages and would enjoy the company.

She said she didn't know how long she'd be gone and told me she felt just like a pilgrim.

When we arrived in Albany she seemed confused again. When we got off the bus and said good bye she looked a little uncertain and nervous at the size of the larger terminal. I watched her for a few seconds as she took a step this way, and then that way, unsure what to do next. She reminded me of a puppy caught in traffic. I knew no one was coming to meet her because I had asked her.

I left her for a moment and went into the depot to call and reserve a motel room near the airport. When I turned back to see if I could help her in some way, she was gone. I walked over to the grimy depot window just in time to see her step into a taxi and drive off. I went out the opposite door. Life goes on.

Robert Buckley, Fellow Pilgrim

ENGLAND

The Coast-To-Coast

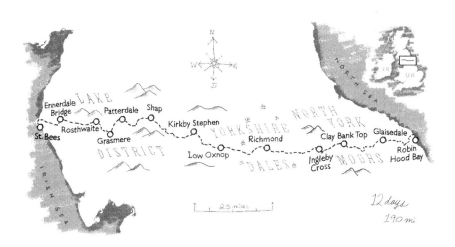

My flight from Chicago landed in London at 11:00 a.m., just 30 minutes late. Jet lag had not yet set in although my biological clock was screaming, *It's 5:00 a.m., stupid, why aren't you home asleep in your warm, comfortable bed?*

It had been almost three years since my first major hike on the Appalachian Trail. I know now that I had made some real "greenhorn" mistakes but that was all part of the learning process. It was a wonderful experience and I'll always treasure it.

But this was a whole different ball game. I was in Europe this time beginning a new adventure – a long way from home.

With no luggage to claim I rushed down escalators following signs to London's marvelous subway system — the Underground

– or the *Tube* as they call it. The airport was packed but I managed to slip into a short line.

"How much to Euston Station?" I hurriedly asked a guard.

"Three and sixty," he shot back.

My fistfull of English coins was terribly confusing. I finally sorted out and inserted three pound coins and three 20 pence coins into an automated ticker machine. (Why were the pound coins so small and the pence coins so large?)

Rushing down the tunnels I immediately jumped on a Piccadilly Line train. No room to sit. I struck up a conversation with a business man standing next to me and asked him what he felt my chances were on making my next connection to Euston Station. He smiled and shook his head. "Doubt it, mate," he said as he got off. "But if you do, don't forget to change trains at Lester."

Lester? There was no Lester station on the map. There was a Leicester station. Did he mean *Leicester*? Hmm. Time was ticking away.

I knew I hadn't much time to make it across town and catch my train north. Any possibility of making the 12:30 connection from Euston Station to Carlisle, a town in the far north of England, looked totally slim. If I missed that train, I knew I'd miss the following connection from Carlisle to St. Bees. If I missed the train to St. Bees I would lose my room reservation. If I lost my room reservation ... etc.

It was like a game of dominoes.

Day One: London to St. Bees

The day I traveled the length and breadth of England with the Vicar's wife

I switched trains at Lester, Leicester, whatever, at 12:25 and barely made my next connection for a short ride to Euston Station where I rushed out onto the platform. There it was! The 12:30 Carlisle train still sitting there at 12:35. Ha! So much for European train punctuality. On I jumped, sweaty and out of breath but feeling very, very pleased with myself.

There was plenty of room in the car. I grabbed an empty seat, placed my bag overhead and sat down and caught my breath. It wasn't long before the public address system alerted everyone there was a *slight* problem up the line. Something about a fire. There was an audible sigh from all the passengers. I didn't care. I was on the right train and I had a seat.

Across from me sat an attractive woman balancing several packages on her lap. We smiled and greeted each other. Her name was Leslie Baden. She agreed to watch my pack as I worked my way up to the dining car and bought a BLT, fries and a can of Stella Artois, a Belgium beer. I had no sooner sat back down when the public address system came back on to announce the delay was now determined to be 90 minutes. This time a *louder* sigh went up from everyone including Leslie.

By this time I learned she was also headed to Carlisle and her husband, Peter, was to meet her at the station and take her to a town very close to St. Bees, where I was staying. She alluded to the fact there might be a ride in it for me.

Just then another announcement revealed the length of delay had become *unpredictable*. Oh no! Passengers began to get off the train. Leslie had already checked her schedule and determined that if we were to get off this train and rush to King's Cross station, just a few blocks up the street, and do it within 10 minutes, we could catch the main East Coast Express to Edinburgh via New Castle where we could get off and transfer to another train that would take us back across England and arrive in Carlisle just a couple of hours late. Whew! Sounded a bit confusing to me.

Either way I knew I would miss the Carlisle–St. Bees connection and quickly threw my fate in with my clever, new companion.

"C'mon – let's go!" she said starting to get off. "It's hard telling how long this train will just sit here."

Off we went, out into the sunshine and up the busy London streets. She was having trouble with her bags so I volunteered to carry one of the largest. It weighed a ton. Knocking into people right and left we rushed headlong down the sidewalk during one of the busiest parts of the day to King's Cross Station.

Again, we made it just in time. We found a couple of seats and settled in. But wait. Here came another announcement: There would be a 40–minute delay until they "can find a driver." A *driver*?

What's going on? Here I was on the crack British Rail System and they lost their driver? We looked at each other and laughed. What else could we do – it was too late to change our minds again. Soon enough they found a new driver and we were moving.

Leslie told me her husband was the Vicar of Workington. She had come to London to visit one of their daughters for a few days and was heading back home. We chatted away as we zoomed along at what seemed like 100 miles per hour toward New Castle. (What's that old saying about … Coals to New Castle?) Leslie was marvelous and warmed to my adventure. She was one of many wonderful people I would meet on my trip.

Soon the conductor came along punching tickets. In the rush I hadn't bought one but knew I could do so on the train. I was expecting to pay around $95 for a one-way ticket. But now, because we were taking a more complicated route, my ticket would be around $130. Ugh!

Leslie felt terrible. I felt terrible. The conductor felt terrible. He hesitated a bit after hearing of my travel plans to walk across the country. He then asked how I was planning to get back to London?

"I was planning to catch a train from York," I said.

45

"Brilliant!" he exclaimed. "We're passing through York on the way up. Instead of a one way ticket for $130, I can sell you a *round trip* for $125!"

(Pause) "Excuse me," I said. "You can sell me a *one–way* for $130 or a *round–trip* for $125?"

"Exactly, but don't ask," he replied, "I couldn't explain if me life depended on it."

Wow – now there's a great deal, I thought. With this new arrangement I actually saved $65 by changing trains and going the long way 'round. Typically English I guessed!

We arrived in New Castle with a little time to kill before catching our next train so I called Mrs. Moffat in St. Bees to tell her I was still coming but would be a little late.

"No problem, luv. There's a comfy room all ready for you and the tea's on."

Leslie then called her husband, Peter, to alert him of our late arrival and informed me I could certainly count on a ride with them to St. Bees. Great! Everything was working out fine.

Peter Baden was waiting for us at the station and off we headed to St. Bees in his tidy little Peugeot. Carlisle was only 15 miles south of the border with Scotland. I had no idea we were that far north.

It turned out that driving me to St. Bees really wasn't that far out of their way – but I was so thankful for the ride. Without it I would have had to spend the night in Carlisle and get a late start on my walk.

We chatted about my trip – and a little about religion. He told me that only about four percent of the people in this area of England attended church on a regular basis. He was amazed when I told him my parish in Iowa had at least 60% regular attendance. Perhaps higher!

We arrived in St. Bees around 8:00 in the evening, three and a half hours behind schedule! They delivered me right up to the front door of The Outrigg House and made sure I was expected before driving off. What wonderful people – right out of a PBS episode of *All Things Great and Small*.

There *was* a pot of hot tea waiting for me. Mrs. Moffat didn't lie. It was the first Bed and Breakfast I'd stayed in for years and a great way to start my trip. It was a typical B&B with a private bedroom, hot bath and a huge English breakfast.

Mrs. Moffat quickly explained the rules of the house before chasing me off to the Manor House – built circa 1679 – for a pint of local ale, a steak pie and a little local chatter.

How marvelous it was to be back in a British Isles' pub with all the lovely accents, heavy wood and brass, and fascinating antique photographs. I loved every minute of it and would have stayed longer – but jet lag was beginning to take its toll.

The bartender (called publicans) became particularly friendly when I told him I was starting on the Coast to Coast in the morning.

"We get lots of Coasters in here," he said. "It's a lovely walk although I've never done it meself. Someday soon, perhaps."

After dinner I bid him good night and walked slowly back up the hill with the scent of a salty breeze in the air. The street was dark and damp with mist by this time. I'd arrived too late to see the ocean – but I knew it was just over the hill. I could smell it and I could hear it. When I reached Mrs. Moffat's I let myself in, took a hot shower, went to bed and immediately fell asleep.

It may have been 10:00 p.m. St. Bees, Cumbria, England time ... but my body knew it was really 4:00 a.m. Marion, Linn County, Iowa, USA time and I had missed a whole night's sleep!

Day Two: St. Bees to Ennerdale Bridge

Hiking to The Old Vicarage with a delightful
interlude at The Fox and Hounds

Breakfast was served in the dining room. When I came down there were a couple of other fellows already eating. It was a typical, huge English breakfast – but I was too nervous to eat it all, much to Mrs. Moffat's dismay. I was most anxious to get started.

The walk I was heading out on is called The Coast–to–Coast Walk and was developed by the late A. Wainwright, a famous and most beloved English naturalist. Now recognized as one of the great walks of the world, most of the trail passes through three of England's National Park Districts: The Lake District, the Yorkshire Dales, and the North York Moors.

Wainwright set out to create a walking trail that encompassed the very best England had to offer. Whenever possible he followed the paths of tenth century Viking settlers who wanted to avoid the long sea journey around Scotland to Ireland. The result is a 190–mile route joining the ancient coastal hamlets of St. Bees on the Irish Sea with Robin Hood Bay on the North Sea.

Throughout the entire trip everyone was curious how I had learned about the walk considering it was relatively unknown at the time even in England. And to be perfectly honest I had to tell them I wasn't sure. All I remember was having read about it in a magazine article a few years earlier and being interested in it ever since.

Although the Coast-to-Coast was not yet one of England's nationally recognized long distance paths such as The Pennine Way — or Offa's Dyke Path, there was no doubt its popularity was increasing every year.

The first stage of the walk crosses England's fabled Lake District, a wilderness that has bewitched generations of artists and

English Romantic poets with its emerald valleys, sky–mirrored lakes, and windswept peaks.

The Lake District is quite compact – 39 miles long and 33 miles wide. But with 1,800 miles of trails and bridle paths, it's possible to walk for days and see few signs of life other than sheep – which I saw in abundance.

There's constant debate whether one should walk east to west, or west to east. One school of thought suggests walking east to west which saves the beautiful Lake District for your grand finale. The other suggests heading west to east to benefit from the prevailing westerly winds at your back. I figured I needed all the help I could get and this is the direction I chose.

St. Bees is a lovely little village although I didn't get to see much of it. I had arrived too late in the evening – and now there was no time. I was on my way.

A Catholic nunnery was established there in the seventh century by St. Bega, an Irish nun, when her ship was wrecked along the rugged English coast. The nunnery survived for two centuries before being destroyed by Danish raiders. Today the village is built along the side of a wide hill sloping down to the Irish Sea. I passed several ancient churches on my way to the start of the coastal path.

I hurried down to the water's edge to get my official pebble. Tradition dictated that every hiker was to carry a pebble with him and toss it into the sea on the other side. Would I even make it that far?

From the breakwater the path climbed steadily along a cliff edge to St. Bees Head. It was 9:30 in the morning and a fairly clear day. To the west – far out in the Irish Sea – you could barely see the Isle of Man and to the north, Carlisle and the hills of Scotland.

I was expecting to be heading east and it was a bit disconcerting at first to follow the cliff a fair distance west and then north before it finally turned back east.

The view from the 300-foot cliffs was spectacular. I could taste the fresh salt breeze. The crashing surf below me and soaring sea birds above reminded me I had come a long way – to *walk* a long way. I took my time to enjoy the scenery but I tried not to dawdle. With only 14 and a quarter miles to walk this first day I knew I had plenty of time but was still hoping to average two miles per hour. At least that was my plan.

Everything I'd read recommended taking 14 days to complete the walk. Fifteen or 16 days would be even better. Unfortunately I only had 12. This meant I needed to average almost 17 miles a day. That was a bunch, I knew. But I had trained for this walk and felt I was up to the challenge.

Soon I was joined by one of the fellows I had met at breakfast at the Outrigg House. His name was Jon Blannin, from Surrey in the London area. We walked along together for a while – but later split up as I stopped to eat a snack and take a short rest. I found him very hard to understand at first. He not only spoke very fast, but his accent and phrases were difficult for me to follow. In the days that followed I had less trouble.

The path along the cliff face was very obvious and easy to follow but as it turned away from the sea and headed east it required more attention. It turned down a lane and through the town of Sandwith (pronounced *san-ith*) and down some more lanes, through farm yards and over open fields.

I should mention that I, as well as everyone else I met on the trip, had special, detailed Coast–to–Coast 1:25,000 Ordnance Survey maps. I carried a good compass, as well. Still, there were times I got lost.

The day turned quite warm and I started to perspire and hit the water bottle early. As I suspected, all the advance walking I'd done before leaving Iowa did not prepare me for the real thing. On I went through the town of Moor Row. It was around noon when I checked my map to discover I had already gone eight and one half miles. Wow, I thought, a blistering three miles an hour! Time for a congratulatory Snickers.

When I reached the village of Cleator I again ran into Jon investigating St. Leonard's Church, a beautiful twelfth century building. We chatted a few minutes and were soon joined by two sisters, Beryl and Sue. We had met them earlier and we all headed out of town together. Directly ahead of us was a tall hill called Dent, part of a deer park centuries ago and today barren of trees but covered with grazing sheep. The path passed right over the summit.

Regarding this point in the walk Wainwright writes: "And dear little Dent, the first hill, is waiting nearby to introduce the wonderful territory that lies ahead."

Well, that should have told me something about the English proclivity to understate. "Hill" indeed. Eight hundred feet almost straight up. It took all of us by surprise. Up, up, up we puffed and climbed until we finally reached a summit marked by a huge rock cairn.

The view was gorgeous in every direction but who was looking? We all collapsed and gasped for air. I don't think any of us were in such great shape yet. I sure wasn't. From experience I expected to get stronger day by day. At least I hoped so.

We rested and ate our luncheon snacks and headed down the other side, into a forest area, towards a place called Nannycatch Gate. The trail got extremely steep as we descended and I soon discovered it was much more painful and difficult walking down that it was going up. I'd acquired enough good sense since my Appalachian Trail walk to have purchased a quality Leki walking stick; adjustable, lightweight and strong. It really came in handy as I planted it in front of me to break my forward momentum.

Breaking out of the forest we came onto a hill covered with gorse – or a very thick fern–like undergrowth which seemed to be taking over the hillside. Sue, who seemed to know a lot about these things, commented that the government was considering introducing wild pigs back into the countryside to help control this kind of impenetrable undergrowth.

In the meantime, we discovered we'd managed to stray slightly off route. Not a serious error, mind you, but not wanting to continue in the wrong direction we saw a man heading up the extremely steep hill toward us so we waited for him. It was a local and he marched uphill as if he were walking on flat ground.

"Excuse us, is this the way to Ennerdale Bridge?" Sue asked.

"Oh aye, aye, ood jist cont larg ay bistrantk," he replied giving us a vague wave of his arm and continuing on his way.

"What? What'd he say?" I couldn't understand a single word.

"My, my," Beryl noted with a chuckle, "now that was a *broad* accent, wasn't it? But at least it seems we're heading in the right direction."

Laughing – we set off, slowly and carefully down the hill. Finally we reached the bottom and turned up Nannycatch Gate, a very narrow cut in the hills. We were only three miles from our destination. Soon we came to a paved road (tarmac), turned left on it, and chatting away, continued down the road. And again we got lost.

"Where be ye 'eading?" yelled out a farmer who was watching us from a nearby farm building.

"Ennerdale Bridge," we yelled back in unison.

"Well, ye'll not get there going that way," he said as he came over and turned us around and 'eaded us back a mile or so in the opposite direction.

We had another good laugh after I pointed out to everyone that we had no fewer than eight maps and six compasses among the lot of us, and yet still managed to get lost twice. And this was only the first day. What were we going to do on the moors?

Funny or not, it was the truth – and it gave me something to ponder.

We arrived in Ennerdale Bridge at 4:00. My B&B was the Old Vicarage and we came upon it right where we entered the village. Beryl and Sue were staying somewhere else in the village and Jon was continuing on to Gillerwaithe Youth Hostel, five miles further on. Ouch! I was fairly tired by then and not sure I could stare another five miles in the face and survive.

The Old Vicarage was just that, an eighteenth century, vine–covered brick vicarage turned into a B&B. I was met at the door, directed to take off my boots, and invited in to the reading room for tea and biscuits. Quite civilized, I thought.

The room was filled with every Ordnance Survey Map and book on hiking that had ever been written (or at least it seemed that way). One wall was all windows and a telescope was placed so you could look up into the mountains. I took a good look. Wow! Those were mountains. So, "dear little Dent" was just a hill after all.

I was shown to a quiet little room and immediately took a hot shower and lay down for a short rest before changing into clean clothes and heading down the lane to find a place to eat.

My small backpack only had room for one change of clean clothes, and things were packed so tightly I was afraid I'd never get every thing put back again. Already I was forced to leave behind an old sweater in St. Bees.

I'd managed to stuff two weeks worth of gear into a newly-acquired 3,000 cubit inch pack that, when filled, weighed just 18 pounds. That included such luxuries as rain gear and tennis shoes. (Again, I had learned something from my first walk when I had struggled along with an overloaded, vintage Boy Scout pack weighing over 40 pounds).

Just as I was leaving the Old Vicarage to walk to the village, I met Leslie and Peter Baden walking up to the front door. What a surprise! It turned out I had left a book in the back of their car and they came all this way to return it to me. It really wasn't all that far and I think they were just curious to see how I had fared the first day. I told them I was just headed out for dinner and they offered to drop me off in the square. What great folks they were.

As far as I could tell, the Fox and Hounds was the place to be. In reality I think it was the only place open in the tiny village. What a wonderful little place it was – filled with snug little rooms and chattering people, dark wood and mirrors. In the corner, a fire was burning and the aroma of cooked food stopped me dead in my tracks. This, I admitted, is the real reason I came on this walk – to enjoy all of this!

I had no sooner entered when Beryl and Sue followed. Although we had barely met it was great to see familiar faces and I invited them over to join me.

I ordered a pint of local, hand–pumped ale and a grilled rainbow trout for dinner. Everything was excellent. I treated Beryl to a shandygaff (A favorite British Isles beverage of beer mixed with lemonade. Ugh!) and Sue a Pils and we had a great time visiting.

Sue is married to a police officer and Beryl is married to a valet. They told me they take an annual walking trip together and this was their first time on the Coast–To–Coast. Because they only had a week's vacation, they were only going to the half way point – to Keld – where Sue's husband was coming up to meet them and take them home.

They lived close to one another – in southern England down near the coast – in Essex. They told me the little B&B where they were staying had run out of water just as they arrived. Not hot water *but water* and they had been so longing for a bath. But they were both great sports and had a wonderful sense of humor. And both of them were better walkers than I was.

By 9:00 p.m. we were ready to call it quits and I left them and headed back up the winding lane to the Old Vicarage.

It was black as pitch when I stepped out of the Fox and Hounds. Suddenly it dawned on me I had forgotten to take a torch (flashlight) with me so I could use it to find the way back up the lane and find the entrance to the drive.

It took me about a half hour to muddle my way back up the road without being run over, but I eventually found the right lane and followed it to the house and let myself in.

One successful day down. Only eleven to go.

Day Two
Ennerdale Bridge to Rosthwaite

I learn the difference between a hill and a fell, stay in my first hostel, and eat my very first Sticky Toffee Pudding.

I enjoyed a wonderful night's sleep and went down to breakfast at 8:00. There were three other hikers there, I didn't recognize any of them.

I would like to say a few words here about the typical B&B English breakfast. It tends to be the same wherever you go and I must admit it got a little monotonous after a few days. It normally consisted of a glass of juice and choice of cold cereals, sometimes hot. Then the inevitable pot of tea with toast and marmalade. Along with the tea is served a platter, not a plate mind you, but a platter covered with two large sausages, a rasher (two or three slices) of Canadian style bacon, eggs, fried tomatoes, and grilled mushrooms and/or baked beans on toast. Sometimes fried bread as well.

It took a little getting used to but I usually ate every bite – every day. After a breakfast like that you could walk a long ways. Today it had to last me 15 miles!

Packing up, I paid my bill and headed to town and the post office. Most towns in England, regardless of how small they may be, have a post office. Unlike the USA, the English post office also serves as a general store and gathering spot for local gossip. I bought an apple, a thick slice of brown bread and a Cadbury chocolate bar. I also carried a 20 oz. water bottle. Sounds rather meager, I realize, but with a breakfast like the one I'd just eaten, it was usually quite sufficient until dinner.

Ennerdale Bridge (a village) is located at the beginning of the Lake District, and at one end of Ennerdale Water, a large lake which drains the nearby mountains.

Writing about the Lake District, the romantic poet Wordsworth penned: "I do not know of any tract of country in which, in so narrow a compass, may be found an equal variety in the influences of light and shadow upon the sublime and beautiful."

Just as the trail started around the lake, I reached an odd rock formation at the water's edge called Robin Hood's Chair. I stopped and studied it a moment. I saw no resemblance to a chair ... or anything else, as far as that goes. Slipping around it, the path followed the lake clear to the end, a distance of three miles and a relatively straight forward hike. Once I reached the end I was presented with the first of several choices of routes; the most challenging of which passes over a famous mountain pass called High Stile. I opted for an easier choice; a slightly longer but more straight forward route. I felt it was still too early in the hike to take any chances.

The path continued through a long stretch of woods, Ennerdale Forest, and passed by Gillerwaithe hostel, where Jon had stayed the night before. There was no sign of him, he was long gone. I thought perhaps I would never see him again.

A bit further I passed Black Sail Hut, one of the remotest hostels in Europe. At this point you are deep into the Lake District and surrounded by dozens of famous high peaks: Pillar, Haycock, High Stile and Great Gable, to name a few.

Past Black Sail the route turned up a very steep and difficult path (called *fells* in this part of the world) named Loft Beck climbing from 1,100 feet to 2,000 feet in a relatively short distance. It was my first serious experience with a real fell and I found it quite difficult. Once you made it to the top, you were at Honister Pass and from there it was downhill all the way to the village of Rosthwaite.

Half-way up Loft Beck I ran out of water. I had planned to fill my canteen at Black Sail Hut – but it was closed when I arrived and would not open until later in the day. I had to press on. Even at this height there were ample signs of sheep. Against all best advice about avoiding water when sheep were around I paused by a little mountain stream and filled my water bottle knowing I'd not be able to make it much further before I had to have another drink.

When I finally reached the top I was able to look back the several miles I had come and see the entire length of Ennerdale Water – over ten miles in the distance.

British Royal Air Force jets on maneuvers were screaming down the valley hundreds of feet below me. It was quite a sight.

At the top I met a hiking couple sitting there admiring the view. They had seen me fill my water bottle and asked if I had anything with which to purify the water. When I told them I didn't, they graciously gave me a couple of water purification tablets to use — just in case. I'd seen Warning Signs of a nasty strain of some disease you can get from sheep in the area – and even though the odds were in my favor, I was glad for the extra protection.

The path down to Rosthwaite was terrible; very difficult and rough and I had to watch every step, especially at this point in the day when I was feeling tired and my legs became a bit rubbery. Eventually I arrived at the village of Seatoller and knew I was only a couple of miles from the Longthwaite hostel, my goal for the day.

It was exactly 4:00 p.m. when, as fate would have it, the path passed a lovely pub right on the route and I thought it would be an excellent opportunity to stop and rehydrate with a refreshing pint of ale. It was a lovely place for a break and I took full advantage of it, sitting and chatting with the locals. I considered returning later that evening.

When I finally arrived at the hostel, signed in and took a hot shower, I was finished. Exhausted. Done. It was after 5:00 by that time and I ran into Paul, another fellow that I met the first morning at the Outrigg House in St. Bees.

Before long, a surprise. Jon came straggling in so I decided to stay and eat with them rather than return to the pub. It seems Jon had taken one of the alternative high routes and had gotten lost in the mountains and had walked several miles out of his way. I would have collapsed and cried. He thought it was all terribly hilarious!

The price of the hostel really wasn't that much cheaper than staying at a B&B. What it did offer was the companionship of walkers like yourself who were willing to share information on the best places to see and stay. And I must say, the food was quite good.

Our evening meal started off with a bowl of thick vegetable soup, a couple of different types of salads and choice of entrées. I chose nut roast – which was like a large slice of roasted nut bread - very filling and well ... different. For dessert I had a traditional English dish called Sticky Toffee Pudding with Custard – which was like a hunk of the nut roast swimming in a bowl of caramel sauce. And of course, there was enough tea to float a ship. All a little bizarre, but good and "terribly nutritious" I was assured by Jon.

We finished eating around 8:00 and I was too beat to attempt the short walk back to the pub for a celebratory pint. Instead I rinsed out my underwear and socks and hung them up in a special drying room you found in all hostels and hit the sack.

In reality, that's what they give you when you sign in; a sleeping sack. You use it on the bunks in place of sheets and pillow cases. A little awkward at first, but very efficient.

The room to which I was assigned had four sets of bunk beds and since all bottom bunks were taken I got a top bunk.

The night passed about like you'd think. Lots of snorts, coughs and assorted body noises from my fellow hostlers. Not terrible, mind you – but not great, either. At one time or another during the night it seemed everyone got up to use the bathroom down the hall. The gent who was in the bunk below me was crippled, however, and used a plastic bottle while standing in the moonlight holding on to the side of the bed. Use your imagination.

Luckily I was so tired nothing much fazed me and despite everything I enjoyed a decent night's sleep.

Day Three
Rosthwaite to Grasmere

I lose my fear of the fells and march whistling into Wordsworth Country via Helm's Crag.

Dawn. Not wanting to chance a cold shower I climbed down from my bunk early and rushed to the bathroom. The sky looked clear so I put on a T–shirt and shorts and when the 8:00 a.m breakfast bell rang, I was at the front of the line. A bowl of Muselix, an extra large croissant with butter and jam, a scoop of yogurt, a pot of tea and I was raring to go.

I walked most of the day with Lisa and Simon, a young couple I met at dinner the night before. Lisa was a graduate student in genetics at the University of Nottingham and had an amazing likeness to Jessica Lange. Simon, her traveling companion, was a graduate student in textiles (I wasn't sure what that prepared him for and was afraid to ask).

The path we took circled around the village of Rosthwaite and headed quickly through the village of Stonethwaite before starting to climb almost immediately. Simon set a brisk pace but Lisa and I had to pause every 50 yards or so to rest and catch our breath. We used the gorgeous views back on Stonethwaite as an excuse – but there really was no hurry anyway. The total mileage for the next two days would only be 18 miles – so we had plenty of time to pace ourselves and enjoy the scenery.

Our maps indicated there was an alternate, more challenging route straight to Patterdale which was a little shorter – but not recommended in anything less than clear weather – and involved some very accurate map reading. Well, the weather was OK – but I'd already determined my map reading was anything but accurate so I decided to make this a two–day trip and make up the lost day later on. Wainwright's notes recommended the same thing. Sound advice I think.

The wind blew out of the east all day – directly into our faces and in exactly the opposite direction we anticipated. The higher we got – the colder it got. Finally I had to take off my damp T–shirt and pull on a dry long-sleeved shirt, sweater and gloves. For some reason my legs felt warm enough – so I continued wearing shorts (much to the amazement of Lisa and Simon who were both bundled up like Eskimos).

When we reached the peak – we ran into another small group of hikers and together we poured over our maps to be sure of the correct route before heading on.

The views were incredible – but it was extremely windy. We were at a place called Greenup Edge, at an elevation of around 2,000 feet. After another two miles scrambling up and down over loose shale we arrived at Far Easedale. From there you could look down into the valley and see the town of Grasmere – way off into the distance. The trail split again here. Straight ahead the route was downhill all the way. To the left was a ridge walk – a little harder and longer – but more spectacular. Since it was only noon, and since we had taken the easy route yesterday, we decided to take the ridge walk. It was a small gamble and turned out to be a good decision.

On we went, climbing over Calf Crag – Gibson Knott – and Helm Crag while looking down the steep mountain sides to the other path, several hundred feet below us. It was a great hike. We took our time – stopping to snack and enjoy the scenery as we inched our way along the narrow ridge line.

Somewhere along the way we got split up. Continuing alone I arrived at Butterlip How hostel at 2:00, the earliest arrival time yet. It was a lovely old Victorian mansion sitting high on a hill overlooking the town of Grasmere. I signed in and grabbed a lower bunk by the window in a huge bunk room. I was the first one there so had the place to myself. After showering, I headed to town.

Grasmere is a real tourist area – and the place was very crowded. Wainwright wrote: "Grasmere is a lovely village in a setting endowed with sylvan grace and dignity, beloved by artists and poets, and because of associations with Wordsworth, it is known internationally and has become a place of pilgrimage."

I stopped at a small shop and bought fresh batteries for my camera, some stamps and a candy bar. I always worry when the first thing I see in a town is postcard racks. There were plenty in Grasmere. I strolled through the twisted, narrow streets and stopped in the Lamb for a pint of stout and the opportunity to write some postcards.

Back on the street I ran into Jon who was shopping for a hiking staff like mine. There happened to be an excellent outdoor supply store in town that had a huge selection.

Shortly thereafter I ran into Beryl and Sue who had just arrived and looked exhausted. They were looking for a place to stay for the night – and were having trouble finding a room because of all the tourists. I wished them luck and headed back to the hostel for a nap.

Lisa and Simon were just checking in when I got back and I filled them in on what I had learned and we made plans to meet up later that night. I enjoyed a long nap and by 6:00 p.m. was ready to head back to town.

I found a delightful pub called Tweedies – and spied Lisa and Simon. I sat and had a pint with them but had seen a more interesting looking restaurant down the street and decided to go there for dinner. By the time I got there it was filled so I walked to the Lamb. It was filled. Back to Tweedies I went and the whole gang was there by this time – Lisa and Simon, Beryl and Sue, Jon and another couple, Derek and Charlie Redding whom I had passed on the trail the day before. They got a good laugh when I, the lone Yank, walked in – still looking for a place to eat.

I ordered a bowl of beef stew which tasted great – even with all the ribbing I received about catching Mad Cow Disease (Sounds humorous now but at the time it was a serious problem in Great Britain.) We stayed and joked around until 10:00 when we finally headed back to our respective lodgings.

The stars were out in full force which was handy as none of us had a torch with us. Beryl and Sue had found a place close by so we all walked back the lane together.

It had been a great day. Short but rich in superb scenery. And to have met such a great bunch of fellow walkers to eat and kid around with was just frosting on the cake. I was having a great time.

Day Four
Grasmere to Patterdale

Walking through some serious mountains
while sticking to the low road.

The walk from Grasmere to Patterdale was the shortest of the entire route – only eight miles. I didn't spot any of my new friends so I left by myself right after a breakfast of cereal, poached eggs, toast, juice and hot tea. Heading up the valley through town – and crossing a small highway – the path immediately began to climb toward Great Tongue. I choose the branch to the right and was soon joined by Jon, Lisa and Simon.

A couple of steep miles further we reached Grisedale Pass – and then Grisedale Tarn. (Tarns are small lakes. Lakes are called Waters). The climb had not been terribly difficult but you did have to watch every step. It was narrow and well–defined, but consisted mainly of loose scree – or small hunks of sharp edged shale.

The walking stick, by this time, had become a part of me and I used it as both a brace going down hill and a pushing stick going up hill. And I felt I was getting stronger.

At the end of Grisedale Tarn the path made a three–way split. The direct route went straight ahead. The famous Helvellyn alternative route split to the left and the newer St. Sunday Crag route split to the right. Both these alternatives are serious detours – stretching the trip only a couple of miles – but extending it by hours. We decided against them. The weather wasn't what you'd call bad, but it was misting and very windy. Higher up it could be quite dangerous.

As I think back upon it, I wish I had taken one of the harder routes just to say I had done it. At the time, however, it was still early enough in my trip to be concerned about being able to finish. And I was still a little in awe of the strain and difficulty of fell climbing.

We skirted around the edge of the tarn and came upon a small group of tents. They were set up in a formation much like a wedge of geese with the lead tent facing down the valley and into the wind which was whistling up through and around them. I couldn't imagine what it must have been like trying to sleep in them. It had to be impossible to get a fire going. You could hardly talk it was so windy. Up on the high trails you could see other hikers struggling along.

We continued down past the tents, past Dollywaggon Pike, Ruthwaite Lodge and Eagle Crag ... down, down, down to the village of Patterdale, a lovely descent.

It was misting as Jon and I entered the village together. Lisa and Simon had fallen somewhere behind us. We stopped at the post office and bought ice cream bars and continued on to Goldrill House, a purpose built hostel, where we arrived by 2:00.

The hostel was originally designed and constructed as a hostel, thus purpose built as they say. Most other hostels are old converted barns, mansions, or churches, etc. This one was great, very roomy and modern and built in the woods on the edge of town beside a deep, clear river. My assigned room was very large and had eight bunks and only three people were staying there.

After a long, hot shower I walked back to the village and into the White Lion for a hand–pumped pint of local ale and a pack of fresh, packaged nuts; the kind you found everywhere in England.

The White Lion was wonderful, filled with dark woods, old photographs, shiny mirrors and lots of leaded glass windows looking out over the lake and mountains. Like most pubs, it featured several snug little rooms lined with chairs and tables just inviting people to come and sit and tell their stories.

Michael Joseph's book regarding this section of the walk reads: "Patterdale ranks in the same high class as Borrowdale, Buttermere, Wasdale Head and Great Langdale in the magnificence of its surroundings. Encompassed by rugged heights and having the lovely lake of Ullswater as a nearby amenity, it is blessed with the typical atmosphere and character of Lakeland. Little has changed to destroy its charm. Visitors here are mainly of the walking and mountaineering fraternity and there are no cheap attractions to delay rubbernecked sightseers. A sojourn here, even if only overnight, is pure delight for lovers of mountain scenery. Patterdale is truly Alpine."

Later that evening, after a wonderful nap, I returned to the pub. The air was crisp and the narrow road damp and slippery with mist. By the side of the road was one of those delightful, red English phone booths and I stopped to call my wife, Lois, to report my progress. The call went through immediately. It was 9:00 p.m. here and 3:00 p.m. home in Iowa.

The White Lion was definitely the place to be that evening; misty and chilly outside, inside it was glowing with warmth and conversation. Two fireplaces were burning. I settled in and ordered a medicinal Jameson Irish Whiskey while I chatted with the local gentry.

Soon Lisa and Simon came in and joined me and we ordered dinner. I had a bowl of pea and ham soup, a mixed salad, and a thick stew of steak chunks simmered in Guinness, with onions, potatoes and carrots. For dessert I splurged with a piece of fresh raspberry pie and ice cream. A disgraceful pig-out but how wonderful it was.

Soon Jon showed up, and Beryl and Sue soon after, and a couple of chaps from Cheshire, Bob Lovatt and Kevin Nairn. Bob is in his fifties, I would guess, and a very decent fellow. Kevin, a younger man in his late twenties was carrying a large pack and was camping the whole way. I first met him at the Old Vicarage in Ennerdale Bridge when he was setting up in the yard.

Finally, in the door came Derek and Charlie Redding, from London, a thirty-something couple we had run into from time to time. I was the lone Yank and a character of intrigue to the rest who were all somewhat curious why someone would come all the way from America to do the walk. I do believe it pleased them.

After the usual light-hearted discussion about the day's walk, the topic of conversation turned to tomorrow's route. The official word was our honeymoon with the weather was coming to an end! Tomorrow was supposed to turn rainy, cold and nasty and the walk would be the longest day yet, 16 miles to the town of Shap.

More seriously, it was going to cross the highest point of the route – Kidsty Pike at 2,570 feet. By that time we all knew that in bad weather, visibility could very quickly drop to zero and it was easy to get lost.

Detailed maps were spread out over tables. Key compass points were written down. Locals came over and shook their heads and clucked to each other. Lots of opinions and options were discussed and, in the end, everyone sort of made up their own minds and headed back to their warm beds.

Oh well, it had been a restful day and the meal truly memorable. Tomorrow was a long way off.

Day Five
Patterdale to Shap

*We pick an alternate route up and over Kidsty
Pike – and into a bloody gale force wind.*

I awoke at 7:00 and quickly ate breakfast. Juice, hot porridge
and a cup of cocoa. The night before I had decided to skip the
community breakfast so I could get an early start.

On my way back to my room, I ran into Jon talking to Lisa
and Simon. They had been studying various maps and had come
up with an alternative route – was I interested in joining forces
and walking together? You bet!

We left by 9:00. It was dry but very windy. We were soon joined
by Harry, a sturdy looking hiker from northern England, right on
the border of Scotland. I *really* had a hard time understanding
his strong English-Scottish accent.

Instead of heading straight up the mountain and risking
missing one of the many tricky turns, we headed out of town
along the river to a nearby, tiny village before turning uphill on
an animal path that we were assured joined the main path en
route to Kidsty Pike. The climb was very hard, ascending from
approximately 500 feet to 2,000 feet in a relatively short
distance.

About half way to the top we passed Haweswater, a beautiful,
lonely looking mountain lake. As with most of the countryside
through which we have been traveling, the hills were dotted with
sheep – but there was very little foliage.

We climbed for at least three hours before we could see, off in
the distance, other hikers coming down the main trail from our
left. It would be some time before we joined up – but it looked
like Beryl and Sue along with Bob and Kevin. After a few days
you began to recognize hikers by the size and color of their packs.

Later we learned Derek and Charlie had taken a completely
different route – around the mountain – longer but safer and a
bit quicker.

By this time of day, everyone had put on windbreakers, hats and gloves. The wind, if possible, had gotten even stronger since we started out, but thank God there was still no rain. The visibility was still okay by the time we joined up and continued together up to Kidsty Pike, the highest point along the entire trail.

It was very difficult to stand erect because of the strength of the wind. Everyone was walking – leaning at around a 60 degree angle. The views were powerful. We stopped at the summit for group pictures and quickly headed on. In the distance, you could see the famous High Street route – but no one was foolish enough to try it today. Far below us was the immense Haweswater Reservoir — the agreed upon destination for our lunch stop.

As usual, going down was harder than going up. One wrong turn and you could easily twist an ankle or knee or worse. In addition the path was covered with slippery sharp stones and if you slipped and fell you would surely gash yourself. My knees, in particular my right knee, was starting to hurt from the constant pressure I was putting on it even though relying heavily on my walking staff.

I heard that if you were injured and unable to continue, you were either carried out by volunteers – or lifted out by helicopter – at your expense. Ouch.

We arrived at the reservoir around 1:00. Both legs were really bothering me by this time so I popped a couple of Excedrin. My lunch was very simple – as it was every day – an apple, a hunk of local cheese, a Scottish oat bar and a Snickers. And canteen water, of course. For some reason hard exercise like this was not making me very hungry. Perhaps that's why I ended up losing eight pounds by the end of the trip, something I'd never done on RAGBRAI, the annual bike ride across Iowa I participate in every year.

The five-mile path along the reservoir seemed very long. Although it didn't climb much higher, it was rough and steep in short spurts. Finally we reached the dam at the end and took a break by a lovely, old stone bridge, Packhorse Bridge, an ancient thing hundreds of years old. By this time it was 3:00 and the walking had become much easier – but the directions had become harder to follow. A few times we were all stumped and had to take several compass bearings to be sure we were headed the right way. We didn't leave until there was some kind of consensus.

At 4:30 in the afternoon – we arrived at Shap Abbey, a monastic religious house built in the twelfth and thirteenth centuries to serve the nearby town of the same name. Simon and Lisa decided to stop and snoop around while the rest of us continued into town finally arriving at 5:00, feeling beat up and very tired.

This was about as late as one would want to arrive at their evening's destination in this part of England at this time of year. By 5:00 the sun was already slipping below the hills behind us. In another hour or so, it would be dreadfully dark.

Shap has been notorious amongst road travelers since stagecoach days. For centuries it had been a main, although dangerous, traffic artery to Scotland. When the M6 motorway opened in 1970, Shap became quiet overnight. The economy of the village is now largely based on the huge, local granite works and limestone quarries.

My lodging was the Rookery Guest House which was right at the edge of the village as we entered. I was the only one staying there. The others were scattered along the long, narrow street that ran from one edge of the village to the other.

My room was quaint, clean but very small – with a shared bath. I desperately wanted a shower – but couldn't figure how to get the ancient thing to work. There were a series of knobs and levers and ropes to manipulate. Finally I gave up and used another bathroom where there was a large, old iron tub.

After resting and cleaning up I headed down the main street to the Crown for a pint and some peanuts. We had made plans to meet there around 7:00 but when no one arrived by 7:15 I started back and ran into them huddled around the village green discussing that very thing. New plans were underway and they were about to send a runner to get me when I showed up. The Greyhound was now the place to go.

Of course, the Greyhound was on the opposite end of the village but was supposed to have the best food and everyone would be there. We were turning into a pack of Vikings.

The Greyhound was, indeed, a popular place. A large wooden sign was hanging outside and looked very old: a lanky, gray Greyhound in mid-stride. It was lighted by a gas lantern.

Another pint, a huge salad and a plate of what they called lasagna and I was on the mend. Everyone had arrived in one piece and was congratulating each other on making it through the rugged Lake District, which had officially ended at Shap Abbey.

A lot of fun that evening revolved around discussions of what happened to people who took shortcuts — or skipped any of the major sights Wainwright pointed out along the route.

Legend suggests that what these laggards could expect was a midnight visit by the dreaded "Wainwright Police" which meant you would wake up in your warm snug bed and find yourself surrounded by a group of Keystone–like cops holding burning pitch torches.

"OK, laddie, up we go," they'd say in grating voices. "Pull on the trousers and boots now. It's back outside for the likes of ye. Took a shortcut across the corner of the field at East Applegarth Farm this morning did ye? Well now, we can't have that, can we? The route's plainly marked there, isn't it now? So it's back we go, laddie, and step lively now. It's back to the farm to do it right this time!" ... and then you'd be dragged kicking and screaming out into the cold and rainy night. Sounded dreadful. But hilarious to hear my trail mates recite the punishment in their best "old English."

After dinner we headed back the mile or so to the other end of the village, the road lighted by an occasional gas lamp. Along the way we came upon a hedgehog waddling cross the road.

"Oh dear," exclaimed Sue, "we must rescue it before it gets flattened by a lorry." She rushed over and scooped it up and safely deposited it in a nearby garden.

I'd never seen a hedgehog before and insisted on taking a picture of her holding it. Everyone got a kick out of that. I suppose it would be the equivalent of them taking a picture of me holding one of our squirrels or rabbits.

I let myself in the Rookery Guest House and barely got under the covers before I fell asleep. What a good night's rest I had.

Day Six
Shap to Kirkby Stephen

The day I leave behind the lovely hills of the Lake District, enter the Yorkshire Dales ... and promptly get lost.

The distance from Shap to Kirkby Stephen is 20 miles, the farthest day's hike yet. With this in mind I arranged to have breakfast an hour early so I could get a flying start and be on the road by 8:15. This would be my earliest departure time yet. I would always have liked to have left earlier but it was difficult to do so without missing breakfast which was normally served at 9:00.

Regarding the country that lay ahead my guidebook read: "The limestone landscape ahead is rarely visited and relatively unknown, almost a blank on the map, yet for the observant a region of immense fascination. Walkers with archaeological and antiquarian interests and students of prehistory may well consider the next twenty miles the most rewarding of all: the ancient Britons had a great liking for this part of the Westmorland and left behind a display of settlements and villages, burial mounds, stone circles and tumuli in amazing profusion."

As fate would have it, the sights I most wanted to see I missed — and the ones forbidden to visit I found with ease.

I headed off by myself and managed to keep up a solid pace, at least for the first hour or so, but then somehow or other I missed a turn and before I knew it I was way out in the middle of a rough moor with no path of any kind in sight. One moment I was right on course – and the next, lost as a lark.

Sadly I managed to miss Robin Hood's Grave (even though he's really not buried there), a wonderful stone circle near the little hamlet of Oddendale, a Roman road, and a few scattered tumuli (grave mounds). But what I did stumble upon was a famous monument called Black Dub ... located on forbidden ground because it rests in a sensitive conservation area. There stands a large obelisk with the inscription: "Here at Black Dub, the source of the Livennet, King Charles II regaled his army and drank of the water on his march from Scotland. August 8, 1651."

Aha! Black Dub was on my map so I at least knew where I was – and that I wasn't supposed to be there. The bigger problem was I still wasn't sure how to get back on route.

I took a reading on what I believed was the right direction and headed off. I was hoping to get to the town of Orton where I'd find someplace open and get something to eat.

Soon I came upon and surprised a couple of local bird watchers out on a hike. I'm sure they were wondering where I had come from. They pointed me in the right direction and it turned out I really hadn't wandered that far out of the way, perhaps a mile is all, so no real damage done.

Good news. The New Village Tea Room in Orton was empty when I arrived – but open. Yea! I ordered a pot of tea and biscuits and settled in by a small fire. Unbelievably, the fair weather was still holding with only an occasional misty rain. But the wind remained constant out of the east ... contrary to how it was supposed to behave.

On the edge of town, in the middle of a farmer's field, there was a wonderful stone circle. I hoisted myself up on a fence to take a picture of it when Derek and Charlie came strolling by from another direction — the correct direction. We joined up for several miles until we stopped for lunch hunkered down beside a stone fence to get out of the wind.

We were sitting there eating when Jon, Lisa and Simon came strolling down the road and joined us. Just like old home week.

We all continued on together – soon passing through an ancient archaeological settlement site called the Severals. (Now there's a strange name.) It's considered a key archeological site and one of the most remarkable in Britain; a complex of stone–walled fields, hutments, dykes and pathways extending over a considerable area. Man lived here in ancient times as a community where no men now live and few men today ever come. To me, the most fascinating thing is that not one part of the entire area has ever been excavated!

Just beyond the Severals are a series of large, rectangular untouched mounds known as pillow mounds – and listed as Giants Graves on maps. To this day no one is quite sure what they are – and what their purpose ever was. Another mystery crying for a spade.

We arrived in Kirkby Stephen at 5:30, later than yesterday and it was near dark. It was a long day of steady walking over relatively easy terrain.

Jon and Lisa and Simon were staying at the local hostel which happened to be a converted church. I had decided to splurge and stay in the King's Arms Hotel – right in the middle of the village. We split up and made plans to meet there for dinner later that night. Terribly convenient, wouldn't you say?

Kirky Stephen is an old market town of pre–Norman origin. A prolonged main thoroughfare gives the impression of a larger town than it really is – but it only extends around a mile, and has little width, the River Eden forming a close boundary on one side.

The King's Arms was ancient and classy. My room was on the second floor overlooking the square. Down the wide halls was a huge bathroom with a monstrous, claw foot, cast iron tub. I soaked long and hard – and later rinsed out my socks and underwear.

Suitably refreshed I walked down the huge spiral staircase into the pub and ordered an appetizer of Brie cheese and crackers and a pint of bitters. I couldn't wait, I was famished. About the time I was finishing – the rest of the group started wandering in and reported on the pros and cons of their respective night's lodging. Eventually the whole gang showed up; Beryl and Susan, Kevin and Bob, Jon, Lisa and Simon. Everyone was starving. I had steak and mushroom pie – savory and delicious.

It was Jon's last night with us. He was planning to stay over and take a railroad trip on a vintage steam engine through the countryside the next day.

That evening everyone took advantage of the sad situation by acting goofy. For example, one of the things they insisted on was teaching the Yank (me) more suitable slang for the rest of my stay in England before I set off on my own. But try as hard as I could, I had difficulty learning the finer points of difference between such useful phrases as, *Sod All* and *Sod Off* ... and *Short Shrift* and *Bugger Off* and *Not on your Sweet Fanny Adams*. The lessons, although lost on me, seemed to be a cause for great hilarity among the locals listening in.

At some point during the evening I was officially given the title, *Sod Off*.

As the night progressed, and the pints flowed, my friends wanted to teach me various, interesting ways to announce when one was going to the visit the *loo* (restroom). I learned, for example, that one could say that one wished ... *to go point Percy at the Porcelain*. Or one could say one was on his way ... *to Shake Hands with the Vicar* ... or *to Wring Out His Socks*, and so forth. I'm sure you get the picture.

If you'll pardon the pun, things quickly got out of hand and before we knew it everyone in the crowded pub was joining in and yelling out their favorite expressions.

With my head swimming in *Englishisms* I *buggered off* to bed around 10:00!

Day Seven
Kirkby Stephen to Richmond

The day we bid Jon farewell
and head into the wilderness again.

Despite the lorry traffic that passed by my window all night I still enjoyed a decent night's sleep. After a hearty breakfast I found all the gang milling around in front of the hotel. Even Jon had come to see us off. I was going to miss his droll wit and good humor and it was sad to say goodbye realizing I'd probably never see him again.

The Coast-to-Coast's official halfway point is Keld (95 miles). Today's route, from Kirkby Stephen to Keld, is a distance of 13 miles. However, since I was already a day behind I needed to make up a half day today – and a half day tomorrow. I needed to go further – clear to Gunnerside if I could manage it.

With Jon standing in front of the King's Arms waving us off, the rest of us headed out of town stopping briefly to visit the parish church of St. Stephen and continued over Frank's Bridge (*Franks's* Bridge?) We soon passed through the nearby, picturesque village of Hartley at which point the trail immediately began a long, three mile ascent out of the valley up the side of a barren mountain thick with boggy moors. We were heading toward Nine Standards Rigg.

You could see them from quite a distance away, standing as if on watch along the ridge. Nine very tall rock cairns. There are many theories about the origins of the Nine Standards, as is usually the case when the truth is not known. Certainly they are very old, appearing on eighteenth century maps and giving their name to the hill they adorn. They occupy a commanding position overlooking the Eden Valley, thus giving rise to the legend they were built to give the marauding Scots the impression an English army was encamped here. More likely they were ancient boundary makers or beacons.

The ridge they occupy is the main watershed of the walk; sort of like the U.S. Continental Divide. Up to this point all the streams and rivers I had been crossing flowed back the way I had come; west to the Irish Sea. From this point on, they would flow east to the North Sea.

As we reached the top we were again stunned by the force of the wind whipping over the summit from the east. We hunkered down behind the cairns long enough to put on hats, gloves and windbreakers before heading down the other side.

There was very little trail to be seen along this hard, barren ground. Rather there were infrequent wooden posts stuck in infrequent patches of boggy ground generally marking the right direction. It was altogether a frightening place. In the rain and snow, it would be very dangerous and easy to get turned around and headed off in the wrong direction.

In a few miles, however, the route opened up to the lush countryside typical of the Yorkshire Dales we had entered and would continually be crossing the next few days.

The rest of the path to Keld was a gentle downhill, cross country walk until we arrived at the edge of the tiny village at 2:30.

The hostel, a converted old shooting lodge, was at the corner leading into the village. It was there I said goodbye to Lisa and Simon and walked across the bridge into the village with Beryl and Sue for a cup of tea before I headed on alone. Already arrived were Kevin, Bob, Derek and Charlie and we had a final chat before I bid them farewell and headed up the river valley.

After seven days it was sad to be leaving them – and I knew I'd miss them all. They turned out to be wonderful companions and great fun to be with. It was particularly difficult realizing I'd most likely never see any of them ever again. However tempting it was to stay with them, I had to keep moving.

At Keld, the path merged with another popular long distance walk called The Pennine Way. I joined it for a few miles following along the River Swale as it headed toward he village of Reeth. I met a few people walking it before it branched off and I was alone again.

The countryside really opened up at this point of the trip and became quite lush and lovely. The gently sloping hills looked as manicured as a golf course, with long rows of perfect stone fences winding off into the distance. And it was along this stretch that I first came across pheasant, grouse and rabbits by the hundreds scampering across the landscape with great abandon. I was so stunned I sat and ate my lunch while watching them. They showed little concern with my presence. It was as if I'd wandered onto a Walt Disney movie set.

The path follows the Swale River clear to the town of Richmond, tomorrow's destination. The Swale is one of the swiftest flowing rivers in England and ranks among its loveliest, winding through a pleasant countryside and adding charm to the beauty of the surroundings.

In a few miles I came to Muker, a lovely little country village with a church, tea house and a typical, laid back, country pub. As I had not yet arranged for a place to stay that night I decided to stop in for a pint and look for a B&B in the area. I had gone around 15 miles at this point and needed to find a place soon.

Because it was the weekend, I had no luck finding anything in town but when I called Oxnop Hall, a farm in the area that takes on lodgers, I was told they had a double room for $35. It was more than I wanted to pay – but I was running out of options and I took it.

Oxnop Hall was in an area called Low Oxnop – not even a hamlet – but a centuries old, family farm just off the route and a couple of miles further down the trail.

Realizing I wouldn't be coming back to Muker after dark, I stayed for another pint and a platter of assorted cheeses and crackers to tide me over until breakfast. The pub was friendly and hosted several small groups of local day walkers pouring over maps. Everyone somehow knew I was a Coast–to–Coaster, and a Yank, to boot, so I received polite smiles and ta's when I finally left shortly after 5:00.

The walk to Low Oxnop was magical. The late afternoon sun cast lovely shadows across the patchwork meadows and stone fences and the rampant screeching of pheasant and grouse was strange to my city ears.

The farm itself was perched on the side of a hill overlooking the valley. Typical of all rural buildings in this part of England, it was constructed entirely of fieldstone and appeared ancient. This particular farm, I later learned, dated back to the 1650s.

I arrived just as it was getting dark and was met at the door by Annie Porter who was afraid I had missed the turn into the farm and was about to come looking for me. She led me to a spotless little room overlooking the courtyard. I even had my own shower and bath. The service tray, which you find in all B&Bs, was filled with biscuits and all types of powdered hot drinks from which to choose.

I cleaned up and took a walk around the property – which was extensive and had many outbuildings — all of which were in excellent shape. The barns, for example, were monstrous – and solidly constructed to last several more centuries, at least.

The view from the front of the house spread out across the Swale Valley and reminded me of a scene from the movie, *How Green Was My Valley*. I half expected to see Roddy McDowell and Maureen O'Sullivan coming hand in hand across the distant fields.

However, once the sun set, it got dark as pitch. I went into the parlor to read for a while and work on my trip notes until I almost fell asleep by the small coke fire burning there. As I got up to return to my room I accidentally knocked over a small lamp and broke the shade. Damn. What was that going to cost me, I wondered, as I quietly tiptoed up to my room.

Day Eight
Low Oxnop to Richmond

My first full day hiking by myself –
lonely and full of pitfalls.

At breakfast I asked Mrs. Porter how far it was to Reeth. She told me she didn't know!

She didn't know? How could this be? You'd think that living in the area for over 350 years you'd have an idea how far the next town was. Even I knew it was just up the road and the largest settlement in the area. How could *she* not know?

After checking my map I saw it was around seven miles. Should I inform her of that fact? Nah – let her live in ignorance. One too many Sticky Toffee Puddings, that one. I wasn't going to Reeth anyway – I was going on to Richmond and had a 17 mile journey ahead of me. Better get going.

The night before I had left a note with the broken shade – and neatly stacked all the broken pieces on the mantle. I told Mrs. Porter how sorry I was and she clucked not to worry one tiny bit but the charge would be $6. Hmm. She knew how much to charge for the miserable lamp shade – but she didn't know how far it was to Reeth? But she was a lovely hostess anyway.

The day was bright and beautiful. I couldn't believe my continuing good luck. Gunnerside was the first village I came to and I quickly passed through it. People going to the church along the road smiled and nodded at me as I passed by. On I went along a relatively flat route on a combination of tarmac and pathways. Around 11:30 I reached the outskirts of Reeth.

Reeth is the capital of upper Swaledale and occupies an open hillside overlooking the confluence of the Arkle Beck and Swale rivers. I stopped at a small grocer's in the village and bought a hunk of wonderful, local, cranberry cheese, a couple of hard rolls and chunk of cake for dessert. They refilled my water bottle. I still had over 10 miles to go so kept on walking to Marrick Priory, another two and a half miles.

Marrick Priory was established in the twelfth century and occupied by Benedictine nuns until it was dissolved by Henry VIII. Today it's become a sad ruin except for the tower which still looks intact. New buildings have been added for use as an Adventure Centre. When I arrived, there were teams of older children playing bonding games similar to what they teach in Outward Bound schools. I sat and watched for a while before continuing into the village.

It was almost 1:00 p.m. when I arrived and came upon another one of those great red phone booths. I decided to call Lois and report in. Again my call went though immediately – but I had forgotten the time difference – it was only 7:00 a.m. Iowa time and I woke her up. Oops.

By afternoon the day turned cloudy and cool and I was sure rain wasn't far behind so I kept plugging away until I reached another hidden little village, Marske, and sat on a small park bench and ate my lunch – sharing it with a curious calico cat and a stray Jack Russell Terrier, a breed very common to the area.

The rest of the day was pleasant enough, with some gentle ups and downs and the constant presence of game birds everywhere. This was particularly true in an area called Whitcliffe Wood. Here the narrow trail passed through the middle of a very dense stand of forest and continued a long, long way while the cackle of pheasants around me calling to one another was non–stop. I doubt I will ever witness anything like it again.

Just before coming in sight of Richmond, I passed under Willance's Leap, not a spectacular precipice as the name might suggest but, according to Wainwright: "... were it not associated with an occurrence in 1606 when Robert Willance fell down the steep slope here while riding, his horse being killed. Robert survived and grateful for his deliverance, gave to the town of Richmond, as a thank offering, a silver chalice, preserved to this day as one of the town's many treasures."

I strolled into Richmond just after 5:00 p.m. and headed immediately for the town square. Seventeen and a half miles in just over eight hours – right on schedule – two miles an hour.

Richmond appeared packed with visitors as I walked around looking over the hotels and pubs. The Talbot, right on the square was priced right so I took a room. My accommodation guide, a necessary tool available to all hikers for a small fee, indicated the price would be $23 but the owner said, no, $25 was the current price. I didn't argue. I should have.

Richmond, with its population of 7,000, is large enough to qualify as the only actual town on the walk. The British Council recently selected it as the typical English market town because of its resistance to modern change (including hotel improvements, I would add.)

In 1071, Norman invaders built Richmond Castle there, an impressive tower or keep guarding the entrance to military buildings within a massive defensive wall. The castle is dramatically poised on a cliff high above the River Swale, and is a monstrous structure. As it was Sunday, it closed at 5:00 and I just missed the chance to tour the grounds but was still able to walk around the cobbled, winding and narrows streets that still surround it.

The pub in the Talbot was dirty and filled with foul–mouthed young people. As I sat nursing my first pint of the day I was toying with the idea of just walking out and finding another place. But I didn't. The man whom I assumed was the owner was trying to get things under control and didn't want to lose the business – he looked rather young and anxious so I stayed. My room overlooked the square and was plainer than plain. The bed had loose springs and the hallways were dark and dingy.

But (and this is important) the water in the bathroom was hot and plentiful – and it looked like I had the whole second floor to myself so I figured I could survive for one night.

Around 6:30 I went out and began looking for a place for dinner. I stopped at the Black Lion Hotel just to check it out and enjoyed a pint of local bitters and watched part of a soccer game. It was also rather empty so I left and finally settled on an Indian restaurant; very common throughout England.

The Shahi Raj was an upstairs affair and the smells drifting out into the street were marvelous. I ordered a glass of red wine and one of the evening specials – a grilled plate of lamb and chicken, a little spicy but not bad, and Indian vegetables and dessert. It was excellent and a welcome change to the rather bland food I had been dining on the last several days.

I ate dinner alone for the first time and I really missed the friendly, good-natured banter of the others. I finished early, walked around town a little and headed back to the Talbot around 8:00. Things had quieted down for the night so I stayed at the bar and sipped a Jameson Irish and watched the *telly* for a while.

But I was tired and oddly enough felt a little uncomfortable in the large city surroundings. Already I was looking forward to heading out in the morning to the quiet of the countryside.

Tomorrow would be the longest day of the entire walk – 23 miles – and I needed a good night's sleep. It was hard to believe I had come as far as I had. And other than dearly missing my trail friends, I was still having a marvelous time.

Day Nine
Richmond to Ingleby Cross

A very, very, very, very, very long walk.
Very long.

The Talbot's owner's wife, a young and very pleasant young woman, fixed me a hearty breakfast and was very embarrassed about the pub crowd that was in the night before. It seems she and her husband had recently bought the hotel and were slowly making improvements. It was hard for them and they appreciated me staying with them so I'm glad I stuck it out. Three sausages, a thick slice of ham, fried bread and fried eggs, toast, coffee, beans and fried tomatoes. Whew!

By 8:30 I was on my way, walking down steep, slippery cobblestones that passed beside the castle walls and across Richmond Bridge and into the low country that splits the Yorkshire Dales and the Cleveland Hills.

This area of England is known as the Vale of Mowbray – a lush, flat farm countryside – with nary a hill in sight. Wainwright wrote: "Don't bother to clean your boots before leaving Richmond. There is mud, glorious mud, ahead."

Mud or not I established a brisk pace and reached the village of Catterick Bridge, a distance of around four miles, before 10:00. Originally a Roman settlement known as *Cataractonium*, there are still sections of the old Roman embankment running along the river by the bridge.

A few miles further I arrived at the hamlet of Bolton–On–Swale where, in St. Mary's Churchyard, is buried the famous Henry Jenkins.

And who might Henry Jenkins be you ask? Ah, Henry Jenkins, believe it or not, was born in nearby Ellerton in 1500 and died in 1670 at the tender age of 169 years!

Mystified after I saw his monument in the village green, erected by public contribution in 1743, I went into the church to read the large marble plaque placed there:

"Blush not marble to rescue from oblivion the memory of HENRY JENKINS: A Person obscure in birth, but of a Life truly memorable for He was Enriched with the goods of Nature and happy in the duration if not variety of his Enjoyments and tho the partial world despised or disregarded his low and humble state, The Equal Eye of Providence beheld and blessed it with a Patriarch's Health and Length of days to teach mistaken men these blessings were Entailed on Temperance Or a life of Labour and a mind at Ease. He lived to the amazing age of 169 was interred here December 6, 1670 and had this justice done to his memory."

Well now, there's an epitaph for you.

Fortified by the knowledge that I also could easily live an additional 100 years, I departed St. Mary's and marched on with renewed vigor.

By mid–afternoon I reached Danby Wiske and came upon a famous watering hole along the route – *The White Swan Inn* – where I stopped for a cup of tea and the opportunity to sign the Coast–to–Coast guest book. There were three other hikers resting there. Two were headed the opposite way, and the third, who I didn't meet at that time, ended up finishing the trip with me several days later.

I don't recall much spectacular about the rest of the day – except it was long. Did I already say that? Long?

Wainwright also wrote about this stretch: "If you are fond of placid rural scenery and have an interest in farming, you might enjoy this section of the walk; but if your preference is for high ground and rough hills, you will find this tedious."

He was right.

I think the most exciting thing that happened to me was when I was walking down a very narrow, mile–long lane lined with poplar trees. Halfway down the lane I heard a truck engine behind me and when I turned to look I was surprised to see a rural library van swiftly bearing down on me. The sides of the van were brushing the trees on both sides of the lane. I quickly squashed myself as far back as I could between the trees as the lorry lurched by with inches to spare and without slowing down a bit. Hadn't the idiot driver seen me? That was close.

By the time I reached A19, a very busy North–South freeway, I had walked over 22 miles and was absolutely whipped. The traffic was zooming by at a very high speed and I had a devil of a time properly timing my crossing. I couldn't get my legs to run – and even had trouble getting them to move faster than a brisk walk. Finally I managed to scoot across during a short lull in the traffic. Whew!

Just beyond the highway was my destination, the twin hamlets of Ingleby Arncliffe and Ingleby Cross. And just beyond them, the hills of the Cleveland Way.

By a huge measure of luck I had made a reservation to stay at a B&B called the Monk's House. It was right along the path as I entered the village. I had called from Richmond the night before and Elsie Backhouse, the owner, told me not to arrive before 5:00 as "... she would be occupied until then." Well, it was well after 5:00 and almost dark and I was bushed – and thank God, she was there waiting for me.

The Monk's House was a gem. By far the best place I stayed on the entire trip and I stayed in some fine places. The oldest home in the area, it had been built in the 1300s to serve the religious community, many of whom died when the bubonic plaque swept across Europe in the fourteenth century! It looked like "the enchanted cottage" and Snow White's house rolled into one. And it was in immaculate condition.

I had half of the building to myself.

Downstairs was a very cozy study, a bath, dining room and kitchen. Upstairs were two lovely bedrooms of which I had my pick. Mrs. Backhouse was extremely neat and gracious and immediately ushered me into the study, which was stuffed with travel books and over 600 Teddy bears (her count, not mine!) She sat me down by a burning fire and served a pot of hot tea and a generous slice of homemade chocolate cake swimming in fresh cream. Wow. A hard place to beat for $23.

"Please use as much hot water as you can," she said. "The pipes are fairly sizzling!"

To my credit I did the best I could – soaking my weary limbs in the tub for a long, long time – and damn near scalding myself in the bargain. She wasn't kidding. The pipes were filled more with steam than water.

Nothing like a hot bath to get you feeling like a normal human being again. It always amazes me how quickly your body recuperates after a hot soak.

Feeling 100% better, I changed into my semi-clean set of clothes and walked down the lane to the Blue Bell Inn for dinner. Of course the place was ancient and very crowded. I met a couple of Canadians and several other Coast–to–Coasters who were also heading east. They had allowed 17 days to my 12 and were using the Pack Horse Service folks, who for a semi–reasonable sum of money, will pick up and deliver your luggage from stop to stop. A very civilized idea I thought – no wonder these people looked so fresh. Today they had only walked nine miles and hadn't had to carry anything except water and cameras. I, on the other hand, had walked 23 miles carrying a pack.

I ordered a pint of local ale, a fresh garden salad and hearty bowl of beef stew. Too late I noticed they had wild boar on the menu. Damn! I wished I had seen it earlier so I could have ordered it. How many places do you find wild boar on the menu?

My knees were killing me as I walked very slowly back to the Monk's House. Before turning in I called ahead for reservations for the next two nights so I wouldn't have to worry about it later. My legs were feeling very tired – and now my feet had also begun to hurt. But no wonder, I had walked 23 miles in nine hours ... averaging 2.6 mph. Way too fast, I thought. I won't do that again. Tomorrow's distance would only be around 14 miles — shorter but hillier.

By 9:30 I was in my big, warm, fluffy bed quickly falling asleep. I hoped the Teddy bears behaved themselves. Nine and a half hours sleep ahead. Yea!

Day Ten
Ingleby Cross to Clay Bank Top

Not much at Clay Bank Top except a parcel of ghosts.

Regarding the stretch of walk I faced today Wainwright wrote: "... this is the finest section of our marathon (outside Lakeland) – a splendid high–level traverse along the escarpment of the Cleveland Hills: beautiful country with far–reaching views. It is also the start of the long crossing of the North York Moors stretching the final 50 miles from here to the coast, heather clad, unenclosed, uninhabited and remote from industry and noise."

Mrs. Backhouse was in the kitchen when I came downstairs, slightly groggy from my long night's rest. She fixed me a wondrous breakfast of scrambled eggs (first time for that), several thick slices of local ham, fresh juice and, of course, hot cereal, toast, marmalade and coffee.

Okay, I thought – bring on those "splendid high–level traverses!"

By 9:00 I was packed and on my way. I took a few photos of the Monk's House and even talked Mrs. Backhouse into posing for me in front of her home. A great stop.

Within minutes I was through the village and beginning the climb into the Cleveland Hills. What I didn't realize at the time was there were five hills I would have to negotiate before day's end. For some naive reason or other I thought I was done with the mountains – hills – fells – whatever. Was I wrong!

A steep forest path climbed past Mount Grace Priory, a fourteenth century monastery built high on the side of the mountain. There I met the Canadian and English couples from the evening before. We chatted for a minute and I learned that all of us would be staying at the same farm house that evening.

The Canadian offered me an extra map showing the way to the farm from Clay Bank Top. I was happy to get it. It was off the route and I was unsure of the direction.

I reached the peak, Beacon Hill, 1,000 feet in elevation, in short order and entered the high moors. Then I climbed down to Scugdale. Then I climbed up to Live Moor, 1,025 feet. Then I went down to Holey Moor. Then I climbed to Carlton Moor, 1,338 feet. And so it went throughout the day. Up and down. Up and down. Beautiful, yes, but very tiring on legs which were beginning to whimper, "Hey, what's going on here? Let's take a break, old man."

Parts of this section of the walk are also shared by two other long distance paths. One is the Lyke Wake Walk, an arduous forty–mile crossing of the North Yorkshire moors. If you finish it within a 24 hour time period you are eligible for membership in the elite New Lyke Wake Club. I met several people rushing along to finish on time.

The other walk is a 107–mile trail known as The Cleveland Way which comes strongly recommended if you only have a week to spend.

Early afternoon I climbed to Cringle Moor, the highest point of the trail remaining at 1,427 feet. I stopped to take some pictures and enjoy the amazing view. I was getting close to Clay Bank Top and looking forward to it. The wind had been in my face all day and my legs were beginning to turn rubbery. Not a good thing to have happen in this country.

Wainwright was right. Other than drop–dead views and dozens of ancient boundary markers and tumuli, there was nothing up there. A misstep going down one of the hills and you could be in deep trouble. Once again, I was very thankful for the hiking staff which had already saved my hide on several occasions.

Clay Bank Top wasn't much of anyplace except a windswept dirt parking area in the middle of nowhere. I arrived around 3:00 and, following the directions on the map, headed down a small road to find the turnoff to the B&B – a place called Malt Kiln House, Urra, Chop Gate, Cleveland. How's that for an address?

Walking narrow country roads was not one of my favorite things to do. It was easy for me to forget the traffic came from the opposite direction. Eventually, after several false starts I found the correct lane and found the farm. It was 3:45 and I was the first one to arrive.

Mrs. Broad wasn't home but Mr. Broad was. I was a little surprised. It's a rarity to meet the "man of the house" in a B&B. Normally the men stay out of sight and leave the guests for the ladies to sort out.

He told me there was going to be a full house that night because of the scarcity of places to stay in the middle of the moors. I took advantage of the situation by taking the first shower and partaking of the ample supply of hot tea and biscuits.

Soon the others straggled in: the Canadian and English couples I had met earlier and another, younger English couple. Everyone took turns cleaning up in the one bath – and gathered afterwards in the upstairs parlor to chat and drink tea. The younger English couple had snacked all day and were the only ones not planning to have dinner. There may have been a restaurant somewhere within driving distance – but certainly not on foot – especially at night.

Mr. Broad, who seemed very uncomfortable, served everyone a glass of sherry and stood around trying to make small talk. Finally, at 7:00 he led us down to a narrow dining room, complete with long, oak harvest table, straight backed chairs, leaded glass windows and glowing fire. It was then we learned Mrs. Broad had spent the entire day over at her daughter's house helping deliver a new baby. She had just arrived back and was completely exhausted. However, in typical English manner, she kept a stiff upper lip and served a delicious bowl of leek and onion soup, followed by a plate of fresh cooked vegetables with beef that was fixed in some strange way, steamed, I think, a little odd tasting to my palate but very tasty nevertheless. Or was it that I was famished? Dessert consisted of ice cream and peaches and fresh whipped cream and coffee. And since this was a Free House (licensed to sell alcoholic beverages), I ordered a pint of local ale while the others split a couple of bottles of wine.

The strangeness and bleakness of the moors monopolized our dinner conversation. At some point in the evening someone brought up the topic of the numerous graves and tombs we'd passed during the last couple of days and this led to the inevitable subject of ghosts.

Of course, with ale and wine consumed, everyone, it seemed, had a ghost story to share. Most of them were fun and kind of silly. But it was the older English couple that had the show stopper. Actually, the husband coerced his wife into telling it as it had happened to her. She was not at all happy to do so but eventually relented when we all insisted.

Her story concerned an event that had happened to her many years earlier. They lived in one of those quaint, ancient little hamlets in the south of England (I can't recall the name) when she, her daughter and a neighbor's daughter were out walking after dinner one evening along a little stream in the area. I don't recall all the details now but it involved an interactive confrontation with a long–dead monk that had lived in the area many decades earlier.

The monk had apparently been seen by numerous others from time to time over a period of many years. But he had never spoken. In this instance, however, he said something to the woman who, at this point in story telling, had grown very agitated and refused to say what it was. She had never told anyone, her husband added, including him.

The tale had enough odd twists and turns to convince me she was telling the truth. At least I have no doubt it was very true to her and it obviously upset her to tell it again and she soon broke out in tears and had to leave the table. No one knew quite what to do. It was rather awkward.

It was all together a strange evening, what with the ghost stories and all, and by 9:30 our little group broke up and nervously retired to their respective quarters.

Outside the wind had picked up off the moors and was moaning sadly as it blew through the few barren trees remaining on the ancient farm. A shutter banged against the side of the barn.

Undoubtedly I wasn't the only one in Malt Kiln House that night busy barring all windows, securing all doors, and placing all religious objects within easy reach. Yikes!

Day Eleven
Clay Bank Top to Glaisedale

*Having survived a night on the dreaded moors
– I foolishly let my guard down in a bathtub.*

Over breakfast Mr. Broad put me on to a little shortcut back to
the route so I wouldn't have to walk back up the road. I always
tremble when I hear locals say "shortcut" because I seldom found
them to be shorter than the long way around. But based on his
skimpy directions, it did seem to make sense.

A quick accounting of my finances showed that after paying
my bill, I would be dangerously low in English pounds. I had yet
to come across an ATM machine on my walk, let alone a bank
that was open. And you would never find a country inn – or B&B
that accepted credit cards. It was entirely a cash deal.

This would be another long day – around 18 miles. The half-way
point would be the famous Lion Inn, a place I planned to stop for
lunch. I hoped they took VISA.

As usual, the day started with a steep climb up a cliff behind
the house to the ridge. By the time I reached the top, my shirt
was already soaked and my heart pounding wildly. As I stopped
to catch my breath and peered back the way I'd come, I swear I
could still hit the Malt Kiln House, almost straight below me,
with a well-tossed rock.

The mist hadn't burned off the moors yet as I walked along
listening to grouse rustle in the surrounding gorse.

Mr. Broad told me the grouse season would be starting soon
and had been a financial salvation for the area since the mines
closed. "Rich Americans now came over and spend upwards of a
$1,000 a day for the privilege of shooting them," he said shaking
his head in wonder.

The path I was walking along was actually a rough shooting
road that led hunters to lines of shooting stands. On this
morning I could have shot all the grouse I wanted with a .22 rifle.

The main feature of today's walk was the abandoned Rosedale Ironstone Railway line which I would be following for five miles. I soon joined it after I reached the ridge and straightened out my direction toward the east.

The Rosedale line was constructed in 1861 when the railway extended its lines by means of a mile–long incline across the high moors at an elevation of 1,300 feet to the ironstone mines in Rosedale. By the turn of the century, ironstone production was in decline and the railroad less in demand. It finally closed in 1929 and the dismantled railway bed left an ugly scar through the moors.

It was a boring, tedious march. Eventually a single hiker caught up with me and I recognized him as one of the walkers I had met at the White Swan Inn a couple of days earlier. His name was Ken Hartley and he lived in Lancaster. He'd retired as a bookkeeper several years ago and had accomplished the first two–thirds of the walk the two years prior.

He told me he planned to complete the walk this time out. His wife, Beth, was following along with their car and would meet him whenever possible for lunch. And at the end of the day, she'd be waiting for him. This explained the skimpy knapsack he was carrying.

Ken was a welcome escape from the boredom and we walked along together for several miles. Suddenly we rounded a curve in the railroad bed and way off in the distance we could see the Lion Inn. Our pace quickened.

The inn went in and out of sight as we got closer and the curves got wider. Eventually we came to a high country road where the inn was supposed to be – but wasn't. We both stopped dead in our tracks, dumbfounded. What in the world had happened? Where did it go? It appeared to have dropped off the face of the earth. It was like an episode from Twilight Zone.

We consulted our maps. Of course! While we were busy jabbering away, we missed a faint side trail that would have led directly to it. Instead we had walked past it adding at least a mile out and a mile back to our journey.

Dating from 1553, the Lion Inn is an abrupt escape from the moor and is the only habitation for miles around. Situated amongst decayed relics of industry, its patrons are no longer ironworkers and coal miners; today it is a port of call for adventurous motorists and walkers.

As fate would have it they did not accept VISA so I restricted my order to a bowl of lentil soup and a hard roll for $3. Sounds rather bleak, I know, but it tasted good and I got by although I missed my hunk of bread and cheese. By this time I was desperately low on cash.

Ken's wife was there when we arrived and they went off to eat by themselves. The Canadians arrived soon after and were staying there for the night. It was early afternoon and I couldn't imagine what they would do once they finished lunch – this was the absolute end of the earth. I'm not even sure they had electricity.

Regardless, I wasn't staying so I finished my meagre meal and left.

According to Wainwright, I would next cross Danby High Moor "... a moor typical of this wedge of high country: now uninhabited and inhospitable but yielding evidence by the excavation of its many burrows or burial mounds of a primitive people who lived here four thousand years ago."

There were tombs everywhere. Some had been dug into, but most had not. I stopped at one. I was attracted to it by a half-hearted wire strand around its edge, apparently to keep you from falling into a vertical 20–foot shaft. Good Lord, even in broad daylight I almost stumbled into it. Pity the poor soul who came wandering this way in the mist.

The walk through the high moors was eerie, but wonderful. Mile after mile of bleak, wind–swept country dotted with ancient boundary markers, stone circles and long–forgotten tombs. Not a comfortable place to be caught in after dark, however.

By mid–afternoon I was well on my way to Glaisedale and the scenery was starting to change again. A mixture of moors and meadows and deep green valleys. Little by little I descended from the high country.

As Wainwright wrote "... upon reaching this point in the trip: The wilderness days are over."

By 5:00 I finally arrived in the village, pleasantly tired but bothered by my sore knee. Although the place was tiny, it did have a bus station and I was elated to find an ATM. I had run out of pain pills early in the day and stopped at the first store I came to and replenished my supply with an English version of ibuprofen.

I had reservations that evening at the Arncliffe Arms, a local pub that rented a few rooms at $23. It wasn't hard to find, right on the trail at the far end of the small village.

The Arncliffe Arms was a little seedy–looking, but my room was clean and as they say, the water was hot. What more could you ask for and anyway, tomorrow would be my last day. My last day! I felt elated and sad at the same time.

I marched into the common room, chatted with Mrs. Westwood over a pint of local bitters and headed up for a shower. And calamity struck!

The oversized bathroom featured one of those huge, cast iron, claw foot tub affairs that must have weighed a ton. It was completely encircled by a shower curtain and featured one of those hand–held spray thingies that never seemed to work very well.

I would have been just fine if my knee hadn't been hurting so much. When I tried to sit down in the tub so I could elevate my knee and spray hot water on it I slipped and fell backwards hitting my head hard on a hidden nozzle at the other end. Wham!

Down I went and there I lay curled up in a fetal position, hugging my head with both hands, cursing the inn owner, cursing myself, and anyone else I could think of. Oh my, did that hurt!

Finally the pain subsided and the shock wore off and I sat up to discover blood everywhere. What was this? Is all this blood mine?

I carefully felt the top of my head and discovered a deep and long gash. Oh no!

So there I sat holding onto my head while dripping voluminous amounts of blood all over the shower curtain, the tile floor and, eventually, the walls. It just wouldn't stop. Every time I'd take my hands down and tried to do something, blood would run down my arms and flip everywhere. I tried turning on the cold water and sat in the ice cold spray – but all that did was freeze me.

Fifteen minutes later I was still standing in the tub, dripping blood, when I heard someone try the doorknob.

"'Ello – still in there?" a man's voice yelled. "'Ow much longer, mate?"

"Out in a minute," I yelled in a panic.

But the bleeding wouldn't stop. Blood was everywhere by this time. Finally I stepped out of the tub and ran over to grab a handful of toilet paper to try to stop the bleeding long enough to get some clothes on and get out of there.

I tried to straighten the place up the best I could but when I looked around before I left, it looked like someone had field dressed a cow in there. What would the next folks think? I left quickly and snuck back down the hall to my room.

Luckily there was a basin in the room in which to drip and eventually I got the bleeding to stop. It took around 30 minutes and I felt I had lost half the blood in my system. Once I got the bleeding to stop I was afraid to do anything that might get it started again so I just sat there holding onto my head and waited until everything sort of dried up in a big, red, hairy glob on top of my head. Ugh. What a mess.

Feeling guilty I did confide in Mrs. Westwood and when I showed her the damage, she gasped and offered to call a vet friend to come stitch me up.

A vet? Was she kidding? She wasn't. I politely declined.

By 8:00 it was dark enough to go out and find a place to eat. Actually, there was only *one* place to go and it was just up the lane in another pub/inn called the Anglers Rest. I wore my cap which covered the worst, but I still received stares from folks mystified by the wad of toilet paper on my head and my rusty red sideburns.

The good news was they accepted VISA and I celebrated that, plus the fact I hadn't yet bled to death, by ordering a medicinal Jameson Irish Whiskey.

Soon the younger English couple I had met at the Malt Kiln House showed up and joined me for dinner. They stared at me, too. Turns out the wife was a nurse so I told her what happened. Of course, she had to take a peek and started to prod around.

"Oh, that's nasty bad, luv?" she said. "You'd best get that stitched up, what?"

"Later," I replied, still thinking of the vet.

Soon, Ken and Beth showed up and we all ate together. Eventually, everyone forgot about my head and we had a great time chatting away comparing our day's experiences.

For dinner I had some kind of ghastly pasta dish, and on Ken's advice, ordered one of the local traditional English desserts which was called, and I'm not making this up, Spotted Dick. It was sort of like Sticky Toffee Pudding – with raisins.

Well, whether it was the Spotted Dick, or the Jameson, or just the joy of having hiking friends to chat with again, I soon felt ever so much better.

Back in my room I carefully wrapped my ruined bath towel around my head to protect the pillow in case I started bleeding again and went to bed. What a strange day it had been – but I had survived.

Day Twelve
Glaisedale to Robin Hood Bay

Wait a minute! This the last day of the walk.
It's not supposed to rain now.

There was no blood on the pillow when I awoke in the morning ... but the towel was a bit of a mess. As were my shirt, pants, shorts, etc. If I could have burned them I would have. My hair was stiff as a board with dried blood but I didn't dare disturb it for fear of opening up the cut.

I felt a little sheepish wearing my hat at breakfast – but it could have been worse. I could have bled to death in their stupid tub.

Oh well, it was my last day of the walk and nothing was going to stop me now. I could almost smell a wet salt breeze blowing toward me as I exited the B&B and headed down the street. As it turned out it was a plain wet breeze I smelled. Rain was finally on its way.

This final leg of the walk was 19 miles.

Wainwright wrote: "This final stage of the walk has a wide variety of scenes: a lovely river and woodlands, heather moors, charming villages, prehistoric relics, a stately waterfall, a forest train, steam locomotives, and to end it an exhilarating cliff path and the North Sea extending to a far horizon."

The day started off just fine, walking down to the River Esk, visiting and photographing the lovely seventeenth century Beggar's Bridge and heading into East Arncliffe Wood. However in another mile I was lost; or to be more precise, temporarily off the mark. Somehow I managed to take another wrong turn and scrambled up a very steep hill and through some fields in the wrong direction thus adding miles to what I already knew was going to be a long day.

No problem. It was still early in the day and I was in a good mood so I simply changed direction, picked up the pace and got back on track.

Soon I reached one of the most beautiful little villages I had seen yet – Egton Bridge. Why hadn't I stayed there night before? It was ever so much more interesting than Glaisedale – and absolutely gorgeous. Too late for second guessing now.

Two miles further was Grosmont, another lovely village and home to the North York Moors Railway Society. It had one of the greatest looking pubs I had yet seen on the trip – the Station House.

Across from the pub was the post office where I stopped to buy some supplies for lunch. Inside was an Australian woman I had been following for the last couple of miles. It turned out she was also doing the Coast–To–Coast walk and had spent the night in Egton Bridge. I wanted to ask her about the town, but she was very standoffish and made it plain she wanted to be left alone.

"Fine," I said under my breath. "When you get lost, don't ask me for help."

I bought some fruit, crackers, cheese and a Snickers and headed up a very, very steep hill out of the village and up to Sleights Moor, an exposed high level heather moor that needed to be crossed before heading back down to Little Beck and into a dense forest area.

It then started to rain.

The Australian stayed well behind me. When I'd stop to rest or take some pictures, she was sure to slow down and stop. If she passed me, she'd never stop or say hello – or ask how I was doing – nothing. Looking straight ahead she'd go barreling by as if I weren't there at all. Very rude and uncharacteristic behavior for walkers.

Soon I had a decision that needed to be made. I was at a point in the walk where I could easily pick up two miles by skipping a loop called Falling Foss Forest Trail.

Earlier in the day, realizing I had already gone miles out of the way, I had decided to skip this part but when I saw the Australian headed that way I'd be darned if I wanted her to think I took a shortcut.

Besides, there was always the possibility the dreaded "Wainwright Police" were real. So in I plunged into a very thick and dark wooded area. Eventually the trail led back up to another high heather moor and the rain grew serious enough for me to stop and put on rain pants and backpack cover. And, for the first time in the entire trip, the wind had finally shifted and was coming from the west – pushing me from behind. My pace picked up and I quickly passed the Aussie with nary a glance nor a "ta."

I later stopped in the middle of the moor and hunkered down in the lee side of a bush to eat my lunch and let the rain die down a little. When it finally did, I looked across the moor and almost fell over. Off in the distance I saw the top of a large ocean tanker slowly moving through what looked like a field of heather.

I continued to stare, dumbfounded. It took awhile before I realized that off in the distance, over the rim of the hill, was the North Sea and I was looking down at the port of Whitby. What a bizarre sight it was! But what a welcome sight, too.

There it was — the North Sea and my goal!

From where I was standing in the Greystone Hills, Robin Hood Bay was only two miles straight east. However, sadist that he was, Wainwright wanted to prolong the excitement of the finish by creating a path leading a few miles north before turning it back east so that you approached the finish along the wild cliffs overlooking the North Sea — somewhat in the same manner he designed the start of the trip by heading you west and north before circling you back to the east.

I hadn't swerved from the course yet and wasn't about to at this stage of the walk. The "Wainwright Police" would have nothing on me!

At 2:30 in the afternoon I arrived at Hawsker, the last village on the route before the big finish; High Hawsker and Low Hawsker were adjoining upland villages which were originally one Scandinavian settlement. It was raining hard again by this time and I was getting wet and chilled. I decided to stop in a pub, the Hare and Hounds, for a precautionary pint before the final assault into Robin Hood Bay.

I can tell you now I stopped all conversation when I came dripping through the front door and ridded myself of pack and staff. The publican, delighted to see me, and a Yank at that, pointed out walkers this close to the end usually charge on to finish and seldom stop in Hawsker.

"That's all right," I replied, "but there's always time for a lovely pint, isn't there?" And this inspired remark earned me a free hand—drawn pint of local ale and pack of peanuts.

It was a wonderful pub and I would have enjoyed spending a bit more time chatting with the locals, but I finished up, thanked them for the pint and headed back out into the rain.

It was after I left the pub when I discovered the rain water running down my face was a bright pink from the blood-caked hair under my cap. I wondered why the men in the pub were starring at me. Too polite to say anything.

Only four miles left.

Those four miles were some of the hardest miles of the trip. Sitting in a cozy, warm pub and relaxing with the boyos had not been such a wonderful idea after all. I started to stiffen up.

After leaving Hawsker I reached the steep North Sea cliffs in about a half hour. The wind and rain along the cliff edge made progress very slow. At the cliff's edge the trail finally turned south and I followed it in a rolling up and down pattern. It was slippery and hard to see where you were going. The wind was howling and blowing up a salt mist from hundreds of feet below.

Way out in the choppy sea a lonely fishing boat kept up with me as we both slowly worked our way along the coast.

At 5:00 I finally limped into Robin Hood Bay. It had been a long day, somewhere over 20 miles, and the light had already started to fade. I was ready for the finish.

The late and famous author, James Herriot, wrote: "Robin Hood Bay is a dream place, so picturesque and scenic that it hardly seems real. It epitomizes the charm of the Yorkshire coast, a wonderful holiday place that still breathes the atmosphere of its fishing past."

Reportedly the former haunt of smugglers, the village is charming as well as small and destined to remain that way because it is falling into the sea: 193 houses have slithered away into the water in the past 200 years! About one a year.

I knocked on the door of Devon House, my chosen B&B for the evening, and Mrs. Duncalfe rushed me inside, clucking about the "wretched weather" and about my "catching my death.' Setting my pack and hiking stick in the corner I started to take off my rain gear.

"Oh no, luv," she admonished, "Ye can't stop now. Take the pebble to the shore and throw it in. It's only a few more blocks. And don't forget to sign the register at the Bay Hotel and receive your Coast–to–Coast certificate. Ta-ta."

Properly chastised I went again, into the rain and fading light, down what seemed to be the world's longest and steepest cobblestone street, to throw my Irish Sea pebble into the North Sea.

Out on the end of a slippery pier I tossed my pebble into the wind and the waves. There wasn't a soul in sight and I felt a little foolish. Even the seagulls were huddling under cover. At the foot of the pier stood the Bay Hotel, an ancient wooden building leaning slightly toward and over the water. It looked like an excellent candidate for slipping into the sea next. I walked up to the door, obediently took off my dripping jacket and cap and entered.

Immediately I was met with a round of applause by a small group of weathered old timers standing around the bar.

"What in the world," I muttered, taken aback with surprise!

But of course, Mrs. Duncalfe had called and told them an American had come all this way to walk across England and soon would be stopping by. They'd been watching me through the window.

In that instant I knew it had all been worth it; the struggle up the steep fells of the Lake District, splish–splashing my way across the rainy dales, and even getting lost in the wretched moors. And somehow I felt deeply touched.

They motioned me into the smoky room and made space for me by the fireplace.

"Well done, Yank," smiled a leathery old fisherman as he handed me a pint of hand–pumped ale, "Well done!"

The walk had officially ended.

THE AFTERMATH

During that last evening in Robin Hood Bay my body seemed to know I had finished the walk and began to shut down. I'd pushed myself too hard the last few days and just didn't realize it at the time. The next day I could hardly get out of bed, let alone get my legs to work properly.

I did see the young English couple in a local pub that last night and they were thrilled to have finished, too.

I also ran into Ken and Beth Hartley and joined them for dinner in an old Victorian hotel high on the bluff overlooking the bay. Hearing of my plans to return to London via York, they offered to drive me to Scarborough the next morning.

Across the dining room I spied the Aussie lass sitting in the corner eating alone. It didn't surprise me.

I did take Ken and Beth up on their offer and rode with them to Scarborough in the morning. From there I took a train to York where I would spend the night before leaving for London to catch my flight back home.

York was magnificent. But I was so beat up and sore I could hardly enjoy it; the tremendous York Minster, the walk along the top of the Castle walls and the twisted cobble streets of the Shambles were wonderful. I hobbled around the best I could but missed so much more than I wanted.

Weeks later I heard from Jon and Lisa and Simon. The three or them had arrived together in Robin Hood Bay the evening of the day I left. For months later, I received cards from them all.

In fact I still receive Christmas cards from the sisters, Beryl and Susan. And Jon Blannin and I still exchange postcards from our wanderings around the world. He still calls me "Sod Off."

It took around three weeks after I returned home to feel normal again. For the first week or two my dreams were filled with episodes of walking. What bruises I had on my hips from the pack disappeared quickly but the callouses I developed on the bottom of my feet made it seem as if I were wearing double thick socks. And I had lost around eight pounds.

But I'm so glad I did it. And yes. I would do it again.

IRELAND

The Head-To-Head

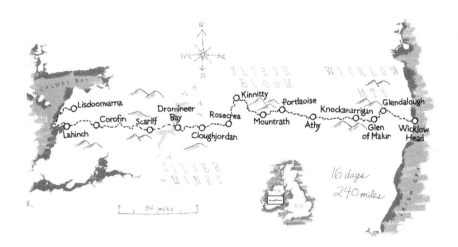

I was exhilarated after my walk across England. It affected me in ways I couldn't have imagined. I talked about it for months afterwards with anyone who'd listen. I wrote articles about it, articles later published in several newspapers and international travel magazines. I guess you could say I was hooked. The following year I started planning another walk, this time across Ireland.

Since there is not a prescribed walk *across* Ireland I decided it would be great fun to develop my own. I ordered OS (Ordinance Survey) maps in several different proportions and pinned them around three walls of our guest bedroom at home. It became my Command Center. When you entered the room you immediately saw taped up maps of the entire country of Ireland, in bits and pieces, stretching from one side of the country to the other and from one side of the room to the other (I still can't believe my wife let me do that.)

For weeks I pondered directions and measured distances and changed and re–changed my route. In summer it finally came together.

This time I would begin my walk in the east and head west. I would plot a route that would take me through the village where my grandmother, Mary McGuire, was born and raised. I would start out about the same time of year. I would do it alone. And so it happened.

The following account comes from my original trip notes and is changed very little. I edited some things out, corrected some things but basically kept it intact. And it starts with a history lesson.

The Irish are going with a vengeance. Soon a Celt will be as rare in Ireland as a Red Indian on the shores of Manhattan.

The London Times – 1848

Over a four year period, from 1845 to 1849, an event that we refer to today as the Great Hunger, or the Famine, or by some historians as the Starvation, over two million Irish people left their homeland. It was during this period that all my ancestors came to America.

It began as a blight of the potato crop that left acre upon acre of Irish farmland covered with black rot.

As harvests across Europe failed, the price of food soared. Subsistence–level Irish farmers found their food stores rotting in their cellars, the crops they relied on to pay the rent to their British and Protestant landlords destroyed.

Peasants who ate the rotten produce sickened and entire villages were consumed with cholera and typhus. Parish priests desperate to provide for their congregations were forced to forsake buying coffins to feed starving families, with the dead going unburied or buried only in the clothes they wore when they died.

The potato crops, upon which the Irish peasant economy was built, totally failed. The crops started off fine. But, almost overnight, they developed black splotches and began to rot immediately. Even the pigs wouldn't eat them they reeked so badly as they putrefied right in the fields. Tragically, the blight came not one but two years in a row.

It had happened before, not only in Ireland but in Scotland and England as well. But in Ireland the consequences were deadly.

Without a doubt the famine was the most dramatic and decisive event in modern Irish history. The experience of mass hunger, disease, death, and emigration had a negative influence on the Irish personality, encouraging despair, insecurity, paranoia, and hatred for all things British.

The Irish census of 1841 numbered its population at 8.2 million. It had been expected that by the next census there would be a little more than nine million. Yet, the actual 1851 census found barely 6.5 million left living in Ireland.

The Irish newspapers were filled with heart wrenching stories for months on end. On January 14, 1847, the Cork Examiner carried this typical article: "... in the parish of Kilmore 14 died on Sunday, three of these were buried in coffins. The Reverend Mr. Clancy visits a farm, and there, in one house, he administered the last rites of religion to six persons. On a subsequent occasion, he prepared for death a father and daughter lying in the same bed."

The Limerick Chronicle of the same year carried this story: "... the starved dogs are being killed like vermin in several parts of this country, as these animals have attacked the barks of trees, bereft of their usual sustenance."

And finally, the Mayo Constitution wrote: "... in the neighborhood of Breaff the following deaths have occurred from starvation and disease: Michael M'Enally, of Roeman, on the 12th; Peter Sworde, of Deerinachrisham, on the 12th; his wife on the 13th; James Gavan, of Ballyshawn, on the 8th; his wife on the 10th ..." and on and on.

The famine deaths, the mass emigration spawned by it and many deaths on the emigration ships, accurately called Coffin Ships, had had their effect.

Conservative estimates place the number of people that died from starvation and disease alone at one million. Current thought places a lot more blame squarely on the English government of the time. We now know, for example, that it not only had advance information about the coming of the potato blight – but was kept constantly informed of the severity of the situation.

One of the saddest facts uncovered in later years shows that at the height of the famine, when thousands of people were dying of starvation every week, excess foods were being exported from Ireland.

At the same time, ships laden with food shipped from America were being turned away from Irish ports of call.

It seems hard to believe this could happen. Here we had people living together, looking the same, with many, but not all, speaking the same language – yet treating each other with such inhumanity. Yet we know it does happen, and it happens all the time. Witness the Holocaust in Germany, the ethnic cleansing in Yugoslavia and African nations practicing racial genocide against each other.

Although the famine did not initiate a mass exodus from Ireland, it did a great deal to institutionalize emigration as a permanent feature of Irish life. Sadly, the people who emigrated were always the most promising. Usually aged between 15 and 30 they were the strongest and healthiest and had the best chances of survival.

And it *was* a case of survival, young children sent off by desperate parents who realized they would most likely never see or hear from them again.

I was told since my childhood in New York that there were two forms of Irish wakes; the first kind was for people who actually died and these were wakes in the more traditional sense of the word. However, the *saddest* wakes were those held for family members who had not died — but were emigrating.

Many went to England first. There were not only more ships leaving from England, but the ships were larger and safer. I've studied many passenger lists and Liverpool is most often listed as the principal port of embarkation to America.

The Irish landed mainly in one of three places; New Orleans, Canada, and New York. My ancestors came to all three. There were hundreds of other ports, but these three accounted for the lion's share.

The stated fare to New York during this period started at £3 10 shillings, or US $17.50, not a great sum by today's standards ... but surely a princely sum for the Irish of the time.

Of the estimated 5,000 crossings made during this period, the average time at sea was two months. Today, one can leave Chicago at 7:00 in the evening, enjoy dinner and a movie on the plane and arrive at Shannon Airport at 9:00 the next morning.

The purpose of this short history lesson has not been to relive the horrors of the Irish Potato Famine – but to review that period of time when all my ancestors left Ireland – none, as far as I've been able to determine, ever to return home again.

This brief account of my journey is in their memory:

Timothy J. Buckley – County Cork
Mary McGuire – County Clare
Dennis Norton – County Roscommon
Mary C. Hughes – County Armagh
Timothy O'Healy – County Cork
Mary O'Donoghue – County Kerry

*Oh Ireland, isn't it grand you look – Like a
bride in her rich adorning?
And with all the pent–up love of my heart I
bid you the top of the morning!*

John Locke – *The Exile's Return* – 1847–1889

The morning breeze sweeping in from the Irish Sea was laden
with a well–seasoned mixture of salt, fish and kelp and I don't
know what else. It smelled glorious indeed! It was early and very
cool and the long, curving promenade extending along the beach
front of Bray was wet with ocean spray.

It was my first morning back in Ireland after many years and the
rush of the sea's breath brought back many fond memories.

Bundled up in a wind breaker I stood on the quay and
watched a young woman working her way along the edge of the
promenade – stopping every 50 feet or so and hoisting a series of
red and yellow signal flags, the type of flags you would expect to
see on the rigging of a ship.

What in the world was she doing I wondered? I walked
towards her and when she stopped to hoist another flag I asked
her what they signified.

"Well now, these flags mean that the surf's brilliant for
swimming and that the lifeguard's on duty," she smiled and
replied in a lovely Irish voice I'd longed to hear.

"Yes, of course. Thank you," I said and moved on looking out
onto a vicious, wave–beaten beach. I couldn't imagine anyone
trying to swim in that surf even if the sun were out, which it
wasn't.

Passing the lifeguard station, which was still locked with no
sign of a lifeguard anywhere, I followed the promenade out to
Bray Head, a distance of two miles before I turned and headed
back along the sweeping bay.

As I walked past the lifeguard station again, I noticed it was
still locked. Signal flags, by this time, were waving madly all

along the beach front and the young woman was hunkered down out of the wind and staring out into the ocean.

"I see the lifeguard station's still locked," I offered as a kind of polite question.

"Well now, today's himself's day off, isn't it?" she replied as if it were the most obvious thing in the world.

"Well, yes, I suppose it is," I stammered, slightly confused. *Himself*, of course, was the lifeguard.

Indeed I was back in Ireland!

Bray, or *Bré* as it's known in the Irish language, is called the gateway to the Garden of Ireland, and the longest established seaside town in the country. One of the most northern towns in County Wicklow, it sits on Ireland's eastern coast, just 12 miles south of Dublin.

Although there's evidence of human habitation from prehistoric and early Christian times, the first permanent settlement came at the time of the Norman Invasion when the manor of *Bré* was granted to Walter de Riddlesford in 1173 and a castle was built overlooking the River Dargle. Henry VIII later gave the manor to the Barbazon family, ancestors of the present Earl of Meath.

Over the centuries the settlement had been constantly attacked by the clans of the O'Tooles and the O'Brynes who had strongholds in the nearby mountains surrounding the town.

By 1854 the railway came to Bray and the main part of the city was laid out much as it is today and it became the leading seaside town in Ireland.

Bray's broad sandy beach is over a mile long and is fronted by a colorful and spacious Victorian era esplanade. Running along the beach, from one end to the other, is a wide pedestrian promenade. During the warmer summer months it's always crowded with strollers, joggers and dozens of mommies and nanny's pushing infant–laden prams. Today however, there were just a few locals out enjoying a brisk fall walk. No swimmers that I could see even if the "weather was brilliant."

At the southern end of the beach the space is dominated by Bray Head, a towering cliff rising dramatically 700 feet above the Irish Sea affording glorious views of both mountains and ocean alike. From Bray Head the promenade turns into a dramatic cliff walk linking the city to the village of Greystones, three miles further down the coast.

Bray is also the town where one can find the address, One Martello Terrace: a home used by James Joyce, the famous Irish author, as the setting for the Christmas dinner in *A Portrait of the Artist as a Young Man*.

I'd arrived the previous afternoon on a DART (Dublin Area Rapid Transit) train from downtown Dublin. I had spent the evening in a large Victorian home two blocks from the ocean costing £20 ... or about $30 for the night. It offered a small, uninspired room, but one convenient to everything. It was the only advanced reservation I had made before leaving home. As it turned out, even that was not really necessary. The tourist season was over and the town was quietly moving into fall, relieved to have survived another hectic summer.

The evening before, Tom McLaughlin and his wife had come down from Dublin to join me for dinner. Tom and I went to Dowling high school together in Des Moines. He's now a retired lawyer and owns a home in Buncrana ... way up in the northwest tip of Ireland, in County Donegal. He and his wife had just returned to Ireland from the U.S. and were on a furniture–buying trip. It was nice to have someone to eat with – but a little awkward as we hadn't seen each other for many years.

It was early September and my walk across Ireland would begin tomorrow. But first I needed to get to Wicklow.

I left our flag–hoisting lass on the beach and walked back to my B&B, packed and headed out. I called the Silver Sands B&B in Wicklow from the train station to arrange lodging for the night.

Mrs. Doyle informed me the station was a couple of miles out of town but thought she might have time to come and pick me up. If not, she advised "... just follow the coast road out toward Wicklow Head."

That was perfect. Wicklow Head was my self–appointed starting point anyway so it sounded like it was going to work out just fine.

I had named my walk The Head–To–Head since it started at Wicklow Head on the Irish Sea and ended at Hag's Head on the Atlantic Ocean. Hag's Head was on the famous and romantic Cliffs of Moher ... some 240 plus miles west. After weeks and weeks of planning I was excited to finally be on my way.

The Bray–Wicklow train runs right along the coast and is a great trip on its own. A lovely young grade school student named Lisa sat by me and studied Irish in her textbook on her way home from school. She told me her parents wanted her to become fluent in the language. She wasn't so sure. Nevertheless, there seemed to be a real push to rekindle interest in the Irish language since the last time I was there.

All road signs and town names were now displayed in both English and Irish. (Or to be more accurate, Irish Gaelic – as opposed to just plain Gaelic which is a bit more ambiguous). All travel brochures were printed in both languages. Even milk cartons carried advertisements for Irish Language tapes especially designed for parents to use to help practice with their children.

The Wicklow train station was deserted when I arrived so I followed a small crowd toward town. In about a mile a car pulled over to the curb.

"Mr. Buckley?" asked the driver, a large, efficient, no–nonsense appearing woman. Mrs. Doyle had arrived.

I jumped in and we sped through town and out the coast road to her home, Silver Sands. It was built on the side of a hill overlooking Wicklow Bay. It was a lovely spot and my room was huge, with two double beds. She warmed to my adventure and recommended Philip O'Healy's Pub for a spot I might want to visit later in the evening. How did she know?

I unpacked and grabbed my cameras and walked out the coast road past Wicklow Golf Club to Wicklow Head. (In those days I carried two heavy cameras; one for slides and one for prints. Digital cameras had yet to become very reliable or popular.)

The scenery was spectacular. A *head*, by the way, is what we would call a point – a steep cliff face jutting out into the ocean with sea birds circling and scolding at the intrusion.

Wicklow Head featured not one, but two lighthouses built in the late 1700s to mark the headland and to prevent confusion with Howth Head, further up the coast by Dublin. Over the years they've been rebuilt and refurbished but it wasn't until 1976 that they were converted from paraffin to electricity.

It was a wild and windy place as I sat and pondered my trip. The sun was out and it was very peaceful sitting there looking across at what would be England's north coast if one could see that far. It had been a little over a year since I had walked across England.

Would this trip be harder or as interesting? Would I have as many great memories when I finished? How many times would I get lost?

I was most excited to get started.

After a short nap, I walked to town and directly to Phillip O'Healy's Pub for a taste of Jameson Irish Whiskey and a recommendation for dinner. I particularly enjoyed the idea I might be related. My mother's maiden name was Haley changed from the original Healy – or O'Healy by her father's generation.

O'Healy's was a marvelous place – full of lovely chatter, dozens of old signs and faded photographs; fishermen and their catches, a local hurling team and famous Irish dignitaries that had visited. There was also a shelf devoted to an interesting collection of old Guinness bottles.

The Bakery came heartily recommended so that's where I went for a bowl of carrot–coriander soup, boiled potatoes and a platter of locally–caught, fried hake, a popular European fish.

After a leisurely dinner I stopped back at O'Healy's for a dinner–settling pint. It was packed with the Wicklow working class by this time. James Kavanagh and his friend, Peter, were there and we met and easily struck up a lively conversation about my trip and my route.

James was sort of a traveling handy man and a local legend in the area and was very familiar with the Wicklow Mountains, it seemed. His parting words were, "When ye cross over Mullacor Mountain and drop down into the Glen of Malure, be sure to stop at the Michael Dwyer Inn and tell them the Gobeen Man said hello."

And with that bit of advice, which I somehow remembered in my slightly foggy state of mind, I struggled up the hill out of town and onto the deserted coast road leading to Silver Sands.

It had gotten dark and misty while I was in the pub and a strong surf was up. You couldn't see it but you could surely hear the wind–whipped waves crash onto the pebble strewn beach.

There wasn't a soul in sight as I walked along. Half way up the hilly, damp road I stopped for a moment to watch, off in the distance, the light from the Wicklow Head lighthouse slowly arc out to sea.

So I have come into Wicklow, where the fields are sharply green, where a wild beauty hides in the glens, where sudden surprising vistas open up as the road rises and falls; and here I smell for the first time the incense of Ireland, the smoke of turf fires, and here for the first time I see the face of the Irish countryside.

H.V. Morton – *In Search of Ireland* – 1830

Mrs. Doyle ran a tight and tidy ship. Realizing I was in such a lap of luxury, I stayed in bed until 8:00. When I entered the breakfast room, it was filled with an Austrian, two Germans, two Americans and an English couple whose curious eyes all followed me as I found a table by the window. Mrs. Doyle must have told them of my plans. But it was almost 9:00 and I was in my marching outfit with no time for idle chatter.

My plan was simple. Head straight west using small country roads or paths and join up with as many natural trails as possible. Avoid busy highways whenever possible and large cities at all costs.

Like my cross England walk, this one would attack the high ground first. The high ground here was the Wicklow Mountains.

Wicklow Town is in the county of the same name. The town dates back over 4,000 years and is abundant in history. The name comes from the Danish words for Viking Meadow – *Wyking alo* – giving you a strong hint to its turbulent past.

There's no doubt that Wicklow is one of the richest areas in all of Ireland when it comes to things to see and do. I, of course, was limited to what I could see on foot, and with that in mind, charted my way to pass through the haunting ruins of

Glendalough – the Valley of Two Lakes. This is where I would head first.

I settled up with Mrs. Doyle and out I went with her blessings, down the coast road, past the statue of Michael Dwyer, the Wicklow Rebel, past Phillip O'Healys Pub and up the road to Rathdrum on the rather busy highway N11, the main route to Dublin. There was a walking path alongside so I didn't mind.

Within a couple of hours I arrived at Mount Usher Gardens, a special spot recommended by Mrs. Doyle. Perfect, I thought. I was ready for a short break and I entered the grounds.

All I could think of as I wandered through these expertly manicured, lush gardens was who paid for the upkeep? Twenty acres of sweeping terraces, superb stone sculptures and wrought iron gates and trellises, a circular pool with soaring fountain jet. Rushing through the middle on its way to the ocean, the crystal clear Vartry River was plump with salmon. I couldn't imagine how much lovelier the more famous Powerscourt Gardens could have been and I didn't care. This was plenty for me.

After an hour's walk around I stopped for a cup of tea and a sweet in the snack and souvenir shop. An elderly volunteer, properly dressed in tweeds, was selling Mount Usher brochures and other keepsakes. I walked up to her and asked her where the restroom was.

"Ehh? What's that ye say? Speak up now, I'm hard of hearing, ye know."

"The *restroom*? Can you please tell me where the *restroom* is," I said louder, not realizing she was that hard of hearing.

"Restaurant? Why ye're in the restaurant. It's right here!" she said, gesturing around the room and looking at me like I was a dolt.

"No, not the restaurant," I stammered, fairly shouting, " ... the **rest–r–o–o–m!**"

"Rest–r–o–o–m? (pause) Oh, ye mean the *toilet*," she screamed. "Ye want to go to the toilet, is that it now? (cackle cackle) The toilet? That's outside ..." (cackle cackle!)

By now, everyone within a square block knew the American with the backpack didn't know the difference between a restaurant and a toilet. I could feel them snickering and staring holes through me as I crept out the door and headed for the road.

They could keep their wretched toilet. I'll take my business elsewhere. I'll show them, all right.

The town of Ashford was the turnoff into the foothills of the Wicklow Mountains. My destination was a place called Devil's Glen where there was a mountain hostel. The total distance from Wicklow Head to the hostel was around ten miles which I felt was about right for my first day.

The road started climbing almost immediately and soon I overtook another hiker. She was a young woman from Warsaw, Poland, who was on a group tour of Ireland and had taken a couple of days to hike around the area on her own. The rest of her group had stayed to shop in Dublin and she had taken a bus down by herself. We walked together for a few miles until my road turned off to Devil's Glen hostel, another mile up a forest path. We wished each other luck and I turned off.

The hostel was closed when I arrived. It was only 2:00 and it wouldn't open until 5:00 – drat! What in the world was I going to do till five? There wasn't a soul around so I decided to press on. Too bad, it looked like an interesting place. I'd read it was part of a centuries–old farm with the dormitory part of the hostel being the main house. There were also several individual, family size rooms converted from stone livestock buildings built around a sort of courtyard. An interesting setup in a unique area.

I walked back to the road and headed west. Eventually I arrived at Laragh, a very attractive little mountain village on the banks of the Avonmore River. I just couldn't walk any further having doubled my original planned distance. Tired and hungry, I decided to stay the night and continue the short distance to Glendalough in the morning.

Regarding long day's hikes and problems with feet: I've had many questions about how to prepare to avoid blisters, etc. My answer is simple. Plenty of padding in your boots. I've never had a lick of problem after my first walk on the Appalachian Trail. This is why: assuming your boots are sized correctly and broken in, I first put on a pair of light-weight polypropylene socks. Next a light-weight pair of regular cotton socks and finally, a good pair of medium or heavy weight wool hiking socks. Snug, but comfortable. That's my secret.

The Laragh Inn was a great stop offering a small but very clean room for only £12 1/2 ... around $18. I left my pack in the room and went immediately to the adjoining pub where I enjoyed a Guinness while talking to couples from Australia and England. After a shower and short nap I returned to the restaurant and devoured a bowl of fresh vegetable soup and a platter of smoked salmon served with fresh soda bread. Lord, was that delicious!

After dinner I sipped a cup of tea and wrote postcards in a little cubicle overlooking the swift clear river that passed below into the forest. Laragh was a nice stop.

It was also a very short distance from there to Glendalough where I planned to hook up for a short distance on the famous Wicklow Way, an 82–mile trail from Dublin to Clonegal in County Carlow.

Knowing I'd have such a leisurely stroll ahead of me, I slept in until 8:30. After a breakfast of juice, coffee and fresh–buttered, hot raisin scones, I found the forest path leading to Glendalough on the edge of town. It was cool and slightly overcast, a perfect day for walking.

A friendly English couple celebrating their 30th wedding anniversary walked along with me. They'd first come to Glendalough on their honeymoon in 1956 and were returning there now. We arrived late morning, a very easy stroll along the Glendasan River through a dense forest which time forgot centuries ago. We tumbled out of the woods and crossed a wooden bridge where I said goodbye and continued on to the hostel. After checking in, and paying my $10 fee, I left my gear and walked back to the famous ruins where I sneaked in on the tail end of a tourist group.

Glendalough was established by St. Kevin in the sixth century, making it one of Ireland's oldest and most famous religious centers. The settlement was sacked frequently by the Vikings but still flourished for over 600 years. Decline set in only after English forces partially razed the site in 1398. It still continued to function as a monastic center for 200 more years. Pilgrims kept on coming to Glendalough even after that, particularly on St. Kevin's feast day, June 3.

St. Kevin was born in 498, a descendant of the royal house of Leinster. He rejected his life and privilege choosing to live instead as a hermit in a cave at Glendalough. He later founded a monastery there and went on to create a notable center of learning devoted to the care of the sick and the copying and illumination of the famous Irish manuscripts.

The age of the remaining buildings is uncertain, but most date from the eighth to twelfth centuries, the most notable being a superb round tower, cathedral, stone churches and decorated crosses. I'm glad I came when I did because during the summer, it's wall–to–wall tourists. Even now, there were still plenty of people enjoying the solitude and peacefulness of the place.

There's no actual town of Glendalough. There is a small Irish Tourist Office, a very expensive hotel, a pub and gift shop and the hostel where I was staying. The hostel was located between the two lakes from which the place gets its name: Glendalough or Glen of Two Lakes.

I took advantage of the location to repeatedly visit the ruins during the short time I was there. The light was beautiful for photography in between the soft rains that blew down the valley off the adjacent, muted green mountains.

That evening I walked to the Glendalough Hotel for a very expensive hamburger, the likes of which I'd never seen before. Perhaps trying to outdo McDonalds, and undoubtedly trying to justify the price, this burger was absolutely huge, at least a pound of meat. Sitting on a platter with a pound of chips (french fries) and tomato and onion slices, I could hardly eat it all. I did my best while watching the pub's *telly* all aflutter with the news of Princess Diana's funeral the next morning. The news was very negative against the English ... and particularly against the Queen Mother who the commentators felt "... did very little, too late."

There was a turf fire burning in the hostel parlor when I returned. The lights were low and an odd smattering of people were sitting around talking softly, and pouring over maps – charting courses to who knew where. The sweet pungent smell of burning peat stopped me and even though I normally avoid parlors and groups of strangers, I entered and acknowledged their greetings. Apparently the hostel warden had told them about the American who was walking alone across the country and they had questions.

I sat and chatted awhile with two women from Holland, two young Scottish lads who had arrived on bikes from Aberdeen, and two English college girls on holiday. They all seem intrigued about my plans; how long did I think it would it take, who came up with the route, was I really doing it alone, etc.

It had been a very lazy day but I knew the work would begin in earnest tomorrow so I said good night around 9:30 and went upstairs to a large dorm room I shared with the Scottish bikers. There must have been bunks for at least twenty or thirty people.

I awoke early Saturday, but forced myself to stay in bed until 8:00. The Scottish lads were softly snoring on the other side of the room when I finally got up and used the shower. The night prior I remembered I'd left my bath towel some where so I snitched a skimpy dish towel from the kitchen and used it to dry off. There was no one else up yet so I walked around the grounds admiring the setup.

The main building I was staying in was very old, probably early 1800s, and slept 50 people according to the warden, although there were only 12 staying the night. It was a very large, vine covered, stone and wood building and must have been a lovely home at one time, with a large parlor, dining room, community kitchen, several bathrooms, a drying room, several dorm rooms and well as a private office and living accommodations for the warden and staff.

In the adjoining courtyard were several private rooms, built, I would guess, from converted stables, and used by family units.

After a quick breakfast, I filled my water bottle and took off, crossing the bridge between the two lakes and joined the Wicklow Way following it up a wide mountain trail. My goal for the day was to reach the Glenmalur hostel, a distance of around nine miles up and over Mullacor Mountain, 1,971 feet.

It was a wonderful walk, not too steep and with lots of interesting scenery. I soon ran into two women, Swedish and English, out for a day's hike. We walked together for a while before I headed on alone. It was obvious I wasn't in shape yet and I started perspiring right away with the strain of the climb even though it was cloudy and cool.

Along the way I came upon a team of two forest workers and their Clydesdale horse thinning out part of the forest. One worker had a chain saw and would cut down a particularly large Sitka spruce while the other would chain it to the horse who would drag it down the steep slope and out onto the mountain road. Hard, dangerous work, I thought.

As I approached the top and passed above the tree line, the path got very sketchy and boggy. The trail soon disintegrated into a sloppy, slippery mess identifiable only by a few marker poles and water–filled boot marks. But, as the saying goes, you could see for miles. Way across the glen, I could see the slopes of Lugnaquilla Mountain, the second highest peak in Ireland, and the one I would have to cross the next day. From where I stood I could just make out the faint zig–zag trails going up its side and disappearing into the cloudy mist.

Passing over the top of Mullacor the trail became more difficult and dangerous as it always does when you're heading downhill. Again I was glad for the support my Leki hiking staff gave me, yet I still managed to take a few soft, sloppy spills.

By mid afternoon I reached the other valley. The Wicklow Way passed right by the Glen of Malure Inn, and remembering the request from James Kavanagh, the man I had met at Phillip O'Healy's pub, I stopped at the inn and introduced myself to the owner, Anne Dowling.

"Achhh, may the good Laird save us," she said laughing. "Ye've been a pub with the likes of James Kavanagh, and lived to tell about it."

She knew her man, all right, so we had a nice visit about my walk. I told her I was heading up the valley to the Glenmalure hostel for the night.

"But, tis closed for the season," she said. "August 31st was their last day now, wasn't it? Ye'll find no place to stay up that valley this night."

"What? Are you sure?" I said. "I thought they were open throughout September."

In reality, however, I wasn't at all sure. The hostel warden in Glendalough wasn't even sure. Since the hostel had no phone, all reservations were supposedly made through Dublin but calls seldom went through. I was acting on hearsay ... and hope.

Not looking forward to walking three and a half miles up the valley to the hostel, which was the absolute end of the line, and finding it closed, I asked Anne about a room there, instead.

At first, she told me no, that they were completely booked up for a 40th birthday party for a "wild bunch" coming down from Dublin. Then realizing I had no other place to stay, she reconsidered and told me she'd find me a room, but that I'd have to put up with some noise.

"No problem," I said. "A little noise won't bother me. I'll take it." (I spoke too soon as you'll see later.)

The Glen of Malure Inn is an early nineteenth century coaching inn which hadn't changed much since the day it was built. It sits deep in a pine forest at the low point of a crossroads surrounded by serious mountains. The road running by the inn is called the Military Road and was used by English troops in the early 1800s.

Across from the inn and over a stream by the edge of the forest stands one of the original, old English barracks. I was told all the other barracks had long since been blown up by the IRA. The locals are trying hard to preserve this one despite periodic, wild–eyed threats by the "... boyos loose on the whiskey."

Anne showed me a small, but comfortable room and warned me that I was directly above the party room.

"No problem," I repeated. "I can sleep through most anything." (Hah!)

Giddy with my good luck at finding a room, I adjourned to Michael Dwyer's, the inn's pub, for a little sustenance and late afternoon chat with the local gentry.

The great Gaels of Ireland
are the men that God made mad,
for all their wars are merry,
and all their songs are sad.

G. K. Chesterton – 1899

Standing in the doorway of the Glen of Malure Inn and looking around at the rugged wilderness surrounding me, I found it hard to believe Dublin was only an hour's drive away.

The mist in the highlands was like a living thing, rolling over the top of Lugnaquilla Mountain and sliding down its slopes into the valley where I stood – like an avalanche in slow motion. The only sound you could hear was the rushing water of the Avonbeg River as it hurried by on its way to the sea.

It was hard to imagine what the trip from Dublin must have been like on these roads 200 years earlier. The inaccessibility of the mountains provided a safe hideout for opponents of English rule. This area of the country was known as the Pale and harbored stubborn rebels for centuries. Michael Dwyer was one of the most famous and I was in a pub named in his honor.

A contemporary of Robert Emmet (after whom I was named by my Irish grandmother), Dwyer and his rebel band took part in the ill–fated 1798 Rising. Unlike Emmet, who was caught, hanged and quartered on the Dublin docks in 1803, Dwyer was never caught but led the English on a merry chase around these very mountains for years.

Tomorrow, weather permitting, I hoped to pass over them and down into another valley. There I planned to stay in Knockanarrigan, a small village where the Dwyer–McAllister cottage still stands.

In the winter of 1799, Dwyer and his rebel band were discovered hiding in the cottage and surrounded by English troops. The situation seemed hopeless. Finally a man named Robert McAllister placed himself in the doorway and drew the English gunfire while Dwyer broke away into the mountains. McAllister was mowed down by musket shot while Dwyer escaped.

The Irish dearly love their heroes and here in the pub were original framed newspaper accounts reporting on Dwyer's bold exploits. And like stories about most Irish heroes, this one has a sad ending.

Because the English troops never caught Dwyer he became a huge source of embarrassment to the English government – and of immense glee to the Irish people. After eluding the English soldiers for many years, he eventually surrendered with the promise of safe passage for himself and his family to America. Unfortunately no one had bothered to check with the American government about this and the last thing America wanted in the early 1800s was another insurrectionist. America nixed the deal.

The English put Dwyer in jail and during the following years of imprisonment he somehow turned into a serious alcoholic. Eventually he was released and banished to Australia. His family tried desperately to join him for years and years but the English wouldn't allow it. Finally, with his health failing, they relented and allowed his family to sail, under guard, to Australia for a visit. He died as their ship was en route.

That's the stuff Irish songs are made of.

The birthday entourage from Dublin began arriving at the inn around 7:00 p.m. and by 8:00 the pub and the dining room–turned–party room was jam packed. Fortunately I had staked out a stool at the bar and had already consumed a delicious dinner of grilled salmon and soda bread.

The pub was rather small as far as Irish pubs go – but it had two identical rooms, side by side and separated by the bar. Each room measured roughly 25' by 15' and was lined with benches and low tables. Packed into each room were at least 100 people, talking and smoking and talking and drinking and talking and singing like there was no tomorrow. Lord, how these people can talk.

I was sharing a key position at the bar with Peter and his girlfriend, Mary. Peter was a 30-something local farmer with a barrel chest, no neck and the arms of a weight lifter. Everyone else was wearing long-sleeved, flannel shirts and heavy sweaters. Peter wore a short–sleeved work shirt and looked quite comfortable. I sincerely hoped he liked Americans. Mary was very shy, had a mouthful of large teeth and smiled a lot. When she did talk, I had a very difficult time understanding what she said so I nodded at everything, hoping I nodded at the right things.

The Dubliners carefully avoided Peter who said very little but liked Guinness enough to drink three pints to my one – and I had three.

At some point in the evening a guitar player showed up and began singing a mixture of Irish folk songs and old Johnny Cash and John Denver tunes. Every time he started an American song, Peter would nudge me with his heavy elbow and smiled for approval. I smiled broadly back.

I don't recall ever seeing four bartenders work so hard for so long. The mandatory closing time of 11:30 came and went. I finally called it quits at 12:30 and edged my way towards the door just as the gang was getting into the swing of things.

Earlier in the evening Anne Dowling had sent a maid down to inform me that, anticipating a potential problem with the crowd, my room had been switched to the other end of the building. I was now in Room 14 instead of Room 2 which, at this stage of the evening, I had a bit of trouble locating. Not all the problem was caused by the Guinness. For some insane reason, the rooms were not numbered sequentially. In fact, there was no Room 13 at all. The Irish are very superstitious.

The party downstairs finally ended at 5:30 a.m. I know because I was kept awake by the noise the entire night even though it originated at the opposite end of the building. It stopped just before daylight with the sounds of several Irish *Bodhrám* drums leading the crowd off into the distance to who knows where and for what evil purpose. Thank God for that and I finally manage to slip in a few hours of nervous sleep.

I woke not feeling so very good. The noise, the smoke, the Guinness and the lack of sleep were not the best preparation for a hike over the mountains. I lay in bed willing my body to mend. I looked around the room and noticed a sort of tassel–rope thingy hanging down from the ceiling. I wondered if when I pulled it, an eighteenth century chambermaid would appear at the door with a cold towel and hot coffee. Nah ... probably not.

I was the only person stirring in the inn at 8:30 when I tiptoed down the creaking hallway, stepping over several bodies, to the bath. It featured one of those terrible shower arrangements that required a mechanical engineer to get working. I just wasn't up to the task and finally gave up and splashed some cold water around, shaved and cleaned up the best I could.

The dining room was last night's room of revelry. It was vacant except for an angry old crone sweeping parts of clothing, musical instruments, cigarette butts, broken glass and Lord knows what else into a large pile in the corner. She obviously disapproved of the enthusiasm displayed at last night's party and the condition in which it left the room. It reeked of stale smoke and spilled ale.

"Good morning," I said, trying to be sociable. "Find any bodies laying around from last night?"

"Well, ye might look under the tables," she muttered, "and if ye see anyone, give 'em a good hard kick! Juice and tea on the sideboard. Flakes and toast if ye want."

And with that she left. Hmm. Perhaps a bit too early for levity on my part. I quickly ate and headed up the valley.

My map showed the mountain road led to the Glenmalure hostel and then dead-ended where a series of trails continued up into the mountains. Not sure of the best route over the top I hoped I would run into someone I could ask for advice.

I was in luck. A mile down the road I came upon a large group of sensibly-dressed, middle-aged folk gathered around a small bridge. I stopped and learned they were members of a Dublin hiking club who were about ready to head up dreaded Mt. Lugnaquilla and that I was welcome to join them.

I showed them my proposed route and the leader told me it might be a little easier but definitely longer, and I shouldn't try it alone in any case as I would most likely get lost, particularly if the rain clouds moved in, etc. Hmm – point taken. I accepted their invitation.

They were a great bunch and an interesting mixture of beginners and experts, around 30 in all. They were very friendly and wanted to know all about my trip. I visited with them as we climbed higher and higher until talking became too difficult. We zig–zagged our way up through open country occasionally stopping for the beginners like me to catch our breath. The group leader was right. I'd never have found the route myself and I was glad for the company and the promise that they'd never leave a hiker behind.

We stopped for lunch around 11:30. Everyone except me had packed sandwiches and hot soup. I, of course, had neglected to request a lunch and dug into my half canteen of water and emergency slice of beef jerky. Making the best of it, I smiled and pretended it was my usual fare. They either thought I was quite the outdoorsman ... or a bloody idiot, indeed.

Another hour back on the trail, we crossed over a high windy ridge and I breathed a sigh of relief. I'd assumed we had reached the top. But no, wait!

"Ah – there she is, lads," exclaimed the trip leader as he pointed up and u–p and UP to what I thought were rain clouds, but what was the top of the mountain, " ... and isn't she a lovely thing to behold, indeed."

My knees buckled as I stared up in astonishment. That's the top? My God, I thought, I'll never make it.

When we did finally reach the top two hours later I was completely out of water and totally soaked.

The wind and the cold caught me by surprise and I quickly put on all the clothes I could find before I froze to death. Lugnaquilla was over 3,050 feet and the second highest range in Ireland ... the highest being in County Kerry. There was a huge rock cairn on top from which you could see for miles in every direction. Wow!

After a short rest I thanked my friends and said goodbye as they headed back another route. I was given a compass setting to use and told to "stay on the ridge and avoid the bogs."

One of the hikers recommended I stop at Fenton's Pub and call her friend, Anne Carpenter, for a place to stay.

It was a bit easier getting back down although I was very tired and it seemed to take forever. I did stray off the ridge once and promptly sank past both knees in an upland bog. I had a terrible time getting out and looked a mess when I did. Definitely something you wouldn't want to do in nasty weather. I see what he meant by "... avoid the bogs."

The area I was passing through was normally used by the Irish Army as an artillery range. There were red warning flags posted during firing times but as it was Sunday, the flags were down and I was told artillery practice was halted. It was.

I finally arrived at a narrow farm lane leading down into the village. I felt very good about things as I strolled down an unusually narrow lane lined with 20–foot tall thorny hedges until I heard a loud crash just behind me. I whirled around just in time to see a white bull the size of a mail truck come crashing through a wooden gate and onto the lane.

"What in the world!" I muttered aloud, backing away and looking right and left for a quick exit. There was none. Through the hedge to the right I could see a field of very attractive cows. "So, that's what he's after," I thought, hoping I didn't look like a cow with my backpack!

The bull stared at me for a minute, snorted, pawed the ground, and, sure enough, began to look for a way through the other side of the hedge to the cows. I backpedaled as fast as I could until I got out of sight then turned and trotted as fast as my shot legs would let me. Whew – that could have turned ugly!

Soon I came to the edge of the village and saw a building on which Glen of Imall Bar was etched on the frosted glass door. Hmm. I thought my hiker friend said I'd come to Fenton's Pub first. Confused I continued on up the road into the village proper but soon could tell there wasn't another pub in sight so I turned around, walked back and entered the Glen of Imall Bar.

Earlier in the afternoon I'd used up all my water so by this time I was dying of thirst and quickly sucked down a tall glass of water, a bottle of Fizzy Orange, a Seven–Up, and a pint of Guinness before I could talk properly. I then relaxed a minute and looked around at what might have been the motliest pub I'd been in yet, complete with dirt floor, sooty, pock–marked walls with part of a dart board hanging on one side. I think the pock marks were caused by bullets. The air was thick with the smell of peat smoke and generations of spilled ale. Behind the bar was a copy of the *Proclamation of 1916* along with various grimy photographs of various Irish heroes and a 1920 vintage photo of the local soccer team.

Sitting around a small table in the corner, a group of silent, old Barry Fitzgerald types had been quietly staring at me since I walked in. Directly behind me sat an elderly lady sipping a cup of tea. All eyes were fixed on me. I must have been quite a sight. Sweaty shirt ... bog dripping pants ... cow dung splattered boots, walking stick, backpack and wearing a Scripps Institute of Oceanography cap. Not your normal Glen of Imall Bar regular by a long shot.

'*Himself,*' the publican, had been slowly moving up the bar towards me in the act of false labor, dusting and washing mismatched glasses and watching me though squinty eyes. The whole pub was silent in anticipation of what the strange Yank might do next.

I felt a little self–conscious at this point but paid my tab, gathered up my pack and politely inquired, "Could you kindly tell me where I'd find Fenton's Pub?"

(The sound of people shifting.)

Himself straightened up, carefully folded the bar towel and said, "Well now, aren't ye standing in it already?"

"I am?" I said, taken aback. "This is Fenton's Pub? But the sign on the door reads Glen of Imall Bar," I stammered.

A sinister smile crossed Himself's face as he said, "That very well may be true but doesn't Fenton himself own it?"

(Snort–snort, wheeze–wheeze from the old Barry Fitzgerald–types.)

Taken aback and realizing I was losing ground rapidly I asked, "Are you Mr. Fenton?"

(Pause)

"Well now, I might be if I'd be dead for forty years," he quipped gleefully.

(Big time snort–snorts, wheeze–wheezes from the old timers.)

Himself had the Yank on the ropes. I slowly gathered what little composure I had left and smiled best I could. I told them I had just crossed over Lugnaquilla and was on my way west.

"And how far west be ye going," jumped in one of the Barry Fitzgeralds.

"Well, all the way to the Cliffs of Moher," I said, turning to the gawking group.

(Pause)

"Where's the auto," asked Himself, a little perplexed and I sensed a little irritated that he didn't know about this. "Ye left it by the bridge, did ye?" he asked.

"I have no auto," I said. "I'm walking."

(Long pause. Sound effects of bodies shuffling in seats.)

"Ye'd be walking ... to the cliffs ... in County Clare?" asked Himself a bit taken aback.

"I am indeed," I smiled. "I started in Wicklow Town and I'm walking alone all the way across Ireland."

This was obviously more than he could take in. He finally stared at me, slowly scanning me up and down. He saw my boots and backpack and staff as if he was seeing them for the first time.

"And all the way on foot?", he stammered.

(Pause)

"Well, it might be on *hand*," I quipped in a moment of genius, "but I didn't wear me gloves."

(Very long and loud snort–snorts, wheeze–wheezes from the Barry Fitzgerald types).

Even Himself smiled.

"And by the way," I added, "do you know who owns the large white bull back up the lane?"

"Why's that?" said Himself looking up with alarm.

"Because it's just broken down the fence and is loose on the lane," I replied.

"Oh, Jaysus, Mary and Joseph! That randy old beast is at those cows again," he yelled as he threw down the bar towel, grabbed a rope and his coat and rushed out the door closely followed by the pack of shuffling, snort–snorting, wheeze–wheezing old timers.

It had surely turned into a grand day!

Grinning, I looked around and, besides myself, there was only the old lady left at the table behind me sipping her tea and smiling widely.

"Musha, you did Seamus a good one," she said with a smile, "That was lovely indeed."

I smiled back and asked if she knew where Anne Carpenter lived.

"I do," she said. "Just up to the first crossroads. First home on the right." It turned out Anne was a dear friend of hers and laid out a lovely table, she added.

Feeling very good about the way things were going, I said goodbye and headed up the road.

Anne greeted me at the door with, "So you did old Seamus a good one, did ye. That's brilliant and welcome for it."

Hmm. Word spreads fast in Knockanarrigan.

Anne Carpenter was a lovely hostess and immediately delivered an immense tray of cheese and crackers, a tin of sardines and brown bread, hot tea and cookies. She even loaned me her bike to pedal down to the famous Dwyer–McAllister Cottage which you could see almost hidden among the larch trees on the side of a hill a mile or two in the distance.

The Dwyer cottage was picture perfect – but locked up tight when I arrived on a vintage Irish Revolution Era bike with very little air in its tires ... or *tyres* as they're known in Ireland.

It had a beautiful thatched roof and when I peeked in the windows I could see rooms I just knew were accurate to the period.

When I returned, my room was pitch dark and I couldn't get the lights to work. After switching bulbs around with no luck, I determined the power was turned off for some reason. I walked over and tapped on Anne's kitchen window and asked for help. She was mortified and rushed over and inserted a couple of coins in an ancient looking electric meter hidden behind some towels in the bathroom.

Apparently my attached cottage had its own electric service which one paid for on an as needed basis. I'd never seen such a thing before or since.

By this time it was around 8:00 and it was too dark to try and negotiate the roads to the nearest restaurant so I decided to forget dinner and stay in and read. I was still full anyway with the food she had served me earlier – and I didn't dare go back to Fenton's ... or the Glen of Imall Bar... or whatever it was called now. Seamus would be armed and waiting for me, I'm sure.

The next morning I slept in – well, until 8:00. But considering how early I went to bed the night before I had 10 hours sleep!

Anne was at the door at 8:30 sharp with a tray of hot and cold cereals, toast (only one side toasted?), coffee and soda bread with fresh preserves. It was slightly cloudy and cool this morning and I turned up the heater for a shower.

Anne was a great lady, in her mid 50s, very healthy looking and a walker it turned out. She surprised me by telling me she had recently returned from a walking trip in the Andes and proudly showed me a walking staff a blind man had made for her.

It was really sad because her husband was very sick with emphysema. I saw him from time to time sitting on a stool outside the back door smoking cigarette after cigarette. He looked more like her father than her husband and I felt so sorry for both of them. He really didn't look like he'll be around much longer the way he coughed and spit up all the time.

Anne took in a couple of preschoolers to earn a little extra money. When the kids arrived I kidded around with them and took their pictures before I left. She looked sad to see me go and as I headed out their gate she shouted, "Be sure to send me a post when you finish."

At the cross roads I stopped at the post office/general store to mail some cards and forward a packet of materials I'd accumulated so they'll be waiting for me with my clean clothes when I arrived at the other side.

"Heard ye did one on Seamus yesterday," the combination grocer–postmaster said with a huge, toothless grin.

"Yes, I suppose I did," I mumbled in surprise and headed up the lane. There were *definitely* no secrets in Knockanarrigan.

In a couple of miles I spied a sign by the road pointing out into a field — *Castleruddery Stone Circle*.

Excited, I climbed the fence and found an ancient circular gathering of large stones in the middle of a farmer's field. I quietly walked around the edge of the interior considering the scene a thousand years earlier. How strange I thought. Druids and ancient ceremonies being played out in the dead of winter. Banshees howling in torment on the forbidden grounds. The stones were huge! Where did they come from?

Around noon I arrived at the tiny village of Grange Con and stopped for lunch in Moorne's Pub. Mr. and Mrs. Moorne were tending bar and happy to meet me. They were fourth generation owners of the pub and lovely people. They wanted to know all about the walk and fixed me a huge toasted ham and cheese sandwich. I took their picture before leaving and as I headed out the door Mrs. Moorne slipped me a pack of sweets for the road.

"Mind the lorries," she yelled. I waved and continued west.

The Irish are fond of strangers, and it costs little to travel among them. When a traveller of good address enters their houses with assurance, he has but to draw a box of snuff and offer it to them; then these people receive him with admiration, and give him the best they have to eat.

Le Sieur De La Boullaye Le Gouz
Les Voyages et Observations – 1653

By mid–afternoon I exited County Wicklow and entered County Kildare and arrived at the village of Ballitore where I stopped at the local post office to inquire about lodging in the area.

My original plan was to stay there for the night. There didn't appear to be any more towns until Athy, an additional eight miles. I had already walked nine.

There was a crowd of women in the post office/general store who overheard my simple inquiry. It created a great deal of spontaneous discussion and prompted a lot of advice.

"Well now," said one, "I've heard Bridget O'Malley over in Glenflesk takes in lodgers."

"No, not any more she doesn't," piped in another. "Not since Thomas, the youngest, popped off to Dublin to live with his Aunt Deidra."

"Saints preserve us," jumped in a third, "ain't ye both daft, did ye forget about the extra room Moira O'Meara now has since Sean, that lout son of hers, left to move in with that shameless hussy in Athlone."

And so forth and so on.

The best I could get out of the conversation was there was nothing between there and Athy.

While the discussion was still going hot and heavy, the postmaster waved me over and offered me a Fizzy Lemon and a ride to Athy. I gladly accepted the Fizzy Lemon and thanked him for the ride offer but told him I'd rather walk.

I left unnoticed with several ladies still waiting in line to put in their two pence worth. I wouldn't be surprised to learn they're still deep in discussion.

I knew I could walk eight more miles in three to four hours so I wasn't much concerned. Besides this stretch was perhaps the flattest part of the journey and I was making excellent time.

After an hour's brisk walking I came upon a handsome, stone well and hand pump along side the road. It was straight across from a traditional, stucco, white Irish cottage of which you've likely seen countless photos: thatched roof, lace curtains in the window, peat smoke coming out of a chimney. I stopped at the well and, without even thinking about it, pumped some water into a little tip cup hanging on the handle. It was delicious and cold. I heard a door open and looked across the road and there stood a woman staring at me with her hands on her hips. She didn't say anything but motioned me over.

Oh great, I thought, now I'm going to get yelled at for not asking permission.

Her name was Irene Supple and she was a tiny slip of a woman, maybe 70 years old, grey hair in a tight bun, and wearing a white apron over a bright, flowery print dress — the kind you see all Irish women that age wear.

"Well now, did ye like the taste of that water, did ye?" she asked.

"Yes I did, indeed, thank you very much. It was very good. I'm sorry if ..."

"Well then," she interrupted, "I suppose ye'd like some fresh porter cake and hot tea now?"

"What? Oh no, thank you very much, that wouldn't be ...."

"Well, come inside then, but mind them boots," she commanded as she whipped around and marched into the house leaving me standing there with my mouth open.

Irene just wanted to talk. I took off my boots and followed her through a spotless parlor and into a tiny kitchen where I was directed to a table and told to "SIT." And then she started in. 'Himself' had just left to help a neighbor load up some market sheep – and wasn't it a lovely day – and where was I headed – and what was in the pack on my back – and what was that stick for – and what part of America was I from – and did I know her brother in Chicago … and on and on. I never did get a word in edgewise.

She insisted I finish the pot of tea with her and made me eat two slabs of warm porter cake slathered with home-whipped butter. Whew!

I finally reached *Baile Atha I* or Athy (pronounced 'a tie') at dusk, a typical old market town of medium size.

Like most market towns, it was stretched out along the main road and split down the middle by a river, in this case, River Barrow. Long and narrow, it was filled with lovely old churches and had a quaint little castle right in the middle of town. Lining the main street were a handful of interesting looking pubs. I really liked the feel of this place.

The Leinster Arms had no rooms … nor did the Castle Hotel, but the proprietor, Margaret, took a shine to my adventure and called around and found me a room with a Mrs. Tims for $24. Happy to know I had a room for the night I stayed and visited with her enjoying a pint before walking the half mile to the B&B.

Mrs. Tims was another lovely hostess and put me in a huge room with three comfortable beds from which to choose and invited me down for tea. There I met an English couple who were also staying with her and who were originally born and raised in Athy. They were back on vacation visiting old friends; they were Sean and Una Murphy now living in St. Leonard's On Sea which they told me was right on the English Channel across from France. After tea and a nice chat I cleaned up and headed back to the Castle Hotel for dinner; a glass of local wine, grilled trout with salad and chips. Excellent.

Just as I was finishing, Sean and Una walked in and invited me over to their table where I treated them to a Jameson – and chatted with them until their dinner arrived and I returned to Mrs. Tims'. It had been about a 20–mile day and I was looking forward to a good night's sleep. I wasn't disappointed.

I woke up Tuesday morning feeling a little queasy in the stomach. Knowing for certain it couldn't have been the Guinness nor the wine nor the Jamesons, it must have been the dreaded fish! Nothing serious, but with very little appetite I managed a light breakfast and bid Mrs. Tims and the expatriate Murphys a fond farewell and was on the road again by 10:00 a.m. A bit late, I thought!

I made good time in this flat countryside and before noon crossed into County Laois. Before I left Mrs. Tims' I'd called and made reservations at a B&B in Stradbally which was only seven or eight miles distance. It would make a short day but Stradbally was the only town of any size along the day's route and I thought it the prudent thing to do.

By early afternoon I realized I would arrive at the B&B way too early so I stopped at an out-of-the-way country pub called The Bleeding Horse so I could call and cancel my reservation. Or, at least I thought it was a pub. Turned out it used to be a pub ... but was now a private home.

You can imagine the stir I caused as, unannounced, I marched in through the front door just as the large family was sitting down to eat their mid-day meal.

"'ello, what's this?"

As things settled down we all got quite a laugh out of the situation. They admitted that only locals knew the pub had closed years ago and they've just not gotten around to removing the sign ... and had become quite attached to it anyway.

They invited me to join them in their meal. I politely refused but asked instead if I could use their phone. With eight sets of eyes glued to me I made a quick call to Stradbally to cancel my room and slipped away as gracefully as I could. I'm sure they're still talking about it.

Stradbally was another long and narrow market town, smaller than Athy, and located along N80, a major highway to Portlaoise. I needed to make a decision.

Originally I planned to bypass Portlaoise and head northwest to a town called Rosenaltis, stay there and head into the Slieve Blooms Mountains the next day. The problem was I'd been unable to locate any place to stay.

The other option was to go into Portlaoise and head into the Slieve Blooms from a different direction. Unfortunately the only way to get from Stradbally to Portlaoise was along N–80. The good news: there was a walking path that followed the highway. Also it was a shorter route and I'd pick up half a day.

I arrived at Portlaoise by late afternoon. It was one of the largest towns I had been in so far and I had to stop and ask directions at the Tourist Office. They directed me to a B&B just down the street. I settled in and asked if there were some place I could do laundry and they pointed out a business just across the street where I could drop off my laundry and pick it up in the morning for only $5.

The B&B was OK ... but nothing to brag about. The room was so tiny I could hardly turn around in it. Normally this doesn't bother me ... but for $35, I expected a bit more. It did have a tiny TV however and small private bath ... so I couldn't complain too much.

Until 1922, Portlaoise was known as Maryborough. Listed as a prosperous commercial centre and principal town and administrative centre of the county, it's located on the main Dublin–Cork–Limerick road. Oddly, the county is named Port Laois ... two words, no "e" and the town is named Portlaoise (pronounced like leash.) Go figure.

Although a sizable market town of over 12,000, the business district was rather compact. After a few false starts, I quickly zeroed in on the Salley Gardens, a lovely pub complete with an ample supply of Guinness and traditional peat fire.

Salley, I'm sure you already know, is from the Irish word *saileach* and refers to the sonnet Yeat's wrote in 1865:

Down by the Salley gardens my love and I did meet,
She passed the Salley gardens with little snow white feet.
She bid me take love easy as the leaves grown on the tree,
But I being young and foolish with her did not agree.

And so forth and so on.

Hmm, where was I? Oh yes, so there I sat soaking in the ambience of the moment — sipping a soothing Jameson Irish Whiskey ... or J.J. as the locals refer to it and catching up on my postcards until hunger again got the best of me.

Down the cobble–stoned street I had earlier noticed a Chinese restaurant, Jade Sisters, which seemed a little out of place but I thought would offer a welcome change from my standard Irish diet.

Mediocre, but expensive is how I'd describe my meal. A bit of a letdown I'd say.

However, the night was still young and at the other end of the street was a lovely looking pub: O'Donoghues.

It had my name written all over it and I briskly set out for it.

When money's tight and is hard to get and your horse has also ran, when all you have is a heap of debt,
A PINT OF PLAIN IS YOUR ONLY MAN.

Flann O' Brien – 1911–1966
At Swim–Two–Birds

At this point I want to share with you my thoughts and observations on the Irish pub.

For years the only Irish pub of which I had any knowledge was the pub shown in the movie, *The Quiet Man,* and, in truth, there are, indeed, many pubs exactly like that, places overflowing with friendly, talkative people; places that are authentically old, smoky and noisy. So that's a good reference point from which to start.

I kept a rough count of the number of pubs I visited during my trek and it came to around 60 – or an average of four a day! Now that may sound like a lot – and I suppose it is but I beg you to consider that pubs are also places to stop for a cup of hot tea, your midday meal or evening dinner, as well as your evening's entertainment. They're the heart and soul of the Irish people! This is especially true in the countryside where even the tiniest hamlets generally have at least two pubs, perhaps three.

Unlike English pubs which have marvelous, fanciful names (The Squinting Cat, a pub in northern England, is one of my favorites), Irish pubs are normally named after the owner – or some famous person. Thus you find an O'Healy's Pub or O' Donoghue's Pub, or Michael Dwyer's Pub, or, such as in Killarney, Buckley's Traditional Bar.

Of course there are always exceptions to the rule. Two of my favorites are the Brazen Head, in Dublin, and the Dog and the Duck, in Athlone. But they are usually the exceptions.

Then there are plain pubs – such as the small village pubs, always interesting to the visitor, but, well, *plain* when compared to the fancier city pubs – like O'Donoghue's here in Portlaoise (Mary O'Donoghue was my great grandmother).

Entering through a heavy wooden door with the name O'Donoghue's etched in frosted glass, I found myself in a large room that oozed age and class.

L-shaped, the bar was huge, and its highly polished dark oak fairly glistened. Upholstered bar stools lined the bar and a thick brass foot rest extended the entire length. Small dark oak tables and comfortable matching upholstered benches lined the perimeter of the room separated for privacy every ten feet or so by an oak panel and frosted glass etched with a flowery scene.

The ceiling was patterned tin painted a tan color. Matching, heavy drapes covered the windows. Everywhere, large mirrors and brass wall lamps covered the walls. Reddish brown was the predominant color.

Behind the bar itself was an amazing array of glassware. There's no such thing as the bartender's nozzle with individual buttons for bar mix so common in the U.S. If you ordered a whiskey and soda in Ireland or England you'd be presented with whiskey in a glass and a separate five-ounce bottle of soda. No ice unless you make a special point of asking.

As a result, behind the bar are shelves filled with hundreds of five-ounce bottles of CocaCola, 7–Up, Sweppes Club Soda, Fizzy Lemon, Lime, Ginger Ale, etc., grouped together by brand. There is also an amazing array of bottles of whiskey, brandy, gin, etc., mostly brands which you've never heard of.

In addition, every pub worth it's salt has several selections of beer or ale from which to choose. Usually there were two "handles" of Guinness to one each of Smithwicks and Heineken. Occasionally you'd have a choice of Carlsburg, Murphy's Irish Stout, a strong Cider such as Bulmer's, and even Budweiser.

You either ordered a pint or half pint; the difference not so much in the savings of money, but the savings of time in not having to wait so long for a refill! A properly pulled pint of Guinness, if done correctly, can take considerable time.

This particular evening there were five people sitting at the bar and the conversation was hot and heavy about turnips ...

Gentleman A: "Of all the things I hate, I'd say turnips and bananas topped me list. I always break out when I eat turnips. I remember eating turnips once and ..."

Gentleman B: "Well now, turnips are lovely when they're cooked right. Ye can surely ruin a good turnip if ye just plop it in a pot of hot water ..."

Gentleman C: "That well may be, but doesn't it depend on the type of turnip we're dealing with? Ye've got to plant them at the right time, as well. Some say ..."

Gentleman B: "That's true, of course, but have ye considered this ...," and so on.

The conversation somehow smoothly switched to the Royal Family and then to the curative powers of garlic, and so it went into the night. With my head spinning with all types of important information I headed back to my room to watch a garden show on the Irish language channel. That finished me off.

The next morning I arranged to stay with Joan Bennett at High Pine Farm near Mountrath. The farm was in the foothills of the Slieve Bloom Mountains where I planned to hook up to the relatively unknown Slieve Bloom Way. As suspected, it was tricky finding a place to stay within walking distance and as it turned out I made a smart move in altering my original route.

I picked up my clean clothes (Yea!), repacked and headed out of town. It was late morning. It was a straightforward walk to Ballyfin where I stopped at the post office and bought apple juice and a package of cookies to munch along the way.

The lane to Mountrath was quiet. I don't think I heard or saw anyone or anything the whole way. It was a small market town and I entered just as the local grade school children were on their way home. By this time in my trip I'd developed a little practical joke I enjoyed playing on the children.

They'd always stare at me – the foreign stranger with the backpack and walking stick – and as we neared each other I'd take out my map, look puzzled and ask in a straight face, "Would this be the town of Dublin straight ahead?"

Well, that would throw them for a loop every time. After a moment's incredulous pause they'd politely say, "No sur, this would be Mountrath (or wherever)." Then they'd look at me like I was a helpless idiot and point vaguely off in another direction and tell me I'm headed the wrong way, indeed.

Then I'd shrug and say something like as long as I'm this close to town I might as well stop for a pint. Then I'd walk on. They'd stand there looking at one another and then back at me and either giggle at the joke or insist loudly that Dublin's miles and miles the other way. It worked every time.

There was a pub called Bennett's on the village square. I thought it might be the same Bennett family as the one with whom I had a reservation so I stopped for a pint and a visit.

"No, no relation a'tall," said the publican, "but you can call them from here if you wish." Which I did.

Mrs. Bennett answered and suggested I have dinner in town and she'd come pick me up around 6:30. She recommended the White Horse Lounge. That sounded fine to me. I was a little tired and a lot hungry. Following her directions to the edge of town I found a comfortable looking inn and enjoyed a glass of wine and a lovely meal of grilled steak and onions, salad and potatoes and strawberry cheesecake and coffee for dessert. Expensive – £13 – around $20, but it was worth it.

Joan Bennett was another perfect hostess, perhaps the best yet. She showed up in an ancient Land Rover right on time and we headed into the hills.

Mountrath was in the foothills of the Slieve Blooms and her home was around five miles away. Not a terrible distance, but I would have had a devil of a time finding it on my own. She took the time to show me some of the local sights along the way and had a great sense of humor.

She and her husband own Beech Hills Farm, an ecological farm with everything natural. No pesticides or herbicides, etc. It really didn't look as much like a farm as it did a comfortable country home and was perched on a ridge about halfway into the hills. A lovely, stone, modern ranch style home.

My bedroom was spotless with two queen–sized beds and a private bath. There were wonderful vistas from two large corner windows.

The lounge was also very comfortable with a peat fire burning in the fireplace, tons of travel books and large picture windows looking out over the wooded valley. The only other people staying were three Germans on holiday who had spent the day "deer stalking."

After cleaning up I took a walk around the property. There was a large field in front of the home with several horses and ponies munching grass. Other than that, some cows and sheep were spread out throughout the hills surrounding their fields of corn and other crops I couldn't identify.

I snooped around until dark and went back to the parlor where I read by the fire for a while, and then turned in early. It was as quiet as a church at midnight.

Thursday, September 11th. I had a heavenly night's sleep. I entered the dining room and found that a place was all set for me. Joan was standing in the kitchen doorway smiling – waiting for me to arrive.

Breakfast consisted of a half grapefruit, a serving of smoked salmon and brown bread, a bowl of granola with stewed prunes, coffee and assorted breads and jams. Very elegant. The Germans showed up during breakfast; a married couple and a friend.

Joan told me they came to spend a week every year and were quite wealthy. Today, they planned to spend the day shopping in Dublin which was only about 90 minutes away by car. Together we spoke some English and some German.

As fate would have it, they were from Nurenberg in Bavaria, where I had spent a year and a half in the army in the mid–50s. I surprised them with my knowledge of some of the famous buildings in the old town; the famous Frauenkirche, Albreck Durër's house, the Heilige Geist Krakenhause and a few others.

Nurenberg happened to be the city that hosted the famous war trials after WWII but we managed to avoid that topic. They, of course, had never been to Marion, Iowa.

I finished the wonderful breakfast and returned to my room to pack, then met Joan in the lounge. We discussed my route through the hills and where I might stay that evening. We decided on a different route that would take me near the town of Kinnity. The only person she knew in the area was a woman at High Pine Farm, another rural location about three miles out of town. She called and set things up for me.

Before I left she invited me into the kitchen to meet her husband — a very rare thing to happen; that is both to meet the husband and to be invited into the private part of the home. He was a very pleasant guy, soft spoken and extremely knowledgeable about the Slieve Blooms.

She fixed us a cup of tea and we chatted for about a half hour keeping comfortably warm by a huge, antique, enamel stove and surrounded by a parcel of sleeping cats. I finally left but promised to do my best to return someday – and I meant it. What a lovely spot.

Joan dropped me off as close to the trail as she could and said goodbye. It was misty cool but clear, and with no rain in sight, so the walking was okay. I passed through mixed terrain, entered County Offaly, and soon came upon some recently harvested peat bogs. I walked off the path for a closer inspection and ended up losing the protective rubber tip of my walking staff somewhere deep in the soft peat. Drat!

The Slieve Bloom Way is described as a unique 48–mile, circular walking trail along forest roads, riverside paths, high bogs, tarmac roads, open mountain and what's traditionally believed to be the ancient road from Tara to Munster. Modest in height when compared to our own Rocky Mountains, the highest peak in the Slieve Blooms is less than 2,000 feet. Yet, on a clear day like this, the view over the tops of ancient spruce and beech forests was spectacular. Energetic walkers can finish the entire trail in three days, but a more leisurely pace would require four or five. I only had time for two so I did what I could and saw some of the best.

My first day was spent going up and down moderate grade hills. Around noon I stopped and ate some cookies and beef jerky and drank some of my water. While I was quietly resting, a herd of fallow deer came by munching on the undergrowth. I'd heard and read about them before, but had never seen any until now. They are tiny compared to our midwest variety and an ancient breed supposedly introduced in Britain by the Romans in the 1st century.

From that point on I found the trail was poorly marked and I inadvertently ended up on a remote forest path and got lost. The map I was using for this section of the country was not accurate enough for these close quarters.

I wandered around for a couple of hours in a huge, dark, damp forest of immense Sitka pines – wandering up one trail and down another before I started to get worried. I didn't want to get caught up there after dark so I did what you're supposed to do when lost, or "off trail" as I prefer to call it. I headed downhill knowing that I'd eventually come to a road or river. The local stories about the Slieve Blooms being the last bastion of the dreaded fairies was starting to work its black magic on me.

Before too long I found another forest road that led into Kinnity where I arrived late in the afternoon. I was saved!

To celebrate I headed directly into the Slieve Bloom Pub which was vacant except for a couple of college age kids. No fun there. I had a quick pint and wandered down to Kiltraps Pub which was also deserted except for a friendly owner who offered me dinner after hearing my shameless, exaggerated tale of getting lost. I quickly accepted and was served a platter of cooked turnips, potatoes, and a stew of meat and carrots. And another Guinness, of course.

When I told her I was staying with Mrs. Lalor out at High Pine Farm she offered to drive me out as she was heading that way on an errand. Again I quickly accepted and was glad I did. It turned out to be three miles in the opposite direction.

Mrs. Lalor was expecting me and brought me a tray of tea, soda bread and cookies. High Pine was a large dairy farm in the middle of nowhere. It was very nice, but I had earlier noticed a small hotel right in town that would have been much more convenient and I wished I had stayed there instead.

Mrs. Lalor was pleasant enough, but distracted with kids running around. I got the feeling she was not particularly enthralled in having house guests this late in the year. Oh well, I'd survive for one night just fine. I settled in the lounge area and watched a little TV. About the only news was about the upcoming National Hurling Championship that was being played on Sunday. I should have paid more attention – but more on this later.

Around 9:00 p.m. she stuck her head in the lounge and wanted to know if I'd be interested in going with her and

"Himself" into town to an "Afters." They were leaving around 10:30. She described an Afters as a party at a bride's home after a wedding and usually just for close friends to get together, have a few drinks and chat – but that I'd be most welcome, indeed. I'm sure she was just trying to be polite but by that time, the stew and Guinness and hot tea was working its magic on me and I was starting to fade so I politely refused.

In retrospect, I should have gone for the experience. How often does a Yank get a chance to attend an Afters?

At breakfast the next day Mrs. Lalor was all smiles and in great humor. The kids had all left for Dublin to see the big hurling match that weekend. Himself (who I never did meet) was out milking and the house was quiet. She told me their oldest son was attending the University of Maryland and they had visited him last year and were very disappointed with Ellis Island. Hmm ... a prosperous farm apparently. After I packed and was ready to go she offered to drive me back to Kinnity to continue my walk. I appreciated that.

I got back on the Slieve Bloom Way and followed it in a southernly direction several miles before I eventually had to leave it behind and head toward Roscrea via the hamlets of Longford and Boheraphuca. Along the way I stopped to investigate a ringfort I'd located on the map. It was in a field opposite a farm and I asked a woman working in the yard if it would be okay to cross her fence to visit the fort. She smiled and said that'd be just fine but didn't I know we were surrounded by ringforts?

"They're everywhere around here, luv," she said as she swept the horizon with a vague wave of her arm.

Irish ringforts, by the way, are ancient stone fortresses built in the form of a circle with houses and other buildings inside. Generally they are in various stages of collapse but considering most date between the fifth to tenth centuries, it is understandable. This one was certainly worth the stop.

Some time during the afternoon I left County Offaly and entered County Tipperary. By this time in the day I'd been caught in a couple of cold rain squalls and my legs had started to complain a bit. After walking for nine days steady I found my pace slowing down. But there was no one around to complain to. A little earlier I had stopped to watch an old man wearing the traditional suit jacket and cap of the Irish working man. He was cutting hay in a large field with a sickle. I bet he didn't complain.

I arrived in Roscrea around 2:30. It had been a wet thirteen–mile day. Tomorrow would be fifteen.

The Tower Inn was a traditional, old fashioned town inn and had the best shower yet. (By this time I was rating rooms by the quality of their showers.) I had gotten chilled during the day and enjoyed a long, hot soak and rest.

Roscrea is one of Ireland's oldest towns and the site of St. Cronan's sixth century monastery. In the thirteenth century, a royal castle was erected to fortify this town's strategic location on the *Slighe Dhála,* one of the five great roads of ancient Ireland. A large medieval market town, it was filled with wonderful old buildings. The Tower Inn, where I was spending the night, was right in the middle of it all.

After a leisurely sightseeing stroll around town I returned to the inn and headed to the bar just off the small lobby where I settled in, had a J.J., and caught up on my log. It was around 7:00 in the evening, still early for dinner by Irish standards and the place was nearly empty. A few people were watching reports of Sunday's big hurling match when I entered the dining room and ordered lasagna for dinner with a large slice of strawberry gateau and coffee for dessert. Brilliant.

Back in the bar, which was very busy by this time, I stopped for an after dinner J.J. and visited with an Irish couple who were in town from the country who wanted to know all about my trip. I shared my plans for the rest of the route, which involved crossing Lough Derg on Sunday on my way to Whitegate, hometown of my grandmother.

When hearing this they informed me that I was most likely in trouble. Didn't I know all Ireland would "come to a bloody stop" on Sunday to watch the great hurling match? They said I'd be lucky to get a ride across Lough Derg with <u>anyone</u>.

That certainly didn't sound very promising.

On the way back up to the room I called and reserved a room at the only B&B I could find listed along the way, an equestrian center in Cloughjordan, a town about half way to Lough Derg.

Saturday morning I woke feeling very refreshed. Settling up at the desk I paid $38 for the room and an additional $16 for the food and drinks. After a light breakfast of juice, coffee and raisin scones I was on my way. (I had grown rather partial to raisin scones by this time.)

It was a very quiet, flat walk to Cloughjordan. I saw only four people the entire day; a couple of workers sitting in an old beat up pickup truck drinking tea, a rural milk hauler and a man working in his garden.

I had switched to a different map system at this point in the trip as the new *Discovery Series* maps I had been using were not yet completed for this section of Ireland. Although I thought I might have some problem finding the right turns I didn't at all.

I arrived famished in the village around 1:30. All I had to eat and drink all day was juice, coffee, a raisin scone and a little water.

The Clough Inn was packed with folks getting ready for a funeral. I felt foolish walking in on them but by the time I learned what was going on, it was too late to leave. Trying to blend in, I headed toward the back and took off my pack and ordered a Guinness and a sandwich. Unfortunately, because of the pending funeral, the kitchen was closed so I had to be satisfied with a couple packs of peanuts. Soon everyone there knew what the Yank was up to.

While I was standing there enjoying my snack, a pleasant woman mourner came up to me and said, "Me husband, who is now dead, God rest his soul, walked the English Coast–to–Coast a year before he died."

When I told her I had also walked it and was now walking across Ireland, she sat and talked for some time. We chatted about the funeral and she pointed out the family. They were seated in a front booth greeting villagers as they stopped by for a "wee drop in preparation for the walk to the graveyard." She told me the deceased was a young mother, whose kids were running wild in the pub.

"Ach, poor thing," she said. "She was killed a day or two ago when a car fell on her."

Huh?

I later found out that was her polite way of telling me the poor woman was on her way home drunk and fell off the curb in front of a car and was run over!

Charlie Swan's Equestrian Centre was three miles out of town on the Modreeny Road. I walked up the drive around 4:00 and almost fainted at the sight of the place.

Here stood this huge, eighteenth century Georgian home set on palatial grounds with stables and its own Elizabethan castle ruins. I was stunned.

Mrs. Swan came to the door. She was a gorgeous woman, now in her 50s I guessed, and a real beauty. The interior of the home looked like a movie set with its own ballroom, formal lounge, dining room, kitchen and private rooms on the first floor and a large winding staircase lined with military memorabilia leading to the second and third floors.

My bedroom on the second floor was at least 25 by 15 feet and filled with eighteenth century antiques. It had two queen-sized beds and small private shower and tons of old furniture. I was almost afraid to move for fear I would either break something or leave mud somewhere.

Fascinated, I spent the rest of the afternoon snooping around my room and all other rooms open to guests. On one of the many bookcases I found a first edition copy of Mark Twain's *Innocents Abroad* sitting next to an autographed Dick Francis novel. And there were hundreds of very rare looking books which Mrs. Swan said had been in the family for generations. She had no idea what was in all the drawers and chests located through the house.

The Swans had been world travelers until fairly recently when they had taken over the family estates. Apparently Mr. Swan, an ex–Captain in the Royal Dragoon Guards, had also been a jockey of some notoriety – as was their son now.

Hanging on the wall were photos of Queen Elizabeth taken with Mr. Swan after he had won some famous race or other. Now, they run this world–famous equestrian centre where well-to–do families send their children to learn how to "properly ride the hounds." I was very impressed.

Lucky for me there was a public restaurant in the original basement kitchen of the house, The Foxes Den. The space was leased by an enterprising, local young couple and gave the area residents someplace elegant to go for a special night out. I entered early as I was famished. The special for the evening was Venison in Blackberry Sauce.

Perhaps it was because I was so hungry but it was the best Venison in Blackberry Sauce I had eaten in ages ... like ever. With the venison I had a bowl of cream of asparagus soup, a garden salad filled with unidentifiable, yet tasty things, hot fresh breads, and a carafe of tangy wine. Coffee and cherry strudel for desert. Afterwards I lingered with an after dinner J.J. in front of a crackling fireplace large enough to park a VW in.

Life was indeed sweet.

I took my Sunday breakfast seated alone at the end of a 20-foot-long, black walnut dining room table in a magnificent walnut paneled dining room while being gazed upon by oil portraits of various Swan family members down through the ages. Silver service, of course. Five different marmalades, stewed fruits, etc. Pretty hum–drum stuff.

I took my leave around 9:00 realizing I'd be hard–pressed to find a place like that again.

The great game of "hurley" – a game rather rare, although not unknown in England – is a fine manly exercise, with sufficient danger to produce excitement; and is, indeed, par excellence, the game of the peasantry of Ireland. To be an expert hurler, a man must possess athletic powers of no ordinary character; he must have a quick eye, a ready hand, and a strong arm; and he must be a good runner, a skillful wrestler, and withal, patient as well as resolute.

Mr. and Mrs. S. C. Hall
Hall's Ireland – Volume II – 1842

It was a quiet Sunday walk with few signs of life. Yet commonplace were posters and banners nailed to trees, fence posts and the fronts of farm houses announcing the National Hurling Championship game later today; County Tipperary versus County Clare. Purple and yellow colored flags were flying everywhere. It was very confusing to me as County Tipperary's colors were purple over yellow — and County Clare's colors were yellow over purple — or was it the other way around?

By 1:00 I arrived at the little town of Puckane, not far from Lough Derg. I stopped at a small pub for a cup of tea and biscuits and inquired if anyone knew of someone who might be available to take me across the lake.

"Well now, that would be Teddy Knight. He's your man," said an elderly gentleman sitting at the bar. "Ask anyone in

Dromineer where to find him. No problem for Teddy. No problem a'tall!"

We'll see.

Another couple of hours and I reached Dromineer Bay — the end of the line until I got a ride across Loch Derg to Whitegate on the opposite shore. The bay sits down at the bottom of a long winding road with the sparkling waters of Lough Derg glittering in front of me as I approached the shore. From where I was at the moment, you could actually see Whitegate way off in the distance.

I entered the Dromineer Bay Hotel and made gentle inquiries about Teddy Knight.

"Well now, Teddy's gone, isn't he," said the man at the desk. "He's off to watch the match in Dublin, you know."

Of course, how stupid of me.

"Best call Teddy's better half," he suggested. "She's the one, all right. Fix ye right up."

I called Teddy's better half.

"Are ye daft?" she said. "No one's going anywhere today, the match is coming on soon, isn't it. Why don't you go up to the Whiskey Still and watch 'Ole Tip' win? Afterwards ye'll get your ride across the lough, all right. The boyos will be lining up to take you across so they can wave their arses at those foolish Clare people once we finish them off. (cackle cackle)."

"But what if Clare should win," I suggested, as incredulous as this might be.

"Well now," she huffed, "little chance of that happening, is there now?" (click!)

I went to the Whiskey Still and watched County Tipperary lose the Irish National Hurling Championship to County Clare by one point.

I paid attention the best I could – but I must admit I had a hard time keeping up with the action. "Ole Tip" was ahead most of the game and the raucous crowd was very friendly and joyous to say the very least. At least the Guinness and J.J. were certainly freely flowing. But, as fate would have it, the tide turned against them in the second half and at the last second, one of those "foolish Clare players" did something magnificent and won the game by one point. Tipperary had lost!

Even though I watched the replay for what seemed a hundred times afterwards, I never could figure out exactly what it was he did. Whatever it was, it sealed my fate. The Guinness and J.J. kept freely flowing but I was destined not to cross Lough Derg this day. No one was in a mood to take me anywhere and I soon quit asking.

It was my granddaughter's fifth birthday. When I left the Whiskey Still, feeling quite dejected, I spied a public phone out in the parking area and called her to wish her a Happy Birthday. Perhaps she could cheer me up.

Since there is a six–hour time delay, it was around noon in Marion while the daylight in Ireland was already starting to dim along the shores of Lough Derg. The call went right through and we were right in the middle of a short, disjointed conversation before she hung up on me anxious to get back to her friends.

Feeling dejected again I headed across to the hotel for dinner and to reserve a room. On the way I made another desperate pass by the harbor and ran into a young German couple who were on holiday in a rented boat, called a river cruiser. I pleaded my case and they agreed to take me across in the morning. Great – I was saved!

Lough Derg is actually a section of the River Shannon where it opens up into a sizable body of water with the towns of Portumna at the north end and Killaloe at the south. Approximately half way down on the east side is Dromineer, one of several towns located in natural harbors around the *lough,* or lake, where I was now.

Two miles straight across is Williamstown Harbor serving the village of Whitegate where my grandmother, Mary McGuire, was born and raised. If I couldn't get a ride across I'd somehow have to work my way all the way around the lake and back down the other side. That would be a disaster and add at least a day to my trip, maybe two!

I could have been stuck in a worse place, however. The Dromineer Bay Hotel was lovely, right by the harbor, which was filled with an eclectic collection of sailboats, large and small river cruisers, row boats, etc. All the owners were either on board their boats watching the aftermath of the game on their own TV sets, or were still drowning their sorrows in the Whiskey Still.

The hotel is family–owned and over 100 years old. Originally it was built as a Coast Guard Inn where Guinness barges and turf boats anchored. Within a stone's throw of the hotel is the ruin of Dromineer castle, an early sixth century home of the O'Kennedy Clan — as in John F. Kennedy. My room on the second floor overlooked the harbor and the castle. Flushed with temporary success of knowing I had a way across in the morning, I enjoyed a Guinness and a wonderful lasagna dinner and turned in.

The next morning was a disaster. It was very windy and so foggy I could hardly see the harbor from my window. Oh no! Could that mean the boats won't leave? I rushed downstairs, ate breakfast and hurried out to see what my German friends thought.

As I suspected the worst, I was not disappointed. No, they weren't going to leave because it was too foggy and they weren't sure of the way without clear vision of the buoys. Great – what else could possibly go wrong!

I asked some locals what they thought of the fog. No one could say for sure, but the consensus was it might lift in the afternoon. I went back in the hotel and called Mrs. Knight back.

"Bad luck, luv," she said. "No boats will be leaving the harbor this day. There's a bloody scamp of a storm headed this way from the Atlantic and the waves will be too rough even if the fog does raise."

Well, that wasn't what I wanted to hear. Deeply disappointed, I went back into the hotel and checked out, got my pack and started to head up the road to see if I could get a lift around the lake. Just then the German girl rushed up to tell me they had decided to leave anyway and I was welcome to come along if I dared. I would, indeed. Hurrah for the Germans!

We headed out into the bay in the 25 foot cruiser. No problem. But once we left the protection of the harbor it got rough. I mean *very* rough! The boat rolled and pitched and I really thought there was no way we'd make it. The way we were tossed around in the small cabin made me more than a little concerned. I couldn't let go of what I was hanging on to long enough to even take a photo.

At this point the German couple were convinced they had made a terrible mistake but it was too late to turn back. We had left the safety of the harbor and the wind had us in its grip. You could barely see the buoys and when we did, we kept getting blown past them before we could make a turn.

It seemed to take forever, but eventually we got close enough to see the other shore. But then we couldn't find the harbor entrance and had to motor up and back several times, while being buffeted by gale force winds before we did. It was the longest two miles I'd ever gone in a boat but we finally made it though it took us well over an hour. Whew! The Germans immediately secured the boat and called it quits.

I bid them *Auf Wiedersehn,* promised to send them a card when I got back home, and headed up the road to Whitegate. While there I was hoping to find someone who could help get a little more information about my family.

Chilled and damp I stopped at the first pub I came to. It was an unfortunate choice. Inside was an alcoholic woman and a slovenly female bar keep. I stayed just long enough for a cup of hot tea and some biscuits. The over-served woman, who was more mean–spirited than drunk, kept asking me insulting questions such as "was I here to mooch off my poor Irish relatives" and "are all Americans as cheap as they look?" It was all together an ugly scene and I got out of there before I lost my temper and headed up the road to the post office.

Several years earlier I had visited Whitegate with my sister, Mary, and a couple of close friends. We had talked with a gentleman, a distant relation, by the name of Tom Hayes who had taken us out in the country to the old ruins of the McGuire farm.

I stopped at the post office and learned Tom had died a few years earlier but his wife, Mary, still lived in the same house. Unfortunately, she was in the hospital in Ennis with a broken leg.

I next stopped at St. Caimin's Catholic Church and was told the priest was on vacation at the time, so I'd get no help there either. So far I was batting zero!

Across the street from Mary Hayes lived the Malones, Peg and her brother, Michael, and I was advised to stop there.

I knocked on the Malone's door and introduced myself and was immediately invited in for ... what else? Why a pot of hot tea and porter cake, of course! Mr. Malone knew about the McGuires and agreed Tom Hayes was related to them, but wasn't sure how. They really didn't have any information that would help but were very nice all the same.

Disappointed I had received such a distasteful reception at the pub and was not able to talk to anyone in Whitegate who could have helped me, I left town in a bad mood.

By mid–afternoon I reached the town of Scariff and decided to stay there for the evening. There was only one B&B open and it was over a grocery store. It was okay, but nothing to get excited about. The town looked quite deserted when I arrived. Even the local pub had only one or two people sitting around. I was puzzled until I was told all able bodied persons had gone to Ennis to greet the victorious Clare Hurling Team when they arrived from Dublin later that night. Apparently half the population of County Clare would be there.

After a light dinner – lasagna again – I turned in early. Tomorrow looked like it was going to be a killer day.

It <u>was</u> a killer day! I was totally unsuccessful finding a place to stay on my original planned route. Seemed there was a pony trekking convention (whatever that is) taking place in the area where I was headed and every available room within miles was taken. I was advised to change my route toward Ennis, instead.

To make matters worse, it had turned cold and rainy as I walked into Tuamgraney to visit its local Heritage Centre. I had to wait an hour until it opened and then was told the person in charge of "the old records" was not coming in that day. It seemed he'd also gone to Ennis to greet the Hurling Championship Team!

I should have known. Things were going from bad to worse.

The only road headed toward Ennis was a busy highway and I really had to watch my step with all the cars and trucks speeding along it. By early afternoon I reached Tulla and stopped for a cup of hot tea in an almost vacant pub. I was offered a room there but it was way too early so I kept going, getting wetter and colder.

Every now and then a car came hurtling down the highway from Ennis wildly honking. All the windows would be open and people hanging out and holding County Clare flags and screaming "UP TIPPERARY" and other things that I assumed were obscure Gaelic obscenities.

After a couple of hours of tough, fast hiking (five miles), a car pulled over and offered me a lift. It was one of the people I had talked to in the pub in Tulla. Ordinarily I wouldn't accept a ride but I had gone so far out of the way, and was so cold and wet, I gratefully accepted.

Ennis was a nightmare. Celebrations for the returned hurling champs were in full swing and the streets were packed even in the rainy weather. Anxious to avoid the maddening crowd — and since it was still early in the afternoon I decided to plod on to Corofin. I consulted my wet accommodation guide and called ahead and made arrangements for a room.

I crossed the River Fergus bridge and headed northeast. It hadn't stopped raining all day and even though it was what the Irish referred to as a soft rain, it was persistent enough to penetrate my rain jacket and pants.

By late afternoon I reached the turnoff for Dysert O'Dea, one of Ireland's great centers of antiquities. Since it wasn't far off the route, I decided to go and visit the famous Romanesque church with it's strange carvings. I was soaking wet anyway – I couldn't get any wetter. A little more rain wasn't going to kill me – and I doubted I'll ever pass this way again.

For a while I was the only one there, wandering through the deserted old buildings, pondering the strange stone carvings. Suddenly, out of the mist, like some alien apparition, I saw a figure drifting my way across the wet fields. No umbrella or rain jacket. It turned out to be a female medical lab technician from Australia who had left a convention in Limerick to come all that way just to see the ruins. She was soaked to the bone. Here I thought I was in bad shape.

Somehow, between the ruins of Dysert O'Dea and the village of Corofin I managed to lose my way again. The back roads were poorly marked and I took a wrong turn somewhere. It always seemed to happen to me on the longest days, when I was dead tired and when it was starting to get dark. By the time I got back on path, I was very cold and shivering.

My B&B, Riverbank House, loomed up in the distance none too soon. It had been a ten hour, 24 mile day. Way too long! The good news was I was back on schedule. In fact, I was now a half day ahead so I could relax a bit.

Riverbank House was on Bridge Street, right on the main road into town. Maura Clancy was expecting me and worried I hadn't shown up. She quickly ushered me into a lovely bedroom with private shower. I got out of my wet clothes and took a long, luxuriant soak and changed into my dry clothes. A Mira 88 Sport was the make of her shower – and they're among the best of the B&B scene, you know. This one merited a strong '9' on my shower scale. It would have been perfect '10' if it hadn't been for a slow drain.

Rejuvenated and again right with the world I headed to Quinn's, a lovely little pub just up the lane to relax with a celebratory J.J. in front of a peat fire. It was followed by a dinner of Irish stew served piping hot in a huge chalice–shaped dish, a large platter of brown bread and butter, a chocolate gateau and coffee for dessert. Soon I felt whole again and walked around town scouting out the location of the Heritage Centre before heading back to Riverbank House and into bed by 9:30.

Mistress Clancy had turned on an electric mattress heater in my absence. While it felt great when I first got in bed, it was so hot I couldn't sleep. I soon had to get up and disconnect it from the wall. A lovely gesture ... but a bit much.

I headed to the Heritage Centre bright and early the next day. I had written to them weeks earlier authorizing a search for specific facts about my grandmother. I hoped they would have some information waiting for me.

When I arrived, the person I wanted to see wasn't there yet. "Come back in an hour," I was advised.

I returned in an hour and Ms. O'Brien was back. She told me she'd found some vague facts about my grandmother's family but she'd not had time to do it justice! I had earlier paid them the requested $100 and I was rather unhappy she hadn't done more than she had. Sensing my disappointment she told me to give her a call in a few days and she'd definitely have more for me. She also promised to follow up with a written report when I returned home.

It was obvious they were overworked. In her defense, her desk was piled high with folders of other people who were looking for information just as I was. During the short time I was there two American couples just popped in expecting to find information about their ancestors on the spot. They were sent away with forms to fill out.

She told me that in the past few years there's been a growing demand for information from America and wondered why. I told her that we were beginning to experience an aging population and as people age they seemed to get more interested in their family history. I also told her there was an increase in the popularity of Celtic music and dance brought on because of the popularity of such grand performances as *Riverdance* and *The Irish Tenors*, etc. Regardless, I left town rather empty handed.

From Corofin my walk to Ennistymon, a fair-sized market town, was along deserted, bleak, country roads. I don't recall seeing anyone all day, just loads of sheep and cattle and a deserted church.

I was getting close to the sea by this time. I could smell it in the wind. Early afternoon I stopped in an Ennistymon pub for a bowl of soup and toasted cheese and ham sandwich. When I paid my bill I found myself almost out of Irish money and headed for an ATM machine to replenish my supply.

When I finally found a machine, I had one of those senior moments and couldn't remember my PIN number. What the hell — how could this happen now? Just give me a minute, I thought, relax and it'll come back to me — but it didn't. I tried several combinations until the machine refused to take the card.

The banks had closed for the day so I couldn't even cash one of my emergency $100 traveler's checks. I was forced to go to an expensive tourist hotel where they cashed it for me and took a liberal commission for the privilege.

On the way out of town I stopped at a butcher shop for an answer to a question that had been driving me nuts for days. It had bothered me in my walk across England, as well. My burning question was: Where were all the pigs?

Every day, in every B&B and pub in the country, two types of pork were standard breakfast items. Yet you never saw any pigs anywhere. There were sheep wandering around in profusion on the roads and in the hills. Yet other than Irish stew, you seldom saw lamb on menus. It didn't seem right. Where were all the pigs?

The clerk behind the counter looked at me like I was crazy and informed me, as if I were a three year old that should have known better, that the pigs are obviously kept indoors and never let out — as if that were even an option! Hmm. I could see her eyes on me as I backed out of the shop.

The road from Ennistymon to Lahinch was busy but short. In no time at all I finally spotted the Atlantic Ocean off in the distance and my pace quickened.

I walked directly through town to the quay and stood and watched the ocean recede during low tide. The salty smells and screech of gulls were a welcome break from the typical farm odors and bleating of sheep I had been around the last couple of weeks. I was also a bit excited as I knew the end of my long trek was in sight.

I wandered around the tiny business district until I finally settled on a place for the night right on the main street — the Admiral Hotel. A bleak little room cost $45 with breakfast or $38 without. I decided to forego the breakfast. After a quick shower I went back out to eat and found a little seafood restaurant facing the ocean. Settled on a stool overlooking the almost deserted beach I ordered a bowl of sea food chowder and slice of apple pie ... washed down with a pint of Guinness. Delightful.

Back at the hotel bar there were several American men who had recently arrived to play golf at the nearby, world famous Lahinch golf course. They were all excited to be in Ireland. I didn't blame them a bit – but for me, the novelty had long since worn off. My excitement lay in the grand finish tomorrow.

Thursday – September 16th – the big finish. I awoke, packed and was on my way by 8:30. I enjoyed a fair night's sleep despite the sounds of pipes banging all night long. The Admiral is an old hotel with steam heat and sounded like a boiler factory.

My route around the bay took me right past the venerable, old Lahinch Golf Course and I stopped in the pro shop and snooped around. It seemed that mostly Americans were there buying rain jackets – called *cheaters* – and other expensive paraphernalia to take home as souvenirs.

Irish golf courses are wild and wooly–looking places with narrow fairways and scary looking roughs. This course ran right along the ocean and I followed it for some time.

It was a lot longer around the bay than it looked and it took until mid–morning to reach Liscannor, the last town before Hag's Head, my prescribed finish. The only place I could find open to eat in was a pub. All they could offer me was a thickly sliced ham sandwich and a piece of apple pie, but that was fine. The two people inside were cleaning the place up and I couldn't tell if they were happy or sad the season was coming to an end. I slipped out of town unnoticed.

The Burren Way, another Irish long distance path, started in Liscannor and continued all the way north to Ballyvaughan. It was my plan to follow it to Hag's Head. Oddly enough I had trouble finding it and had a couple of false starts before I finally spotted one of the small trail markers.

It turned out to be a very poorly marked trail and I thought, a very dangerous one. It followed along the very edge of the cliff face which left little room for error. The ever present slate fence rows followed the cliff face, as well, and the trail was on the outside of them leaving only a very narrow walking path. To make it even scarier, because of the crashing waves, the cliff face was concave–shaped so you were actually walking along a ledge, usually only a few feet thick, separating you from the ocean some 600 feet below. I hugged the fence line and slowed way down!

By 12:30 I reached the point along the Cliffs of Moher called Hag's Head. I had made it! My walk was officially over.

Wicklow Head to Hag's Head – 240 miles in 15 days. Ta da!

The wind was strong along the top of the cliff and the day had turned cool and the sky overcast. Yet I still felt great. Looking down into the gray ocean I watched a fishing trawler slowly crisscrossing the point. Way up the coast line I could barely make out the ruins of O'Brien's Castle, a famous tourist spot where the road came close to the cliff face so people could visit the area in comfort. Eventually I would make my way up there but for the time being I stood alone basking in quiet victory.

I had the place to myself for a while and was serenely munching on hard cheese and brown bread when four American college students came hiking down from the castle. They were feeling pretty cocky having left their tour group behind and braved the cliff walk this far. They were a bit surprised to find me there and asked how I had gotten there ahead of them. I told them I had come from another direction.

"What do you mean," a young man asked. "What direction?"

"Well, today from Lahinch," I replied. "Before that from Wicklow. I just finished walking across the country."

They just stood and stared at me.

That's as close to a brass band as I ever got.

I'm bidding you a long farewell,
my Mary, kind and true!
But I'll not forget you, darling,
In the land I'm going to.
They say there's bread and work for all,
And the sun shines always there,
But I'll not forget old Ireland,
Were it fifty times as fair.

Lady Dufferin – *Lament of the Irish Emigrant* – 1860

My walk across Ireland may have been over but I still had a long way to go before I found real civilization and a place to sleep. After an hour at Hag's Head I continued hiking north along the beautiful and famous Cliffs of Moher to O'Brien's Castle which was still swarming with tourists.

I must have looked quite *earthy* arriving in shirt sleeves, backpack, walking staff, muddy boots and soiled pants. Everyone else was wearing wool hats, heavy sweaters and jackets and long, sensible pants. But I was used to the cool weather by this time and felt quite comfortable in the bare essentials. The college boys must have told them about me. They stared and backed away for fear I'd brush up against them. Can't say I blamed them.

By late afternoon I reached Doolin, Irish music capital of the world, where I naturally gravitated to O'Connor's Pub for brown bread and a bowl of soup. And a Guinness, of course. It had been a long time since I'd last been in O'Connor's, and I don't think they'd emptied the ashtrays since. It's still a grand pub, nevertheless, and as colorful and popular as they come.

Sure enough, there were a handful of old timers sitting around playing the flutes, fiddles and tin whistles for drinks. They were good, too. Of course, it was still early. Lord knows what they'd sound like by dark. I'd have loved to have stopped right there but I still had eight miles hiking before Lisdoonvarna where I would stay the night. I had to catch a bus to Shannon Airport the next day, so I finished up and left, heading up the Old Doolin Road.

Somehow, my mind took the trouble to notify my body that the walk was over. It started to react accordingly during those final long, long, l–o–n–g eight miles. As if on cue, my legs started cramping and my feet started hurting and my back and neck started tightening up. This same thing happened to me when I finished my long walk across England. It's almost as if your body was preprogrammed. By the time I finally reached Lisdoonvarna around twilight I was stiff, cold and dead tired.

In fact, I knew I was dead tired because I started looking for excuses to stop. I found one as I entered town and halted to watch two men working on a beautiful thatched roof. It was a real masterpiece and you see fewer and fewer of them in the country these days. Apparently it's quickly becoming a lost art like the age–old craft of stone fence building. If I hadn't been so tired and had paid closer attention I'd have realized it was my B&B they were working on.

I continued on quite a ways into town before I stopped an elderly woman coming toward me and asked for directions.

"Well now luv, ye've already gone too far, haven't ye?", she said. "Come along with me and I'll take ye there myself as isn't that the way I'm also going, Saints Be Blessed."

I obediently followed her as she took me several blocks right back to the house I had been admiring earlier. I felt a little foolish, but also relieved that I was finally done walking and could relax at last.

It was a lovely place, half ancient, half modern with very accommodating people who took great pleasure in hearing about my trip. After inquiring about a special place to celebrate my victory dinner they immediately suggested Sheedy's Spa View Hotel.

"A bit dear," they said, "but ye'll find it worth every pound and pence."

So Sheedy's it was.

Lisdoonvarna is a funky place. It's best known as the village people have come to for generations of matchmaking, and it's still known for that today. In fact the Annual Matchmaking Festival was in full swing while I was there and is considered the largest singles matchmaking festival in all of Europe. (I'd best stay on my guard.)

Besides matchmaking, there are ancient mineral springs in the area and since the eighteenth century, the local hotels have been catering to folks interested in sulfur baths, massage, wax treatments, etc. Sounded tempting, but expensive.

I wandered around for a bit, had a couple of drinks here and there and worked my way to Sheedy's. The second I entered, I knew they'd sent me to the right place.

Diedra McNamara met me at the door and led me to a proper coach room where she said, "Ye'll be summoned once the table is ready." (But ... but ... there're only six people in the dining room?).

I didn't blink an eye and took a seat and waited "to be summoned." Thankfully, it wasn't long.

The hotel had a tremendous menu. I was starved as usual, and ordered a bowl of the soup d'jour along with a tossed salad with toasted pine nuts. Soon a basket of fresh breads arrived steaming on the table.

The main course was your basic rack of lamb with a Tikka Crust and Polenta, Courgette and Tomato Tian on a Rosemary Jus served with a bouquet of fresh vegetables and requisite boiled potatoes.

I agreed to the suggested half bottle of tangy, rich wine. Marvelous. Dessert consisted of Dark Chocolate Marquis scented with Tia Maria on a Strawberry and Coffee Bean Sauce.

Coffee and Petit Fours came with the bill, but we don't need to talk about the bill. It was "dear" all right ... enough said! I left Sheedy's knowing I'd had a very special meal and indeed it *was* worth every pound and pence.

It was late by the time I headed back to my B&B. Half way through the village I heard the faint sounds of Irish music coming from a small, nondescript alley pub.

"Why not?" I said to myself.

I entered into a small, darkened and smoky interior and worked my way up to the bar. No one was talking. They were all paying strict attention to a hauntingly beautiful young woman who was singing and accompanying herself on guitar. She was dressed in a long woolen knit black dress. Her hair was a deep, dark red. Off to her side a white-haired and bearded gentleman who could have been her grandfather sat on a wooden stool accompanying her on a penny whistle. It was obvious they had captivated the small crowd.

Standing and sipping an after dinner J.J., the music was lonely and sad as only Irish music can be. I felt really caught up with the mood and the realization I would soon be leaving this lovely land.

It was quite late by the time I left and the town seemed strangely deserted. The narrow cobblestone streets were quiet and shiny wet from a mist that had moved in from the Atlantic during the evening. Ancient street lamps glowed amber as I slowly walked down a steep road to the bridge crossing over the inky black Aille River.

As I approached the bridge I met an elderly gentleman coming toward me smoking a pipe. I smiled and bade him, "Good evening."

"And good evening to ye, fine sur," he replied, tipping his cap. Then he paused a moment and said. "But – wouldn't 'lovely' evening be a better choice of words in view of the soft weather we've been having, praise God."

Gosh ... I'm really gonna miss this place.

SCOTLAND

The West Highland Way

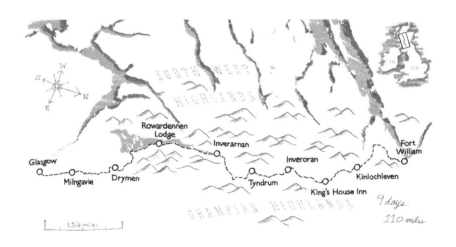

Lady Login's Famous Haggis Recipe, 1856

1 cleaned sheep or lamb's stomach bag
2 lbs dry oatmeal
1 lb chopped mutton suet
1 lb lamb's or deer's liver, boiled and minced
1 pint stock
Heart and lights of the sheep, boiled and minced

1 large chopped onion

1/2 teasp. each: cayenne pepper, Jamaica pepper, salt and pepper

Toast the oatmeal slowly until it is crisp, then mix all the ingredients (except the stomach bag) together, and add the stock. Fill the bag just over half full, press out the air and sew up securely. Have ready a large pot of boiling water, prick the haggis all over with a large needle so it does not burst and boil slowly for 4 to 5 hours. Serves 12.

Our 10:20 a.m. flight from Chicago to Scotland landed at Glasgow's Abbotsinch Airport right on schedule. In no time at all we grabbed our luggage, passed through customs and were on a bus speeding toward the city center.

After a few years break I was back in Europe for the third time and about to embark on another long distance walk. This time I was not going alone but was hiking with an old friend, Jim Giesen. Jim's married to my first cousin, Judy Haley (originally O'Healy). Her dad and my mom were brother and sister.

Although we always have kept in touch, Jim and Judy live in Dubuque, Iowa. We rarely got together except for an occasional visit when one us passed though our respective towns, and for weddings and funerals, of course. Yet at some time, and I'm not quite sure when, we met and discussed my next walk and Jim expressed interest in accompanying me. And so it happened.

I'm sure Jim was as curious as I was how well we'd get along together over the following days. We would be in close quarters walking The West Highland Way – a 110-mile cross country trail leading from downtown Glasgow north to Fort William.

It turned out we need not have worried at all. We got along famously!

We exited the airport bus at the Buchanan Street station, Glasgow's main bus depot, and headed up Renfrew Street to the Victorian Inn, several blocks distant. I had contacted them several weeks earlier and reserved a room for our first night. It was the only prior arrangement we'd made before leaving home.

The weather was overcast – cool and agreeable to us as we lugged our bags up Glasgow's steep streets. We were excited to be in Scotland and had not let jet lag bother us. Once we got squared away we planned to head out and look around.

The downtown district was only a few blocks from the inn and our first stop was the Willow Tea Room ... a beautiful, old fashioned, formal tea room decorated by Rennie Macintosh, a famous turn of the century Glasgow artist who left his mark throughout the town.

Fortified with tea and fruit scones floating in whipped cream, we walked down to see the River Clyde. It was in this early industrial area near the river that the city made its name for building railway locomotives and ships exported all around the world. "Clyde–built" came simply to mean "of the very highest quality." But that was years earlier.

After WWII, Glasgow fell into decline and developed a reputation for crime and poor housing. In the 1980s, however, the city began to reverse the trend and has slowly built up a new reputation of being one of the UK's cultural, artistic and social hot spots.

Jim and I both thought of Glasgow as "strong and stark." Not necessary ugly, but plain. Although there are notable exceptions, the majority of buildings were constructed of huge stone blocks and appeared able to withstand anything, including the severest of earthquakes.

Much renovation was going on in the city centre and we saw several major projects where only the original fronts of buildings were left standing, heavily supported by scaffolding while the rest of the building was being reconnected on the back as new construction. An attempt to preserve the design of the original building, we assumed.

I'd read a description of Glasgow portrayed as a hard working, fun loving construction worker, while Edinburgh was a wealthy old dowager going out for the evening with rouged cheeks and lovely hair, but wearing a wrinkled dress!

It was obviously the quote of a Glasgow native, who by the way, refer to themselves as Glaswegians (pronounced like Norwegians). They are dearly fond of their city and would be prone to exaggeration, I'm sure.

The reputation of the Glaswegians being exceptionally friendly is certainly very true. Everyone we spoke to (and could understand) went out of their way to be helpful and kind. They asked us all kinds of questions about how we liked their city, where we were going, and where we were from.

Edinburgh natives, on the other hand, have the reputation of being snooty to a fault. Glaswegians described them as being "a bit posh," and accompanied this revelation with a flick of the index finger off the end of the nose.

From the River Clyde we walked to George Square, ringed by imposing buildings and with a statue of Sir Walter Scott in the center. From there we continued on to Glasgow Cathedral, a stunning thirteenth century building noted for its unusual upper and lower church, the latter of which contains the tomb of the city's patron saint, Saint Mungo. (He would never have survived in my high school with a name like Mungo!)

By this time we had started to fade and jet lag was starting to set in so we took one of those touristy, red double–decker buses back up the hill to the Victorian House for a short nap and shower before heading out for our proper evening's nourishment and entertainment.

The Griffin and the Horseshoe were two places recommended by several friendly Glaswegians as places we might enjoy visiting so off we went at 6:30 – refreshed and ready! Rain looked imminent but the temperature was a comfortable 70°.

The Griffin was conveniently located just a few blocks from our inn so we walked there in eager anticipation.

Strategically positioned at the ample bar rail, Jim started sampling the famous single malt Scottish whiskeys while I had my old standby: Jameson Irish Whiskey; none of which we felt were very reasonable in cost. The going price for a carefully measured shot was around $4. A pint of beer or ale was only slightly cheaper.

For dinner I had a small salad and a Scottish Pie; a pastry shell filled with a layer of mashed potatoes – covered with a layer of some type of minced meat – covered with a layer of beans! I'll not do that again. Of course, when washed down with a pint of Tennant's White Thistle Ale, anything can taste good. And usually did.

After dinner, off we went looking for the Horseshoe Bar – home, supposedly, of the longest, continuous bar in all of Scotland, perhaps the world!

It was definitely long – and ringed with the Glaswegian working class who had packed the place by the time we arrived. We tried, in vain, to talk with some of them but for the life of us could understand, at best, about a third of what was said. It was exhausting work trying to carry on a conversation – and somewhat embarrassing for both parties.

Compared to the English or Irish, the accent of the Scottish people is very pronounced and takes quite a bit of getting used to. It was several days before our ears became tuned to the quick, sing–song rhythm of their talk. Even then, it was only when they made a special effort to slow down and enunciate for us that we could really understand what was being said. When talking among themselves, it was impossible to pick up a word. I often thought they were talking in Danish or German!

We asked people on several occasions if they had any trouble understanding us – and the answer was always "no." They were always mystified that we had any trouble understanding them.

It was raining lightly when we left the Horseshoe and headed back to our room. We were glad to have our rain jackets with us. Walking down the wet, dimly lighted, city center streets we heard the faint sound of bagpipe music playing nearby. Sure enough, standing all alone in the rain, half way down one of the dim side streets, we saw a young man playing the pipes.

It was 9:30 – and dark. We walked slowly toward him as he kept playing, eyes closed as if he were in a trance – off in some distant, mournful memory. A small tray for donations was on the sidewalk in front of him. It was empty. We listened for a few moments and walked over and dropped in a few coins. No reaction. He was miles away. We left quietly.

Day One

Leaving Glasgow In Our Dust

The West Highland Way is Scotland's first long distance walking path. Opened in 1980, it's now become one of the most popular walking trails in all the British Isles. Running from Milngavie (pronounced mull–guy), a small town north of Glasgow, the path winds 100 miles north to Fort William – from the outskirts of Scotland's largest city to the foot of the highest mountain in Britain. If you begin your trip in Glasgow, as we did, you can add ten miles to your trip.

After a hiatus of a few years, it was my third long distance walk in the British Isles – and it turned out to be the most beautiful by far!

Jim rose early, showered and headed down to breakfast before I managed to get up. I soon joined him for our first full Scottish breakfast: a glass of juice and dish of fruit, coffee and toast, scrambled eggs and mushrooms, a generous portion of bacon and sausage, a potato scone and fried tomatoes. Whew!

By 9:00, we were packed and raring to go. The weather was undecided between blue and cloudy – and a comfortable 65° as we headed up Sauciehall Street to join the Kelvin Walkway.

In short order we came to Glasgow University – a beautiful concentration of buildings up a hill overlooking the city. One of the places on our must-see list was the Hunterian Museum and it was located there.

The Hunterian Museum was different! Filled with an oddball collection of strangeness, it was wonderful yet weird and small enough to see in the hour we stopped there. Lord Kelvin – hence the Kelvin Walkway – was a museum feature. Jim "the Engineer" Giesen correctly identified him with having to do with temperature and cold thingies. All I knew was they named the Kelvinator refrigerator after him. As a kid I seem to recall our kitchen at home having one. I guess you could say when it came to "cool," he was the man. Of course, he was also quoted as once saying, "Heavier-than-air flying machines are an impossibility."

There were two things I remember best about the museum; one was its wonderful collection of monies, including a dramatic display of a horde of rare gold and silver Roman coins discovered nearby.

The other was watching (and listening to) a teacher instructing her class of grade school students seated on the floor. She was talking in a Glaswegian accent so thick we couldn't understand a single word. Those kids didn't have a chance!

As we exited the museum and loaded up our packs – a young woman came up to us and offered to take our pictures. It was a typical Glaswegian gesture! Shortly thereafter, another gent came up and almost wore us out with questions about our travels and how we liked Glasgow and on and on. He was one of those people who came up and parked himself very close to your face and talked and talked. He reminded me of Kramer in a *Seinfield* episode. Very nice – but strange.

We continued through the city and soon found ourselves out on the fringes of town passing through the suburb of Maryville and crossing the line of the Antoine Wall, built by the Romans in AD 142. From here on, the path, which up to this point had meandered along a lovely stream and public gardens, deteriorated into a soggy, wet slog for much the rest of the way into Milngavie, the official starting point of the trail.

We arrived around 3:00 and immediately zeroed in on the Cross Keys pub for a celebratory pint of Guinness and bowl of soup. I gave Jim the honor of finding us a place to stay for the night as it was his idea to wait until we got here to worry about the likes of such mundane matters as a room over our heads.

It was rather amusing watching him fumble through the strange coins and British telephone system in what turned out to be an unsuccessful attempt to find us lodging.

"There's nothing available anywhere in the area," he announced in shock. Apparently there were several business conferences being held in Glasgow and the spillover was affecting the nearby towns and villages. It appeared we were victims of the working class.

We ended up taking the very last room available at the Black Bull Hotel – a rather posh spot we had earlier eliminated because of the $119 price tag. It was, by far, the most expensive place we stayed our entire trip! It was that – or walk back to Glasgow.

I do believe they gave us a special rate as it was – so we really couldn't complain. As we were checking in, a business man rushed in and begged the clerk for any room and was willing to pay any price. Too late – thanks to us.

Unfortunately – the only bed in the room was a double bed. We flipped to see who got the honors – and I, gallant to the last, lost. The hotel crew felt sorry for us, however, and rolled in an old beat up cot that was so broken down, I ended up sleeping on the floor anyway.

Our room was Old World – not plush but very comfortable. Main thing was it had a private bath but a rather tricky system to get the shower to work. It even had one of those heated pants pressers so I took advantage of the situation by rinsing out my considerably muddy trousers and tried to dry/iron them with the pants presser. It didn't work. All it accomplished after thirty minutes of outstanding steam production was to make some very dangerous electrical sounds. I ended up taking the pants down to the front desk and whined for help. They were kind enough to throw them in the hotel's commercial dryer for me.

After we became presentable again we sauntered back to the Cross Keys where I swiftly devoured a steak pie and a Jameson Irish Whiskey. Jim, a self-proclaimed Scotch aficionado, was in seventh heaven.

Not wanting to suffer the same lodging problem the next night I spent some time calling our next stop, the village of Drymen (pronounced like women) where I found a reasonably priced B&B. That done we were all set and could relax and enjoy ourselves, and we did!

Day Two

The Adventure Begins In Ernest

I had a ragged night's sleep on the floor. Groggy, I headed into the dining room and was quickly resuscitated by breakfast. It was very fancy. Strong coffee, croissants, a variety of fresh squeezed juices, fruit dishes, sausages and eggs. We'd better enjoy these plush surroundings while we could.

Except for us, all the people staying in the hotel were there on business and were properly attired in suits and ties, or smart tailored dresses. I, of course, was wearing my one and only plaid shirt, boots, and slightly soiled, plentifully wrinkled, but comfortably dry, pants. I felt right at home.

President Clinton was in the news! All the tabloids were running full page, late–breaking stories about his shenanigans with a Ms. Lewinsky – and the European papers were pulling no punches.

People throughout the country were talking about the affair everywhere we went, but would discreetly hush up when the Yanks appeared on the scene, too polite to discuss it unless the subject was brought up by us. It was embarrassing and made the good old USA a laughing stock!

Before we left the village, Jim and I attended to a few details – mailed a few postcards and met in the center of town where there was an obelisk marking the official start of the Way.

It was pleasantly cool – with the promise of a sunny day. A good way to start.

The guide book we were using divided the first day into two parts: Milngavie to Carbeth, 4.25 miles, and Carbeth to Drymen, an additional 7.75 miles for a total of 12 leisurely miles and described it as "... a relatively simple start on footpaths, tracks, lanes and an old railway with no major climbs. An easy day's walk." And it was.

In no time at all we left the village far behind and marched into the countryside along a very wet and sloppy path through a dense forest called Mugdock Wood.

At the entrance to the wood we ran into Chris, a young student doing volunteer work as a stone mason on his day off. It was nice to realize some of the old trades such as stone masonry and roof thatching were still being taught in trade schools. Lord knows there are miles and miles of stone fences throughout the British Isles falling down with very few people left who really know how to properly repair them. The same thing holds true for thatched cottages which are becoming rare and harder to find every year.

Soon we passed another wooded area which featured Duntreath Castle and the Neolithic age Dumgoyach Standing Stones out in a nearby field. Since it was so boggy, we limited our visit to a view from afar and continued on, instead, to the more user friendly Glen Goyne Distillery – Est. 1833 – where we could devote some meaningful tourist time.

It was our first break in the walk. We inspected the huge copper vats and visited the display room but decided not to wait for the next tour even though it meant passing up the free samples. Gasp! We stayed long enough, however, to take advantage of the facilities and ate our snack lunches on a sunny bench on the grounds.

The rest of the day was uneventful until we reached the outskirts of Drymen when we passed a few of the famous stocky and long-haired highland cattle grazing in a nearby field. We paused long enough to take a few photos and trudged on into the village arriving around 4:00.

Drymen is a delightful village typical of the picturesque little places hidden away off the beaten paths throughout the British Isles. We stopped at the city library/town hall/tourist center building and learned our B&B was close by. Off we went and soon were stopped by a white–haired gentleman leading a small dog on a leash.

"Are you the Americans?" he asked.

Well, we were indeed, and he directed us to his home. His name was Dick Lander, a retired engineer, a weekend sailor, and our host for the evening.

"Just go on in and make yourselves comfortable," he said. "My wife's off for the day and I'm out for a bit of a walk. Take your choice of bedrooms – there are a couple of German lads who'll be arriving later but you're here first and get first choice. I'll be back shortly to fix a pot of tea for us." And off he went.

Later in the day, over a cup of tea, and after we'd cleaned up a bit, a fishmonger came to the door with a basket of freshly caught salmon. Poor Mr. Lander was a bit short of cash and asked if it would be acceptable if we paid for our room in advance so he could buy the fish.

"No problem," I assured him. We paid for our room and asked his advice where a good place would be to go for dinner. Without hesitation he directed us to the Clachan.

The Clachan was a marvelous pub – and reportedly the oldest licensed pub in Scotland, dating back to 1734! Before that it was a private home. Clachan is Gaelic for hamlet and was originally the home of a Mrs. Gow, a weaver, who also happened to be Rob Roy McGregor's youngest sister. Mr. Lander later confirmed all this and told us Rob Roy's grandmother lived there for many years as well.

Rob Roy, you may recall, was immortalized by the famous Irish actor Liam Neeson in a movie by the same name. It was a sobering thought to be sitting in a pub which he had visited many times himself. (Rob Roy that is. Not Liam Neeson. Well – perhaps Liam Neeson, too.)

We arrived early and settled in on the bar side of the small building for a pint, wrote postcards and listened to the locals. I particularly enjoyed it when one man entered with his sheep dog and walked to the bar and filled a large ashtray with water for his dog who drank it down, ashes and all, and settled in under the bar stool to wait for his master to finish his pint.

Later I had a wonderful lamb casserole for dinner. We shared a small table with an English couple we had met at the distillery earlier in the day. They were doing the entire walk as well and we had a wonderful chat with them. It had been a good day.

Day Three

Climbing Conic Hill and Reaching Loch Lomond

Another restless night. Not as bad considering this time I was in a bed. I had not yet gotten into the rhythm. It will come. My body was still adjusting to the time and food difference and, of course, the walking.

Jim and I got up and dressed and waited for the German lads to appear. Soon we all filed into the dining room where Mr. Lander stood at the ready with prepared pots of tea, coffee, and was taking orders – yes, fixing breakfasts as we wanted. That was a rarity. I still have no idea where Mrs. Lander was.

Our destination today was the Rowardennan hostel. We called to make sure there was room.

"No problem, laddies," the warden said. "Simply oodles of room. Come straight away. Thank you very much."

We enjoyed our tailor-made breakfasts, packed and were on our way by 10:00. We only had 14 miles to go and were in no particular hurry. My estimate of averaging two miles per hour was proving correct so we should be at the hostel around 5:00 at the latest.

Our guidebook describes this day's walk as featuring "... good paths most of the way. The first major climb is over Conic Hill (1,074 ft.) near Balmaha."

I was particularly excited as this would be also the day we reach Loch Lomond and I was dying to let loose with song having committed the verses to memory!

Conic Hill was a fairly steep, hog's back ridge. It was the first major climb of the trip, and as all these climbs turned out to be – it was tough going up, but once accomplished, did not really seem that bad after all.

At first the path remained very visible but soon turned rocky. Perhaps because it was Friday and the beginning of the weekend – or just that we were in a popular walking area, but we saw quite a few people along the trail, or at least along this portion leading up the hill. The name Conic Hill comes from the Gaelic *A'Coinneach*, which means the moss or bog, which surrounds the hill on the north side.

We slugged our way to the top where the vista was stunning. Loch Lomond was spread out in front of us and to our sides vast heather-covered hills raced off into the distance. We stopped for lunch and enjoyed the view as well as the sunny weather we had come to appreciate. We counted our lucky stars so far. No telling how far behind us the rains were.

Taking advantage of the stunning scenery and the attentive sheep surrounding us, I stood and in my best Irish tenor voice sang all three verses of *Loch Lomond*. I have the feeling the dear animals were left weeping in the hearing of it.

Down we went to the shore of the loch and into the edge of the resort town of Balmaha, a town named after St. Maha or, depending on who you believe, St. Mahew, a companion of none other than dear old St. Patrick! It was still a little more than seven miles to the hostel so we didn't tarry long but went into a small little shop in search of slide film and snacks.

From this point on the path became very difficult. Steep, slippery and choppy with loose rocks as it wound its way north along the side of the famous loch. It stayed this way the entire afternoon – climbing through a thick forest area and then descending to the loch edge – and back up again. We found it very challenging.

By 5:15 we finally arrived at Rowardennan hostel, tired but happy and close to schedule. The hostel was a lovely, centuries old brick building, most likely a converted house of some rich farmer. We checked in and were placed in an upstairs room facing the loch. Our window looked out over a large lawn that sloped right down to the edge of the water. Behind us were steep hills – and in fact, the path leading up to the famous mountain known as Ben Lomond.

We relaxed, cleaned up and began inquiries of where we could eat. The hostel didn't provide evening meals. The only place we could find open was the Rowardennan Lodge which we had passed a mile or so earlier. Back we went, hungry and thirsty.

The lodge was one of those ivy covered, stone structures built right along the shore with a long wooden pier sticking well out into the water. Very Old World and sturdy – and seemingly deserted.

The large dining room, except for massive stag heads mounted on the walls, was empty so we checked out the adjoining lounge area. There were only a few people there; a sailing couple, a traveling salesman, two fellow hikers and the publican, a disheveled looking man with a large nose ring. We sidled up to the bar for a celebratory libation and a chance to relax a bit before dinner.

I asked about a large, scale model lifeboat sitting on the bar and was told the boat was a collection point for donations from patrons. It seemed lifeboats were the primary means of rescuing climbers and walkers on this side of the loch. There were no real roads and other than helicopters, boats were the means they used to come and collect injured people.

There was a compelling little handwritten sign by the boat: "Please Support The Loch Lomond Rescue Boat Team. Only our boat can get swiftly to the upper East Shore. We aid walkers injured or ill. We help fight forest fires. We even rescued from a pot hole a walker's dog, which promptly bit one of our crew."

Loch Lomond is the largest body of inland water in Britain and one of the longest and deepest of the Scottish lochs; some 23 miles long and 623 feet deep!

The West Highland Way follows the eastern shore for around 20 miles and so far we had walked to about the halfway point.

It is also this part of Scotland that divides the Highlands from the Lowlands – thus, according to our guidebook, creating: "... a corridor of movement and a zone of conflict. While the people of the low country at the foot of the loch were settled farmers on land rented from titled magnates, those inhabiting the rough terrain to the north were small clans of lawless cattle traders and reivers (robbers); the interaction of the two kept the region in a state of tension for centuries."

On a whim I asked the young barkeep if he knew the words to Loch Lomond. I thought we might break into a duet or something to give the small crowd a delight. Of course, he didn't. In fact, he'd not even heard of the song! Why wasn't I surprised.

I was raised in New York, over 4,000 miles away, and I knew all three verses. He was from Glasgow and didn't have a clue. I suspect he didn't even know it was Loch Lomond staring him in the face every day. What do they teach these kids in schools any more?

He informed us the dining room was closed – but the kitchen was open and we were welcome to remain in the lounge and eat. Perfect. We ordered the honey–glazed chicken breast, boiled potatoes, salad and, for me a Guinness and for Jim, some obscure scotch. For desert we had a chocolate Gateau with whipped cream for dessert. It was lovely. We were famished.

After a late, moonlit walk back to the hostel I called Tyndrum – our destination a couple of nights ahead. We had been warned that lodging would become harder to get the further north we journeyed. I was able to book two single rooms in the Invervey Hotel. We had already reserved a room for the following night at Inverarnan (Hard to keep your *ins* straight) – so we were in good shape at least for the next two nights!

That evening I discovered I had left the book I was reading back at the Black Bull Hotel. I called them. They said they'd look around for it. Fat chance I'll ever see it again.

I was bushed when we got back and I quickly turned in. Jim braved the hostel's laundry room to do some washing – but I was out of it!

Day Four

The Walking Gets Tougher!

Our guide book described today's section of the walk as: "... by far the roughest of the Way, particularly north of Inversnaid where the path makes a tortuous route along the side of Loch Lomond with many ups and downs. A full, hard day's walk but the scenery is superb."

Jim and I were both up and outside by 7:30 taking photos of the surroundings and then back inside for a very meager breakfast. Everyone was grumbling about it. The hostel had quite a few people staying there. I'd guess about half were walkers – and the other half had arrived via car or motorcycle or bicycle. I really don't think there was much of a road in the area – maybe an old, gravel drover's path. We quickly straightened up the room, packed and were on our way by 9:00.

   The distance from the hostel to our night's lodging in Inverarnan, at the head of the loch, was 14 miles. Inversnaid was about half way. We planned to stop at there for lunch. As a matter of fact, there was no other choice. From the hostel north there was no road at all and access to this side of the loch was only by boat or ferry from the other side.

The guide book was spot on. The road was tortuous – much more difficult than the previous day. Up and down all morning and more than a little dangerous. We really had to be paying attention to where we were stepping and certainly didn't want to slip. I was getting concerned since the guide book warned the path from Inversnaid on was supposed to be even worse.

   We struggled into Inversnaid around noon, totally bushed. All there was to see was the well–regarded Inversnaid Hotel spectacularly located beside a lovely waterfall flowing down from Loch Arklet, one of many highland lochs in the area.

The English poet Wordsworth who once passed this way wrote a nine–word poem celebrating Inversnaid: "The cabin small, the lake, the bay, the waterfall." My kind of poem.

Crossing over a small bridge by the famous waterfall we met other walkers, many of whom were carrying full packs. They quickly collapsed into little piles getting their breath back.

The Inversnaid Hotel was another one of those unbelievable, Old World hotels. It was built in 1790 for the Duke of Montrose to use as a hunting lodge. It has been blessed since with many distinguished guests including Queen Victoria. Today its cafe is most commonly visited by hikers on the West Highland Way. Walkers were welcome – but were directed to remove their boots and leave their packs by the servants' entrance. (I bet they didn't make the Queen remove her boots!)

We unloaded our packs, dutifully rid ourselves of our messy boots and walking sticks and traipsed into the dining room expecting to see royalty. Sorry, just a bunch of bedraggled hikers.

Jim and I quickly commandeered a sunny table by the leaded glass windows facing the loch. I ordered a tureen (not a bowl, mind you) of tomato soup, hard rolls, hot tea and a pasta salad. We felt quite elegant sitting in this sun–drenched dining room with the sparkling waters of Loch Lomond flashing before us. In the far distance were towering hills which appeared dusted with white powder. The first snow of the season had fallen in the high country the night before. It was quite awesome.

We finished lunch and lingered as long as we felt we could in the security and warmth of the dining room before we forced ourselves back into our boots and packs. We weren't looking forward to the rest of the trail; which was reportedly the worse segment!

By 1:45 we were on our way – closely followed by a group of *Wandervögel*; a band of healthy-looking German youth carrying killer–size packs. They didn't look very happy either about the prospect of the trail.

Expecting the worse, we were delightfully surprised to find it was not as difficult as the morning portion. In fact, it was quite a bit easier. Not necessarily easy, mind you, just easier.

After a couple of miles, we came to Rob Roy's cave, slightly off trail and down a steep embankment. The cave was supposedly where Rob Roy hid from English troops who were out to run him down. Given his association with this area, and the fact that his house was burnt by his enemies on more than one occasion, it is quite possible that he very well may have used the cave for shelter. In earlier days, however, it was known as King Robert's Cave, in the belief that Robert The Bruce had used it in 1306 while also a fugitive. We climbed down long enough to look the place over, made sure neither were there, and kept walking.

Keep in mind that the popular movies, *Rob Roy* and *Braveheart*, had been recently released and both Jim and I had seen them. Rob Roy McGregor and William Wallace were both natives of the highlands through which we were now passing.

It was further along this stretch of trail that we came upon a herd of feral goats lurking in the woods. Large, sinister looking thugs, each with a massive set of long twisted devil horns associated with the evil doings of witches and devils. Very strange. We passed by. Quietly.

Eventually we arrived at Inverarnan – our destination for the night. Our Drymen host had called and arranged rooms for us at the Stagger Inn.

There were two inns in Inverarnan – and nothing else other than a camp ground down by the river. Directly across the road from the Stagger Inn (a play on the word *stag,* by the way, just so you don't get the wrong idea) was the famous Drover's Inn – built, believe it or not, in 1705!

We checked into our tidy little room, bathed and changed into our "evening attire." This place did not have a shower but a very narrow and very long cast iron tub with one of those hook– on shower hose thingies.

Jim warned me about the hot water temperature – and I'm glad he did. It was as close to scalding as could be and still come out of a hose. Yikes! Those things were dangerous. Hadn't these folks ever hear about the McDonald's hot coffee law suit episode? Probably not.

We decided to go to the Drover's Inn for our celebratory pre-dinner cocktails and return (across the road) to the Stagger Inn which, our Drymen host assured us, would be a culinary experience. Sounded perfect so off we went.

The Drover's Inn. Hmm. How should I put this? Well, for one thing it was different, yes, *different*. And well-used perhaps.

I believe Jim summed it up best when he observed that after the inn was built in 1705, it appeared the cleaning ladies quit in 1706. The word *dusty* would be woefully inadequate.

The bar was packed when we sauntered in. I have no idea where all the people came from as there were very few cars parked outside. I recognized several hikers from the hostel – and I'm sure a good share of the people were locals, down from the hills to stare at the hikers, and vice versa. It was so dark and smoky inside, it was hard to tell who from who.

The three bartenders were wearing kilts although I suspect that was part of the show, so to speak. But maybe not. These guys were huge, all well over six feet tall and built in such a manner there would be no kidding about the kilts, I can promise you that. I couldn't imagine anyone, no matter how "over served" they might have been, trying to sneak a peek under one of them. Instant death and into the fire I would imagine.

And there was a fire burning in a huge open hearth at one end of the room although I don't believe there was a chimney. The windows were too filthy to see out of and the sashes were piled with windrows of dead flies. Grimy walls were covered with the heads of dozens of various animals so moth–eaten they had lost their charm centuries ago.

Immense salmon and record-sized northern pike were mounted around the main room and hallways but mostly missing parts of tails, eyes, fins, etc.

Collections of ancient armor and weapons, which I believe were all authentic, were clustered around the room, available, it appeared, to anyone who wanted to take a swing at someone, say with a mace and chain – or to pin a mouthy opponent to the wall with a 12–foot pike. Large candles burned everywhere which really surprised me because of the obvious (at least to me) fire hazard in this old wooden tinderbox.

It was all together an amazing place – kind of like a pub, a tarot reading, a history museum and third world zoo run amuck.

I wandered around in amazement and followed one of the bartenders outside to the back of the inn. He seemed to be a wee bit tipsy and in a bad mood about something. He opened up a shed and started pulling and poking on very old electrical wires connected to some obscure–looking piece of machinery. I asked what it was and he muttered something about the steam boiler not working and people complaining about lack of heat in the rooms today. He admitted it had been that way since March, but now with the cold weather coming on ... grumble, grumble.

I later spoke to some hikers who were staying there and was informed it was ... *a sincere adventure*. Apparently there was no heat, the windows were impossible to open, the plumbing really didn't work very well, the beds had books under the legs to level them, etc. But they loved it.

"After all," one bearded hiker said, "how often do you get to stay in a 1705 inn?" Good point.

Centuries earlier, inns like this, and like the ones we'd be staying in further north in Tyndrum, Inveroran and King's House were mainly used by drovers (old time cattle and sheep drivers). All these places offered a *stance* which was sort of like a large animal yard, where they could rest their beasts overnight and find grazing for them. Old records show that every year 70,000 sheep and 8,000 to 10,000 cattle moved south along this route. From the looks of this place, it appears quite a few of them found their way in the back door and settled in.

When I came back inside I found Jim talking to a guy named Roger, from Rhode Island. We'd met him earlier in the day. He was the only American we'd seen walking the trail – and, as it turned out, he'd be the only American walker we would ever meet.

We first saw him back in the Inversnaid Hotel where we had lunch. He seemed completely dejected as he sat with a huge backpack filled with brand new camping equipment. He told us he didn't think he could make it all the way. Apparently he was recently divorced and going through, in his own words " ... a difficult mid–life crisis. I just think this type of trip will straighten me out and give me a chance to get my life back together ..."

So here he was again, seated by the smoky fireplace, telling all the locals about his mid–life crisis, and how he was dealing with things on a day–to–day basis, etc. Strangely enough they seemed interested in his story. Granted – he was buying the pints.

Back across the road, the dining room at the Stagger Inn was still packed with a huge Saturday night crowd. The English couple we'd met at the distillery was there. A young Danish couple I'd helped get room reservations at the Rowardennan hostel were there, too. Visitors and locals alike were mingling together anticipating the skills of the chef – who also happened to be the our landlord for the night.

The menu was amazing – filled with an interesting selection of wild game: grouse and partridge, venison and wild pig, and salmon, of course. We ordered pints of the local lager and studied the menu in careful detail.

What's this? Is that *haggis* they're offering as a starter? Indeed it was and Jim and I felt inspired enough to start off dinner by sharing an order. Perhaps we should have skipped the earlier libations.

A word about haggis. It seems that every country has some type of national or regional dish for which it's known. Sweden, for example, has its *lutefisk*. Not many people would eat it on a regular basis, if they're even close to sane, but it's something you might try once just because it's there! (Although why anyone would eat good fish after being soaked in lye is beyond me.)

The Chinese have bird's nest soup – equally disgusting, I think, but also a delicacy, I'm assured.

When I visit Oaxaca, Mexico, I enjoy their regional delicacy called *Chapulines* – better known in your yard as grasshoppers. I like them. Go figure.

So here we were in Scotland where haggis rules! Haggis, you may recall from the user–friendly recipe found at the beginning of this particular journal, (and one I'm confident you plan to treat your family to someday) is one of those dishes you may wonder how it ever got started. I mean, c'mon – why would anyone even *think* of cooking anything inside a sheep's stomach in the first place?

The haggis at the Stagger Inn contained, in addition to Lady Login's ghastly ingredients, cooked apples and other secret spices that made it delicious. And I'm not just saying that because I was half–crazed on highland lager. It really was very tasty in a sort–of mixed up oatmeal, apples and corn beef hash kind of way.

Mercifully the helpings were small and we managed to keep them down amidst cries of encouragement from the kitchen and dining room staff. With that behind us I went on to order a main dish of seared wild salmon with fresh highland salad and boiled potatoes. Excellent! Jim ordered the wild hare and lived to tell the tale (sorry).

Feeling rather native by this time, we finished up, paid our bill (which somehow managed to exceed our night's lodging bill) and marched back across the road to the dreaded Drover's Inn for an appropriate nightcap.

"Mid–Life Crisis was still there seated in the same place by the fire and spinning the same personal tales of woe to a brand new bunch of people. His voice was louder and mightily slurred.

There were a few more hikers we recognized who waved us over. They found out poor Roger had not walked there at all – but taken a ferry across Loch Lomond from the Inversnaid Hotel – and caught a bus from there to the Drover's Inn. His secret was out and the hiking crowd was now avoiding him like the plague.

It had been a wonderful day. Tomorrow we would enter the highlands proper.

Day Five

We Reach The Trail's Halfway Point

Last evening's chef prepared our breakfast. Again something different. Poached eggs over smoked haddock. Very traditional we were assured but a bit foreign to this Yankee palate. After a quick but potentially dangerous bath we were off.

Today's plan was to reach the village of Crianlarich by noon – a distance of six and a half miles and then on to Tyndrum, another six and a half miles. The guide book suggested this would be a pleasant walk with a height range of 400 to 2,300 feet. The best news was the sun was still out. We couldn't believe our good fortune with the weather and we left town in great spirits.

Shortly on the way, just as we started up the mournful Glen Falloch, who should we come upon sitting alone by a large boulder on the side of the trail but "Mid–Life Crisis." He looked very sad – and hung over. He assured us he felt fine and was just resting, although we could see his campsite from where we stood, fewer than 100 yards away. His pack looked like it had grown overnight and I felt sorry for him. We left him sitting there with vague promises to meet again somewhere up the trail. I doubted we'd ever see him again.

Soon we arrived at what's called the Old Military Road – built by English troops back in the 1700s as a means of transportation into the highlands to help crush the feisty highlanders during the Jacobite risings of 1715 and 1745. It's called a road – but was really more like a wide walking path used for years by drovers to bring their sheep and cattle down from the high country. It was hard packed ground which, I'm sure, hadn't changed much in appearance in centuries.

The views were wonderful today. We passed numerous waterfalls and fast running, clear streams. Around noon we came to a junction in the trail which led down to the village of Crianlarich. We had reached the half–way point in the trail!

We could see the town from an opening through the trees. Crianlarich is from the Gaelic – *craobh an lairig* – or *the tree by the pass*. It sits nestled among some serious mountains and is a popular departure place for hill walkers. From where we stood it was all downhill – and then back up, of course. Jim and I both had plenty to eat with us so we decided against going down and kept walking.

By early afternoon we reached the ruins of St. Fillan's Chapel. According to our guide book, there is no other single spot on the West Highland Way that holds so many historic and romantic associations. There's not much left today, only a few sections of walls and some burial markers. However since it was Sunday, and seeing we had not attended Mass, we stopped and paid our respects.

St. Fillan was an Irish monk, active as a missionary in the area during the eighth century. In the twelfth century, the site became a monastery and later, in 1318, was raised in stature to a priory by Robert the Bruce and thereafter enjoyed some measure of privilege and protection from the Kings of Scotland.

St. Fillan's bell is one of two relics that have survived the centuries and now is found in the National Museum of Antiquities in Edinburgh. Originally the bell was kept here in the chapel where we visited. It was supposed to be a key object in a sure-fire cure for insanity.

Here's how it worked: Sufferers were dipped in a pool by the nearby River Fillan called the Holy Pool, then carried to the chapel, and left overnight bound by a tombstone, with St. Fillan's bell over their head. In the morning it was expected they would be found cured.

A parish minister in the mid–1800s took a wry view of these proceedings and was quoted as saying: "We have no proof of any one being cured; but the prospect of the ceremony, especially on a cold winter evening, might be a good test for persons pretending insanity." Amen to that.

Feeling adequately purified after our visit, we continued safely on to Trydrum arriving around 3:30 that afternoon. Thirteen miles in six hours. A good, brisk pace.

Trydrum means simply *the house on the ridge*, the ridge in this case being the main east–west watershed of Scotland – sort of like our Continental Divide.

The town was something of a service center for the cattle driving trade during the eighteenth and nineteenth centuries when the small, shaggy cattle of the highlands were moved south to the lowland markets where they were sold to English dealers.

I think a good comparison for Trydrum would be with one of our own western towns during the mid–1800s during a cattle drive – a place like Dodge City, for example. The main difference here would be the towering mountains the cattle came from rather than the flat grazing lands in the western part of our country.

From this point northwards, the mountains dominated the landscape in every direction.

Tonight we decided to splurge and get separate rooms. We even had little TV sets of our own. The bath was down the hall, of course, but that was fine with us.

I took a quick shower and slipped down to the hotel bar for a Guinness before taking a short nap. Back up at 5:30 I started calling for accommodations in the King's House area – a very sparsely settled part of the country. I had no luck! I was told to call back in an hour.

Jim and I met around 6:00 for our celebratory drink and dinner. I ordered a bowl of lentil soup, a platter of spaghetti and glass of wine for dinner. Very good! The young couple from Holland were also there and told us they were also having trouble getting reservations. For us, the challenge was even more severe as we needed either two single rooms – or a room with two beds, something that was becoming harder and harder to find in the remoter parts of the country.

After dinner I walked back up the deserted, dreary road where they had one of those red British phone booths. I called my wife who reminded me that today was our granddaughter, Taylor's, seventh birthday so I also gave here a call.

Taylor was in the midst of an exciting birthday party. The conversation went something like this:

(My son's voice): "Taylor – come to the phone. Grandpa's calling from Scotland! (pause) **Taylor**! Grandpa's on the phone!"

(Pause. Taylor's voice): "Hello Grandpa."

(My voice): "Hello Taylor, I'm calling from Scotland to wish you a Happy Birthday!"

(Taylor's voice): "Thanks, Grandpa. Gotta go. Bye."

(My voice): Wait, wait, Taylor. Don't hang ..."

(Click)

It was 8:30, cold and dark here in the highlands. I called the King's House again.

"Call back at 9:00," I was told.

I called back at 9:00.

"Sorry, mate. All we have left is one double room at $60 and one single at $40. You might try a widow who lives 15 miles up in the hills that sometimes takes in walkers."

I called the widow.

"Yes, I have one twin room at $90. But I'll have to charge $15 to drive down to pick you up and take you back to the trail."

Damn, what to do? I was in a spot and took it.

Walking back to the inn my math caught up with me. Wait a minute, I thought! That's $105! It would have been cheaper and less hassle to have taken the two rooms at King's House. I rushed back to the phone to call. Double damn. I was out of coins so rushed back to the inn for change and then back to the phone booth.

I called the King's House again but before I had a chance to say anything, the manager, who was, perhaps, exasperated at hearing me call again for the fourth time, blurted out that they would give us a family room that normally goes for $100 but charge us only $75. Hooray for the Scots!

Then I called the widow back and canceled. Whew – this room reservation thing was getting to be a tough job.

Flushed with success I went back and turned on the TV and switched back and forth between the colorful "President Clinton Affair" and a local sheepdog trial. Soon I couldn't tell one from the other and went to sleep.

Day Six

Heading Into True Wilderness

I joined Jim in the dining room at 8:30 – another leisurely start to what promised to be another lovely day. The view from the window indicated very few trees from this point on. Just wide open expanses of bog and heather and mountains. And believe it or not the sun was still shining!

We sat next to a table with a middle aged couple from Wisconsin. They had heard us talking and figured we were Americans and asked how we were enjoying our holiday and immediately began to tell us about theirs. They were on a circular driving tour around the country and were on their way back south toward England. I told them we were heading to Ft. William and when they said we should be there in a few hours I added "not likely" as we were walking.

"You're walking!" they exclaimed as if we were from outer space. "What's the point? How can you see anything on foot?"

We just smiled.

We packed and headed out of town around 10:30. Today would be the shortest walk of the trip – only nine miles. Before leaving I was able to buy some slide film at a small gift shop – along with my standard noontime snack supplies – an apple, a hunk of fresh cheese, a couple of hard rolls and my daily fix of a Snickers bar. I was all set!

The road climbed gently most of the day as we passed through the foothills of some serious mountains – first Ben Odhar on our right, then Ben Udlaidh on our left, then Ben Dorain on our right – and on throughout the day. Although our path stayed on the Old Military Highway, we occasionally crossed over Highway A82 and the railroad tracks of the West Highland Line.

People became scarcer and scarcer as we went further north – in direct proportion to the growing numbers of highland cattle and sheep we saw dotting the hillsides.

On our map the settlement of Bridge of Orchy appeared to be larger than it was – but upon arriving turned out to be a few houses, a school and a hotel in the midst of largely uninhabited countryside.

We paused at the local, one-room school when entering the village. The school's entire enrollment of nine children rushed over to ask us questions as we passed by. Sports questions from boys – movie star questions from the girls. We had fun chatting with them for a few minutes before they were summoned back inside. We continued into the village for a spot of tea.

In 1730, a disgruntled visitor described the Bridge of Orchy Hotel as: "... shabby to the point of scandal, no better than a common tavern, smoke blackened, smelling of the reek of peat and mordants used in dyeing cloth; lit by cruisies, going like a fair with heavy traffic from cattle drovers."

Today's guide book was a bit kinder: "Gloriously relaxing, a timeless getaway destination hotel, deliciously prepared and presented modern Scottish/European cuisine, in amazing scenic location amidst the majesty of the Scottish central highlands - on the doorstep of Glencoe, flanked by Rannoch Moor, Scotland's last wilderness, and a staging post for the famous West Highland Way, possibly the best long distance scenic walk in the UK. A truly superb touring destination base."

That was good enough for us. We paused on our march for pots of hot tea, apple-cranberry scones and a rest by the fire. Purely elegant. Covering the dark walls were photos of the hotel taken over the decades, many depicting snow scenes in which trains, sleds, and hikers were struggling through waist–high drifts.

Sharing the lounge with us was a young German couple we had last seen in one of the hostels – a rather unpleasant, taciturn young man and his drop-dead gorgeous, raven haired female companion. We were to cross paths several times during the remainder of the trip.

Leaving the hotel we needed to make a decision; either take the low road – easier yet longer and leading around the edge of

Loch Tulla – or take the high road up and over Mam Carraigh and down to the Inveroran Hotel, our evening's destination.

Properly fortified with tea and scones we took the high road, of course.

We climbed out of the village for a full mile until we reached a rock cairn at the highest point, 3,000 feet, where, according to the guide book "... in good weather (which it was) this is one of the Way's most dramatic viewpoints. The whole range of the Blackmount Forest is spread out to the west and north, a wild tangle of long ridges and deep cories, with bold granite peaks and craggy outcrops ... and shimmering below the waters of Loch Tulla."

One nice thing about climbing a mile is the amazing views you'll always find when you reach the top and we were treated abundantly. The other nice thing is you get to descend a mile which, if it's not too steep, can be just as exciting.

By this time the German couple had approached us from behind and appeared somewhat disappointed to find the scene disturbed by our presence. We pressed on so they could be alone.

Soon we could see our night's lodging choice way off in the distance. The guide book talks about this inn and the fact that it's been sitting there for over three hundred years: "... facing east and close–sheltered by trees, it appears the very epitome of a snug haven in the wild country around."

It also refers to Wordsworth's visit there during his tour of Scotland in 1803, and talks about the fact that although they were made very welcome, his party found the: "... barley cakes fusty, the oat–bread so hard we could not chew it, and there were only four eggs in the house, which they had boiled hard as stones. Seven or eight travelers, probably drovers, with as many dogs, were sitting in a complete circle round a large peat–fire in the middle of the floor, each with a mess of porridge, in a wooden vessel, upon his knee; a pot, suspended from one of the black beams, was boiling on the fire; two or three women pursuing their household business on the outside of the circle, children playing on the floor; There was nothing uncomfortable in this confusion: happy, busy, or vacant faces, all looked pleasant; and even the smoky air, being a sort of natural indoor atmosphere of

Scotland, served only to give a softening, I must say harmony, to the whole."

The drovers had left by the time we arrived and we found the old inn – built 1708 – sparsely occupied. Our room had a twin and a double bed and Jim, still feeling guilty about me sleeping on the floor our first night out, graciously offered me the larger bed. In other words, he lost the coin flip.

We spruced up a bit and headed for the bar to find the lovely German girl and her miserable companion just finishing up a cup of tea and leaving for their camping spot 200 yards down the road. We couldn't believe that this beast was subjecting that lovely, young thing to the indignities of a tent. We didn't say anything and let them pass unchallenged.

The inn was like a tomb. I only ran into one other couple staying there, a textbook English couple who proudly informed us they had journeyed up every year to fish for salmon. They were wearing heavy tweeds and quietly kept to themselves.

The only place to go, other than a very small bar, was the sitting room which featured several overstuffed chairs, a peat fire, walls filled with photos of salmon fishing scenes, stag hunting, or various full color etchings of Scottish military officers from a multitude of eras.

There was the community television set with extremely poor reception and a writing table. Strewn about were dozens of copies of obscure and outdated magazines with fascinating titles such as: *The Polite Garden ... Sheep Trials Quarterly ...* and *The Successful Moor Walker.* Jim settled in with his book and I stayed long enough to write a few postcards before heading off to bed.

Day Seven

Entering the Dreaded Rannoch Moor

Today was another short day – nine and a half miles to our remote lodging at the King's House. At this point in the walk we cut across the western portion of the famous Rannoch Moor – one of the largest and most desolate moors in the British Isles and one which our guide book describes as: "... very exposed in bad weather with no shelter of any kind. Magnificent scenery but in poor conditions, a tough stage."

Again the weather was clear – though decidedly cooler and a little overcast. We were assured by the locals that "weather was coming." We interpreted that to mean rain was surely on its way.

Leaving the inn we crossed over Abhairn Shira, a picturesque upland stream draining Loch Tulla. The path led us around an old shooting lodge and up into the Blackmount range. The guide book suggests the word Blackmount refers to the peat hags on the moor – but neglected to tell the reader what a *peat hag* is. At any rate, I assume we passed them in profusion as we trudged through the lonely countryside.

Jim caught my attention and pointed behind us where we finally saw rain clouds gathering in the distance and slowly moving our way. I could appreciate what the book talked about if caught out here in a bad storm. There wasn't a stitch of cover anywhere as far as the eye could see. Neither were there any signs of roads, people or animals. It was a little disconcerting.

Eventually we crossed Bà Bridge and a nearby ruined cottage called Bà Cottage and knew we were in the remotest part of the West Highland Way. It was here, on the bridge, where we paused for our snack lunch and a few commemorative photos, that I flirted with disaster.

Somehow, in a rare moment of neglect, my backpack, which I had left resting on the sturdy stone railing, became dislodged and fell over the side of the bridge into the River Bà below.

I rushed down the embankment amidst Jim's whoops and hollers of glee to rescue it from the mercifully shallow water. Whew! That could have been a disaster if the water had been deep and running swiftly as were most of the streams in this area. My pack would have been somewhere in the North Atlantic by now. As it was, I got it out of the water before too much damage was done. My boots got wet and my socks were soaked, of course, and I had to change them quickly. I'm glad my loyal mate, Jim, was able to enjoy it.

By mid afternoon we could look down on the King's House – (shown on many maps as a Mountain Rescue Post) way off on the horizon. Then, one of those strange events occurred.

As we descended the hill we came upon a middle–aged American woman standing next to a rental Toyota parked off the side of what appeared to be a seldom used road.

She was in anguish because her husband had damaged the car and had wandered off looking for a tow truck. (Where he was going to find a tow truck, I have no idea.) She was from Montana, and asked us if we could possibly help. We were the only sign of life she had seen in hours.

It turned out the clutch was ruined. It was a manual shift car and yet, you could shift through all the gears without using the pedal. That car wasn't going anywhere. It was trashed. She admitted her husband didn't really know how to drive a manual shift. We dutifully looked under the bonnet and crawled under the car hoping some linkage might have come loose – but there was nothing we could do. He had stripped the gears in the transmission.

When I was seated in the car playing around with the gear shift and trying to get it to react to anything (which it didn't) I just happened to spy a postcard stuffed under the dash with the name Mel Davis written on it.

I don't know what got into me – or prompted me to do it – and I should be ashamed of myself – but as I got out of the car I said to the poor, distracted woman that unfortunately *we* couldn't do anything for her and it was a pity that Mel Davis weren't here as *he* could surely fix it.

Well, she just froze and her mouth dropped open and she stared at me in disbelief and fairly shouted, "You know Mel Davis? From San Diego?"

"Well, not very well," I stammered. "At least, I think ...."

"Oh my God, wait till Ed returns," she interrupted excitedly, forgetting all about the car. "He's not gonna believe this. Here we are in the middle of nowhere and who should we run into but *another* friend of Mel Davis! Oh my God, can you believe this! And how do you know Mel?"

"Oh, I may have met him once," I managed to choke out, thinking wildly. "I think it was ..."

"But how did you know we were friends of Mel?" she blurted out trying to connect the dots.

(Things were getting out of hand.)

"Well, I just had a strange feeling," I said, starting to back away ... look we've gotta get going."

Jim was standing to the side, staring at me in total confusion and wondering, How *did* I know Mel Davis? And who was Mel Davis anyway?

"Oh, wait – wait a minute," she sputtered grabbing for a camera. "I've gotta take your pictures. Oh my God, this is just too much. Wait till we call Mel! What did you say your names were? Are you from California or something?"

We quickly backed away as she took our pictures and shouted more questions.

We hated to leave her alone – but we were confident old Ed would show up sooner or later. I'd have loved to have been there to hear her tell him about the American strangers who knew Mel Davis – and somehow knew that they knew Mel, too.

"What the hell was that all about?" asked Jim as he followed me across the road. "Who in the world is Mel Davis?"

"Later," I said. "I'll explain later. Let's get outta here."

We soon arrived in the safety of the King's House. They were expecting us and showed us to our room. It was huge – at least compared with what we had become used to. I won the toss again and thus, the queen bed! I was on a roll.

On a whim I asked the clerk if he had heard anything about an an American couple in the area with car trouble.

"Oh, aye, aye," he said. "Gent came in earlier and we fixed him up with a tow. No problem a'tall."

The view from the window was a picture postcard view of the valley and mountains. The sky appeared clear with large billowy clouds rushing over the summits of the nearby mountains – being chased by black, meaner looking clouds.

Our bathroom was spacious and complete with towel warmer – a chrome sort of contraption that was plugged into the wall and over which you draped your towels so, I presume, they would be toasty warm when you stepped out of the bath. Quite civilized, I felt, and much better fitted to our stations in life.

The hotel's water, on the other hand, was running a distinct peat brown color and gave one the feeling they had bathed in a mud creek. A little scary to fill one's canteen and drink from it, but we managed.

Looking out the window, we could tell rain was almost upon us – and the temperature had dropped considerably. We cared less, of course, as we had a toasty little room with a towel warmer to retreat to for the evening.

Heading down to the inn's snug little pub we passed the German couple in the midst of a heated discussion. As best as I could surmise with my fractured German, they were balancing the pros and cons of shelling our their earned money for a room while the great (and free) outdoors beckoned. Eventually the overbearing toad of a boyfriend won out and we witnessed him march out into the imminent storm followed by her poor, dejected, Teutonic loveliness who turned in despair and glanced back furtively to the warm hotel lobby. The wind had picked up a couple of notches. Our hearts went out to her.

With compassionate sighs, we turned and continued to the pub for our well–deserved celebratory treats and a chance to review the evening's menu amidst the hotel's fascinating surroundings.

Feeling particularly adventurous this evening, I broke with tradition and ordered a jar of *Oban*, a 16–year old Single Malt Scotch highly recommended by my Scotch knowledgeable companion. I followed it with a pint of *Old Speckled Hen,* one of the local lagers. Slowly sipping away, comfortably seated by a peat fire, I found out more about this amazing inn.

Built early in the seventeenth century, the King's House is believed to be one of Scotland's oldest licensed inns. The building was used after the Battle of Culloden (1745) as a barracks for troops of George III, hence its name. It was George's task to keep the rascally highlanders under subjection and to capture their elusive champion, Bonnie Prince Charlie.

In spite of its isolation, the King's House, being on the main route between Fort William and Glasgow, received its fair share of passing traffic. At the turn of the century, work began on the Black Water Reservoir, and the King's House was the last port of call for hundreds of *navvies* – itinerate Irish laborers – making their way to the dam via the dreaded Devil's Staircase. Many who had imbibed too freely in the pub got lost and perished in the hills, while others filled the byre (barn) and stables only too pleased to get a roof over their heads.

The reference to the Devil's Staircase was not lost on us as this was the same route we were to follow in the morning!

The inn was a large, rambling sort of affair that had been modified and added to on numerous occasions over the centuries. With severely sloped floors, twisted staircases and mysterious locked rooms I heard the inn had its share of ghosts, which was not hard to believe. There were 23 bedrooms of varying sizes, a formal, elegant dining room, a proper sitting room, and a drying room. There was also a delightful, large pub, the latter offering a warm fire and an abundance of long benches and tables and eating spaces. This is where we ended up – and, as expected, ran into small clumps of other walkers, some of whom we recognized, sitting around discussing the day's walk.

In 1803, our friend Dorothy Wordsworth, usually very tolerant of primitive accommodations, wrote this about the King's House: "Never did I see such a miserable, such a wretched place – long rooms with ranges of bed, no other furniture except benches, or perhaps one or two crazy chairs, the floors far dirtier than an ordinary house could be if it were never washed. With length of time the fire was kindled and after another hour of waiting, supper came, a shoulder of mutton so hard that it would be impossible to chew the little flesh that might have been scraped off the bones."

Happily, most all of this is in the past. The accommodations had improved greatly and the cuisine was stunning. In fact when I looked at the menu I was startled. Here's an abbreviated sample of what was offered that evening:

STARTERS

Cullen Skink – £3.95 – A creamy broth using the finest west coast haddock.

Lochaber Venison Liver Pate – £3.75 – Served with cranberry sauce & oatcakes.

Cornet of Smoked Salmon & Prawns – £5.50 – On a bed of mixed leaves, with lime scented mayonnaise.

Breast of Pheasant – £5.95 – Pan fried with red onions & mounted on a wedge of black pudding, with brandy cream.

Fillo Pastry Shell – £4.95 – With goat's cheese and fresh sorrel, on a pool of red current coulis.

MAIN COURSES

Saddle of Venison – £13.50 – The finest cut of venison, pan fried with thyme, flamed in whisky and finished with a rich port wine sauce .

Breast of Duck – £9.50 – Baked with a honey glaze, and served with a lime & almond sauce.

Roast Pheasant – £10.50 – Coated in an apricot & apple compote.

Poached Salmon – £9.50 – Served on a pool of fresh dill & lemon butter.

Wild Mushroom Cassolet – £9.50 – On a bed of basmati & wild rice.

Goodness. The difficult part was everything looked and smelled marvelous and our appetites were always in high gear by this time of the day. When you're this hungry, it became easy to forget that we're talking Scottish Pounds here, not good old American greenbacks. In other words an order of Saddle of Venison was, in reality, $22.95, not $13.50!

The good news was the same meals you'd order in the main dining room were always much cheaper if ordered in the pub. Sometimes, by as much as 50%! And in the pub, you could order just starters if you wanted. That's what I did. I ordered the venison paté and another starter that was only available in the pub ... a large grilled sausage and rolls and fresh vegetables. Coffee and a pastry for desert. Marvelous!

Unlike in Ireland and England, most pubs in Scotland are locally–owned. You can always tell the difference by the lack of commercial advertising items on display. For example, there were no Guinness beer coasters on the tables. And there were very few brand signs on display behind the bar. Another clue was the wide variety of beers and ales available on tap. It made for a much more interesting visual display – as well as an intriguing choice of liquid refreshments.

I studied the choices available at this pub, for example, and discovered the following handles: Moreland Old Speckled Hen, est. 1711; Caledonia Brewery 80s/ est. 1869; Alloa Export 80s/ ale; Carlsberg Lager; Guinness Stout; Kilkenny Irish; Strongbow Dry Cider; and Lowenbrau Premium.

And these were just the ones on tap. There were many others available in bottles. This was typical of most Scottish pubs we visited throughout the trip.

The rain started while we were eating. Lightly at first but steadily picking up. After dinner Jim and I adjourned to the sitting room with mugs of coffee as a herd of wild red deer suddenly appeared out of the rainy mist and approached the front lawn of the hotel. We quietly watched as they cautiously munched on scattered patches of grass until a distant car came sputtering down the road to scare them off. They were very large, wild looking creatures that we were told lived freely in the surrounding mountains.

As it got darker and darker you really developed a sense of the solitude and loneliness of this place. Soon it was totally black.

Back in our room and snug under warm covers, the wind outside was whistling and the rain pelted our window with a vengeance to get at us. I sleepily shivered at the thought of those hardy walkers huddled outside in their tents; especially that foul German lad who had the nerve to subject the precious young lady friend of his to such indignities.

Day Eight

We Spot Brigadoon Through The Mist

The address of The King's House is simply Glencoe, Argyll, Scotland.

Glencoe – or the *Glen of the Weeping* – is one of Scotland's most beautiful – and famous of glens just a few miles to the west of the King's House. It was there, in February, 1692, when the infamous Massacre of Glen Coe took place in the lower, inhabited part of the glen.

It seemed all the clan chiefs had been required to swear allegiance to King William III by January 1. Not untypical, some highlanders procrastinated.

On February 12, troopers who were members of the Campbell Clan in King William's pay and who, at the present time, were guests of the MacDonald Clan received orders to put all under the age of seventy to the sword.

During the night they crept up on their sleeping hosts and slaughtered 37 of them. Some 200 escaped into the night and snow covered hills – where many subsequently perished. Even to this day, according to our guide book: "This massacre has enshrouded the whole region with a black pall of shame."

It was still raining when we woke in the morning. The wind had picked up even stronger than the night before. Visibility from our window toward Glencoe was very poor. Gratefully Jim and I had enjoyed a marvelous night's sleep – almost ten hours – and were ready to face the day.

Our destination was Kinlochleven, only nine miles distant. The guide book described today's route as: "... potentially serious in bad weather; there is no shelter at all on the exposed upper part of the Way – not so much as a tree or a standing wall. On these hills, to sit down and wait for the mist to clear away is an invitation to exposure in any by the mildest weather; the party should have map and compass – and skill in their use."

Hmm. We had maps and compasses all right, but it was the part about "skill in their use" that gave us pause to think.

I'm not sure exactly what they meant by bad weather but I do know that after several dry days we were finally able to put our rain gear to the test.

We battened down the hatches and were on our way by 9:30. We sadly left the warmth and security of The King's House and soon passed several tents that looked on the verge of being blown away. We shuddered at the thought of having to get out of warm sleeping bags and pack away all that gear in the wind and rain. Our poor, wretched *fraulein*!

The trail climbed steadily for an hour until we reached the dreaded Devil's Staircase; a section of the Old Military Road built in 1750. After a long, sluggish uphill climb in winds which we estimated hit gusts of 50 miles an hour we finally arrived at the highest point in the trail. In the deep of winter it must have been a terrifying experience, and even now with temperatures hovering around forty, it was dicey enough.

At the top was a saddle (a lower part of wall) crossing over into the next glen, and if the sun had been out it would have been something to see. As it was, we were trying to keep from being blown away or slipping on the sharp, exposed rocks so we didn't pause long enough to look around.

After an additional hour of steadily slogging along, the rain and wind slowly died down and we could see patches of blue skies off in the distance. The temperature started to climb as well. Yea!

Soon, a magnificent, full rainbow appeared through the mist and curved down from the heights where we stood looking down on what we assumed was either Lerner and Lowe's fabled *Brigadoon* – or at the very least Kinlochleven. It all seemed so magical, we opted for *Brigadoon*.

Eventually we passed the Blackwater dam and reservoir, an immense facility in the middle of nowhere. The dam alone measures over half a mile long and 75 feet high. It was built between 1905 and 1909 to serve as power source for the now defunct, aluminum smelter at Kinlochleven. Up to 3,000 men were employed in its construction and it was one of the last great engineering projects built by *navvies*, the tough itinerant Irish manual laborers whose muscle power created the canals and railroads of industrial Britain.

It was not the first time I had heard the word *navvies*, and when I later made inquiries of people we met, they all seemed familiar with it and believed them to be mainly Irish. Apparently they were a "hard working, hard living, hard drinking bunch" and the squalor and lawlessness of their lives was something to behold.

Our guide book mentions an autobiographical novel by Patrick McGill called *Children of the Dead End* which describes his life as a *navvie* during the building of the reservoir. When I returned home, I acquired a copy.

He writes of gangs of five men working 10-hour shifts on drilling – a task whereby one man holds a steel drill between his knees while the other four struck it with their sledgehammers in rotation: "... it is really a wonder that more accidents do not take place, especially since the labor is often performed after a heavy night's drinking or gambling. A holder is seldom wounded; but when he is struck he dies." Lovely!

During the five years of construction work, a number of bodies were found in the area of the Devil's Staircase and in the wilds of the Rannoch Moor; the remains of *navvies* who had set out for the reservoir and had been caught in bad weather, or of some who had made an expedition to The King's House for whisky and lost the path back in darkness, mist or snow. They were usually found during the spring thaw!

Soon we had reached the outskirts of Kinlochleven where Jim had arranged lodging for us in Edencoille Guest House. For as small a village as Kinlochleven was, we had a terrible time finding the place – but by 4:00 – damp and tired, we finally located it on the far edge of the village.

According to a brochure describing the guest house: "... the rooms are equipped with foot spas and are all immaculately decorated in an attractive country style."

Translate that to mean Edencoille had cornered the Highland market on frilly lace, plastic meadow flowers and creepy stuffed animals. We were too discreet to inquire about the proper use of foot spas.

Kinlochleven is not an attractive place. It reminded me of scenes from the old classic movie *How Green Was My Valley*, which dealt with a similar–looking Welsh mining community. There were spirals of smoke from coke fires rising from chimneys all through the village. Unique to the highlands as a factory town, it remained an extremely isolated place until the 1920s. Even today, to go there by car or bus would require a long, out–of–the–way trip around the banks of Loch Leven. Recent years have made matters worse because of the declining labor force.

We decided to have our evening meal at Edencoille as they offered an interesting looking menu. Jim went for a starter of kiwi and apricot on half melon, fresh rolls and grilled trout, salad, beets, potatoes, creamed broccoli and carrots. I choose a smoked Salmon salad starter, followed by an immense helping of tuna casserole – plus the same vegetables as above. Chocolate cake and coffee for desert. It turned out to be way too much food – and we were hungry!

We were joined during dinner by a construction crew from Glasgow who were working in the area. They were very pleasant young men who were fairly easy to understand until they started talking among themselves when we lost them completely.

After dinner Jim went to the sitting room to catch up on some letter writing and reading and I headed down the hill to work off some of the superb dinner. I remembered passing by the Tailrace Inn when we first entered the town and it promised to be a popular place to head for a well–deserved, after dinner drink and a bit of light–hearted chatter.

I was halfway down the hill when suddenly – there, in all the bleariness of this stark Highland village, I caught a glimpse of her gorgeous Germanic loveliness standing on the porch of a shop across a narrow ravine. She was all alone, staring sadly up into the mountains. Her miserable male companion was nowhere to be seen.

I stopped and in a loud voice, shouted out in my best German, "*Guten abend, fraulein. Wie gehts mit ihnen?*"

Her head snapped around and stared at me a moment and then, wordlessly, she turned and walked inside. Not a word. Nary a smile. Can you believe that? Whatever her beastly male companion saw in that tasteless hussy was beyond me!

Soon enough I heard the soothing sound of rushing water and there stood the Tailrace Inn. I entered, found a comfortable seat by the fire and ordered a dinner-settling Jameson. It was wonderful just to sit and relax by myself for a while.

Suddenly I heard a familiar voice.

"And so here I was in a failed marriage and I found myself in a mid–life crisis so I threw caution to the wind, went out and bought some hiking gear, packed up and headed for Scotland ..."

Good heavens – there on the other side of the fireplace sat "Mid-Life Crisis" spilling his tale of woe to a group of semi-interested locals. The publican told me he had been in there most of the afternoon, having arrived on the noon bus from Glencoe.

I quietly moved over to the other side of the room, quickly finished my drink and slipped out the side door.

It was almost pitch black as I threaded my way back through the twisty, damp lanes to Edencoille. Dark as it was I could still make out the silhouettes of the steep mountains surrounding the village. Dotted sparsely on the slopes, I could see flickering lights of a few cottages. The only sound I could hear was the river rushing down the spillway into the loch. The stars were out in force and it even looked like tomorrow might be another sunny day – perfect for the big finish!

Day Nine

A Victorious Entrance Into Fort William

The final walk into Fort William was 14 miles. Here's what the trail guide said about it: "... today's trail involves a steady climb from Kinlochleven on a good track over the Lairig Mor and another climb through forestry into Glen Nevis, both reaching a height of about 1,000 feet and giving fine view of Ben Nevis and surrounding hills."

After a hearty breakfast, we packed up and headed out and down the hill towards town. It was 9:00. We stopped to buy some snacks for the trail – crossed over the mill trace bridge – and almost immediately began a rather steep climb.

The day was brilliant and the view back across Loch Leven got prettier and prettier the higher we went. By the time we reached the top of the first rise we had stripped down to tee–shirts and were huffing and puffing!

When we left Kinlochleven we entered Lochaber, one of the ancient provinces of Scotland. There was no doubt that we were now in the North – and not just the north of Britain, either, but in the generic North, where the air was crispier, the light paler, and, for much of the year, there was snow on the distant mountains. I believe at this point we were at about the same distance north as Juneau, Alaska!

The rest of the day was a march through pristine wilderness – crisscrossed by sparkling clear mountain streams – and through patches of forests so dark and dense that if you wandered in a 100 feet you would find yourself in total darkness and absolute isolation.

Toward mid-afternoon we finally caught our first glimpse of Ben Nevis, the tallest mountain in the British Isles. It truly looked massive; a huge hump–backed brutish mass of stone. Although we didn't realize it at the time, we were fortunate to even see it on one of the rare clear days in this part of Scotland. At the foot of the mountain lay Fort William – and the end of the trail.

Our pace quickened. We were beginning to meet small groups of hikers heading our way, out for a day's climb. And we started to pass other day groups that were on their way back to Fort William. I recall passing one poor woman who was walking along (limping actually) in her stocking feet. She was carrying her boots over her shoulder and complaining how her feet were killing her. I could hardly believe it.

By this time Jim's feet weren't in great shape either and were a bit bruised and bleeding. But to walk only in stockings was a foolish thing to do and could do serious damage to your feet.

We kept up a steady pace all day and were getting excited for the finish. When we got to the edge of Nevis Forest, the outlying buildings of Ft. William were just becoming visible. From here on the path was a steady, yet difficult, downhill descent.

We forced ourselves to slow down. The path was slippery and stony and the last thing we needed at this point was a twisted knee or ankle.

By 4:00 we had finished! Ta-Da! As the trail entered Fort William we stopped and took our pictures by the stone obelisk marking the trail's official end. We had walked the entire West Highland Way – 110 miles in nine days.

We were both ready for our well-deserved liquid treats.

The Guisachan House was located on Alma Road, the same road that led down from the mountains. We checked in and took long hot showers and changed out of our hiking clothes for the last time. After a celebratory toast to each other in the small bar area we headed the few blocks into town and ended up at the Indian Garden, a Tandoori Restaurant, which you find in every decent size city throughout the British Isles.

Fort William is a fair-sized town, and very scenic with an immaculate shopping area and beautiful homes, the most elegant of which were spread along the banks of Loch Linnae which provided a direct link to the Atlantic Ocean. We made plans to hike to the top of Ben Nevis in the morning – weather permitting.

In case that didn't work out, we had a back up plan of taking a scenic steam train ride to Mallaig, a small, coastal fishing village.

Jim was interested in finding a way to go from Mallaig clear down to Glasgow by boat; a task which, after multiple inquiries, proved impossible to put together. Too bad, that would have made a delightful return trip.

After dinner we slowly wandered back to the Guisachan House, and stopped in its small pub where we met two very pleasant vacationing Scottish couples who, once they learned we were Yanks and had just completed the West Highland Way, insisted on treating us to what seemed like two or three hundred rounds of their favorite brands of single malt Scotch whiskey ... *well, now laddies, you seemed to like that one well enough. Now let's move onto the Speyside Malts and here's a lovely one you must try – MacFlatery's Underwear – with a taste of the distant hills hidden under the heather* – or words to that effect.

Thank goodness our room was just up the stairs.

Winding Down and Heading Home

We never made it to the top of Ben Nevis. Typical northern Scottish weather had moved in during the night and the next morning we could only see the base. The other 90% was hidden in a thick fog.

The walk may have been over but we still had a couple of days before our flight home so we decided to head back to Glasgow via the coastal villages of Mallaig and Oban.

Oban is the jumping off spot for the Inner Hebrides Islands which lie off the West Coast of Scotland. We spent a day visiting the famous island of Iona – the *Sacred Isle*, the historic cradle of Christianity, where we paid our respects to the long-deceased Scottish King's buried there, including Macbeth.

We arrived back in Glasgow by bus, passing by many of the places we had seen from the path. We walked up to the Victorian House where we had stayed our first night – to a large, family–sized room for the same price as a regular room. But the really great news was CLEAN CLOTHES. That's right, our bags were there waiting for us filled with clean underwear, clean socks, clean shirts and pants. Hooray!

There was even a special surprise for me. the Black Bull Hotel, in Milngavie, the village where we had spent the first night, had found my missing book, *A Civil Disobedience*, and mailed it back to the Victorian House for me. A grand gesture and a typical Scottish thing to do. I was very impressed.

But then, everything on the trip impressed us; the superb scenery, the friendly people, and the unique meals.

What a marvelous time we had! Not sure we could say the same for "Mid-Life Crisis."

WALES

The Pembrokeshire Coastal Path

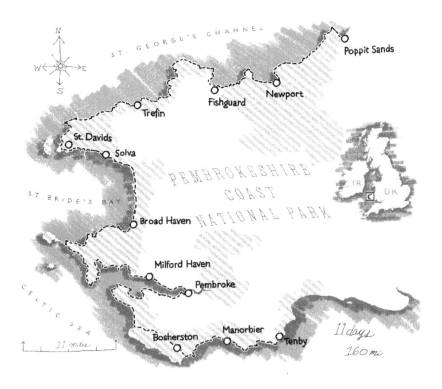

It was close to noon when my train crossed the border and entered Wales. And a quiet crossing it was. No large *Welcome to Wales, Mr. Buckley* sign to signal my arrival. No billboards exclaiming, *You Are Now Leaving England And Entering*

Wonderful Wales. Just a smooth transition from one country to another.

No one else on the train seemed to pay much attention, but I was hyped! It was my first time ever in Wales and I was sitting on the edge of my seat staring out the window.

It had been several years since my last long distance walk: The West Highland Way. This time it was the Pembrokeshire Coastal Path, a 186-mile cliff walk along the southwest coast of Wales.

Of course my friends and family, particularly my wife, thought I was suffering from a severe case of late life crisis.

I reluctantly saw their point. I had just celebrated my 70th birthday and secretly wondered if my legs and feet were up to the task. I felt great and what few aches and pains I did have were not a big deal. I figured if the good Lord didn't want me to go, He would have figured out a way to keep me home.

I approached this adventure as I did with every other challenge I met. If I didn't do it now, when would I? So I did.

I boarded the Westbound Express at London's Paddington Station a couple of hours earlier and although it wasn't a "bullet train," it was fast and smooth. I was heading to a B&B on the Wales coast via a bewildering combination of trains and buses.

I'd be in Swansea in half an hour. There I needed to switch trains for Carmarthen.

The scenery had changed dramatically since leaving behind the hustle and bustle of downtown London. Now the landscape was covered with green fields, stone fences, cows and sheep. Everywhere you looked, small twisting roads had replaced busy, traffic-saturated streets. Stone, single story farm houses had replaced tall office buildings and apartments.

This time I did it right. I spent the first night in London, thanks to a great British Airways promotion which offered, besides an attractive fare, a free night's lodging in my choice of several three-star hotels. Unlike earlier walking trips when I was always in a hurry, this time I managed to get a solid night's sleep before heading off into the "wilderness."

It was a good thing, too, as my flight from New York was an hour late. By the time I arrived at my hotel, Thistle Kensington

Gardens, it was already early afternoon. I quickly checked in, showered and changed for an afternoon on the town. It was a balmy, sunshiny day; a rarity in London this time of year and I planned to take full advantage.

Ticket sellers for the Big Red Bus Company were on the street right in front of the hotel and I decided to buy a ticket and see what I could. It turned out to be a marvelous idea. These great tour buses traveled past the most popular tourist sites in the city and you could get off and on again whenever you wanted – plus it included a short river cruise down the Thames – right through the heart of London.

In the next few hours I saw many of the major sights: Piccadilly Circus, Trafalgar Square, Tower of London, Big Ben and Westminster Abbey.

By the time I finally returned to the hotel, around 7:30, I was beat. After a quick shower I walked up the street to the Black Lion pub where I bellied up to the bar and ordered a lovely pint of one of my all-time British Isle favorites, Old Speckled Hen. Hey – any beer with a name like that has to be respected.

Relaxed and happy I sat back and enjoyed the atmosphere. It was great to be back in the British Isles again and I was so looking forward to my fourth walk there.

Riding the Poppit Rocket
to the Well of the Cuckoo Bird

So that was yesterday and here I was now, deep in Wales getting off the train at Swansea and boarding a shorter, drabber country cousin kind of train to Carmarthen for the second leg of the trip. The clientele changed radically.

The London–Swansea train had been filled with business people talking on cellphones, reading the financial news and working on computers. Now, there was a colorful collection of farmers and tradespeople and immediately across from me, a bike–riding preacher who started lecturing to me the second I sat down. I understood about half of what he said. He seemed to be visibly shaken by the drunken antics of the local cricket fans in anticipation of the weekend's long-awaited sports competition for the Ashes.

"The Ashes?" I said. "What in the world is the Ashes?"

He looked at me as if I were an alien and shoved a newspaper in my hand. "Here mate, read this!"

Two men stood vigil overnight at the Oval to ensure that the most eagerly anticipated match in English cricketing history goes ahead at 10:30 am today. The pair guarding the pitch were part of a 500–strong security operation surrounding the final and deciding test in the summer's pulsating Ashes contest. England's players, who will take to the field to a rousing rendition of Jerusalem, lead the series 2–1. They need to win or draw to regain the Ashes which have been held by Australia since 1989.

"Sorry," I said. "What's cricketing?" (I was having fun with him, now.)

That was definitely the wrong thing to say. He grabbed his bike and wheeled it to the other end of the coach to find someone else who had more common sense than I had. (Days later I learned more about this mega event ... and I'll bring you up to speed, but for now you'll have to wait!)

Soon a young woman came down the aisle and sat next to me and, in a nervous voice, asked if I would mind answering a few questions for a survey she was taking.

"Sure," I exclaimed, glad to have a diversion from the biker-preacher man.

She was taking some type of travel survey and wanted to know about my choice of trains today, how often I rode it, where I was heading, etc.

Seeing this was the first time in my life I'd been in Wales, let alone on this train, I'm afraid I skewed their statistics a bit but she didn't care. She just seemed relieved to have someone agree to be interviewed. We talked for a few minutes and then she left.

I picked up the biker-preacher's discarded newspaper and browsed the headlines. Amazing. Here are three that caught my eye (and these were for real):

Wheelbarrow thief is caught in two mph chase.

Local police hot on the trail of the poisoned pigeon fancier.

Liver rich diet bad for bones, warns watch dog.

The train arrived in Carmarthen right on time and I walked a half mile to the bus station to catch a bus to Cardigan, the next stop on my journey.

When I got to the station I found there was a five minute discrepancy on the posted bus schedule. When I innocently pointed it out to a group of locals, it started quite an uproar.

It soon was like the train scene in one of my all-time favorite movies, *The Quiet Man*. People started checking their watches and looking at my ticket and rechecking the posted schedule and arguing among themselves about what it all meant.

Man 1: "Well now, that can't be right? Five minutes off? Can't have that, what?"

Man 2: "The ticket's wrong! That bus always leaves at 1:20, never 1:15!"

Woman 1: "That's altogether a terrible error!"

Man 1: "Computers! That's the bad of it all."

And so on.

The bus came and I left at 1:20 while they were still standing around discussing it. I loved it.

Another hour and a quarter and I finally arrived in Cardigan with two hours to kill before my last bus, the Poppit Rocket, left for Poppit Sands, the final leg on my trip. (Poppit Rocket ... really? Yes! Poppit Rocket.)

In Cardigan I walked to the middle of town and stopped for lunch at the Priory. Steak pie, chips and tea costing the equivalent of $12. It was at this point I realized I was not going to get by very cheaply in Wales. It was a hot, filling meal ... but $12?

Of course I could have ordered the daily special for $10. But something about eating Ceredigion Faggots in Gravy did not ring my bell. (I later looked up *faggots* and found they were a traditional dish in this part of the world comprised of your basic mixture of pig offal. Ugh!)

The Poppit Rocket left right on time and, as earlier advised by Mary Cave, my hostess for the evening, I asked the driver if he would drop me off at her lane. He was happy to oblige and I arrived at her B&B, *Fynnon Gog*, at 5:00. Dusk was upon us as Mary stood waiting in the yard – all smiles.

She led me into the "conservatory" where a pot of tea and a tray of biscuits (dainty cookies) were waiting for us, then lots of small talk. She told me that other than an African mother and daughter who were visiting friends in the area, I was the only other person staying there.

And why wasn't I surprised, with the house up a nearly deserted, winding, narrow lane two miles out of town where there was nothing to see or do anyway? (Unless you craved faggots.)

Mary Cave was a gentle widow just trying to get along, a common reason for opening up one's home to guests. I asked her about the name of her home, *Fynnon Gog*. She told me it was an old Welsh term that meant *Well of the Cuckoo Bird* because of the large number of the nasty creatures that lived in that particular area of Wales. (I didn't realize there *were* actual cuckoo birds – other than on clocks.)

My original plan was to walk back down to the local pub for a pint. However the weather quickly turned cool and misty so I settled in my spotless little room and unpacked my suitcase and packed my backpack.

After a hot shower, I read awhile and turned in early. It was quiet as a morgue outside with nary the sound of a cuckoo bird or anything else. A light rain started to fall.

Spectacular coastal scenery
all the way to Newport
with nonstop ups and downs

I enjoyed a marvelous night's sleep with only the sound of rain dripping off the tree outside my window to complement the absolute quiet. Mrs. Cave announced breakfast at 8:00 so I came down to find everything waiting. Juice, corn flakes and scrambled eggs on toast.

The plan was to leave my luggage with her and pick it up when I finished the walk. She looked over my backpack carefully, nodded sagely when she saw my walking staff and asked a few questions about my preparations for the trip.

"This isn't a stroll in the park, mind ye," she admonished. "And I hope your boots are waterproof and you've got a sound set of cheaters packed away!"

They were and I did.

I was relieved when she offered to drive me down closer to the trail because I knew it would save at least an hour's hike. The rain had stopped but it was misty and overcast when we parted company. She wished me luck, slipped a small bag of sweets in my hand and waved me along. I was finally on my way.

The Pembrokeshire Coastal Path follows 186 miles of wild and rugged coastline along the southwestern peninsula of Wales. Secluded beaches, castle ruins, rocky coves and sleepy fishing villages were the type of sights I was looking forward to on this walk which skirts Pembrokeshire National Park.

Mrs. Cave left me off as close as she could to the trail. I suppose a "purist" would have backtracked a mile to St. Dogmaels where the trail officially began but I'd decided that was just plain silly. As fate would have it, I immediately got turned around and walked a mile the wrong way before I got straightened out. Poetic justice, I suppose, and not a particularly impressive start.

How in the world could a person get mixed up on a coastal walk, I wondered? I mean the basic idea was keep water on the right, land on the left. How hard can that be? Well, harder than it sounds, as it turned out in the days ahead.

After slipping and slogging my way along the wrong path I finally arrived at the coast line where the scenery stopped me short. It was startling! Rugged cliffs running miles up and down the coast – and hundreds of feet straight down, a churning surf.

The trail runs right along the edge of the cliff: mostly boggy, wet and spongy in this part. A narrow hedge of gorse was all that separated the walker from the edge. And on this particular section of the path were hundreds of huge, brownish black slug-like creatures. Yikes! Happily, they were a rare occurrence.

Mrs. Cave was correct. Right away I discovered it was definitely not going to be "a stroll in the park." From the beginning, the trail climbed up and down – from the top of the cliff down to the ocean – from the ocean back to the top of the cliff – and so it went the entire day.

Unfortunately, I had not properly trained for this walk. I had bought a trail guide, but hadn't read it very carefully. I had *assumed* that cliff walks were along the *tops* of cliffs, gently undulating, perhaps – but for all practical purposes – flat. An unwise assumption for which I would dearly pay the price.

My guide warned hikers that the first few days were the most difficult. The first day alone involved over 3,000 vertical feet of climbing. But I felt fresh and excited and up to the challenge so I kept plodding along enjoying the scenery.

I guess it was a blessing it was misty and cool. I had no idea how tiring this constant climbing and descending would be. Of course, in short order my shirt became drenched and I had to take lots of breaks. But that's okay, the scenery was spectacular.

Later in the the day I met an English hiker from the Midlands. Nigel was his name. We passed each other several times during the day and we'd stop and visit now and then and ended up finishing the first day together.

Nigel, at age 73, was a highly experienced walker and could have walked me into the ground. He was only going as far as St. Davids before he had to return home. I told him I had done the English Coast-to-Coast walk a few years earlier hoping that would impress him. He informed me he had done it three times. Hmm. So much for one-upmanship.

We reached Newport in a light rain (not to be confused with the more famous and larger town of Newport on the southeastern coast of Wales). We arrived just in time as I was bushed.

According to the guide: "Newport is a marcher borough. Owen, in 1603, described it as one of five Pembrokeshire boroughs overseen by a portreeve. It retains some of the borough customs such as electing a mayor, who beats the bounds on horseback every August." (I hope you got more out of that than I did.)

In any case, I was quite pleased with myself. I'd managed fourteen miles in seven hours, and a tough 14 miles it was, indeed. Two miles an hour!

Nigel and I split up as we headed into the village. I was staying in a local hostel and he was staying in a B&B.

It was around 4:00 when I reached the hostel and discovered it would not open until 5:00 so I quickly adjourned to the Golden Lion for a pint of local ale and some chatter with the craggy old timers sitting there. When I told them I was staying in the hostel for the evening that really started them going. It turned out the hostel is a converted schoolhouse where they all had attended as children back in the 1930s.

The hostel was wonderful. I was assigned to a large room, all to myself, and was able to spread everything out to dry. Hostel prices had gone up considerably since last time I was in the British Isles when I recall spending around $15 to $20. Now, the cost ranged from $25 to $30!

After a long, hot shower I headed back into the village center for dinner at the Castle Hotel. It was still early and the place was almost deserted, but I was famished. I ordered a glass of wine while I checked over the menu. Soon Nigel entered and came over to join me.

I ordered lasagna and fries for dinner which together with a glass of wine cost around $18! It seemed every entree on the menu cost between $15 and $20 with deserts extra. I decided at that point I had to stop worrying about the costs. I not only had no control over them, I only paid for one real meal a day.

Normally breakfast was included with the price of my room. For lunch I was able to buy apples, cheese, hard rolls and scones for a few bucks. Those, along with a Snickers bar, were plenty for me. If I got too hungry, I could always find a tea room or pub and get a pot of tea and some biscuits.

Over dinner Nigel and I chatted about the walk as well as other walks we had made. He had completed most of the long walks in England and, like myself, was working on the rest of the British Isles. He was impressed that a Yank would come all that way to do the walk, especially alone.

It was a relaxing evening but I was dragging and by 9:00 I was back in my room reading. Tomorrow was supposed to be a little easier hiking. I sure hoped so.

You must believe me
I did not push that cow over the cliff

I woke at 7:30, stiff and disoriented. The hostel was like a tomb. I was the only one astir. This was one of the rare instances when I stayed in a hostel that did not provide any meals whatsoever.

I dressed, left quietly and walked into the village to buy a banana, sweet roll, bottle of milk and an orange and returned to the hostel to pack and eat.

By the time I returned, there was a Danish couple in the community kitchen heating up some food. They both spoke excellent English and we exchanged brief greetings. In the days that followed we ran into each other several different times and by the end of the walk we became quite good friends and finished together.

Packed up and feeling better, I headed out and immediately ran into Nigel. He was going back the other way to look for an archeological site somewhere near the entrance of the village. I kept going. The day was cool and cloudy but no rain in the forecast.

Newport is described in my guide as: "... an ancient and proud little town with much to be proud of." I'm sure it was but I was eager to get going.

The walk was still hard. Perhaps just as hard, if not harder, as the day prior. There were just as many ups and downs and they seemed even steeper. Before long my shirt was again soaked. I had to remind myself this was just the second day, and I was not used to it yet. At first I thought it was just me. But later in the day, I ran into Nigel and he, the much stronger hiker, was huffing and puffing as much as I was. It was just plain hard.

I thanked my lucky stars I had my trusty Leki hiking staff with me. I used it by sticking it in front of me to help going down – and behind me to help push me up the steeper parts of the path. I'm not sure I could have made it without it!

It was shortly after noon when tragedy stuck.

I was walking along minding my own business when I saw ahead of me, standing on a narrow stretch along the cliff face, a fully grown cow blissfully munching grass, apparently without a care in the world. The problem was it was not supposed to be there. It was taking up most of the narrow path.

Several feet further I passed a broken down section of wire fencing where it must have gotten through and wandered out on the path, oblivious to the edge of the 600-foot cliff, a foot or two behind it.

Perhaps it was because of a thick growth of gorse along the edge that this cow thought it was safe. Did it think the grass was really greener on this side of the fence? But do cows think much?

I stopped walking to observe – reviewing options in my mind. The cow just kept eating. I moved ahead slowly and it moved back slowly. I thought maybe I could scoot around it, but it wouldn't let me get close enough. This went on for several minutes before I heard and saw a farmer running towards us from across the field to my left. He was screaming at me to stand still which I did, of course. He then climbed over the fence and tried to get the cow turned around and headed back towards me and back through the broken fence section.

It didn't go well. Not at all. I backed way up past the opening to give the stupid cow plenty of room. The nervous farmer became panicky and tried to slip a rope over her head. The cow got agitated and started to turn around, but it was turning the wrong way. To the horror of the farmer, and discredit to the cow, it started shifting towards the cliff face.

It happened in a heartbeat! Her large rear end suddenly slipped over the edge and she dropped, temporarily caught half on, half off the cliff edge. For a heart-stopping second or two she was hung up on her belly, mooing rather loudly with wild eyes flaring and head whipping right and left. Then ... all of a sudden, nothing! Whoosh! She was gone.

I froze in horror – as shocked as the farmer. You didn't need to run and see what happened (although the farmer did). We could both hear what happened. Several seconds of frantic mooing followed by a frightful sound. The tide was out. Just piles of large, ugly rocks at the bottom.

The farmer lost it and rushed past me to make sure there were no other cows out on the path. (At first I thought he was thinking of pushing me over as well.) I took advantage of the situation to beat a hasty retreat before he returned and decided to take out his frustration on me!

It was a long way down to the rocks at the base of the cliff and I snuck a quick peek as I hurried around the bend. It was rather messy ... yet sorta cool at the same time. Sorry.

Pondering this weird event I kept moving, eventually climbing down to a small bay where there was a country restaurant – *Pwllgwaelog* was the Welsh name. (Sort of rolls off your tongue, doesn't it?) I stopped and ordered a bowl of Cowl Soup (a Welsh dish of potatoes, carrots, leek and hunks of sweet lamb) with a hard roll and glass of lemonade. I told them about the cow incident. They didn't seem very shocked and informed me that happens quite frequently along this stretch of coast. One toothless old fisherman nursing a pot of tea remarked that a friend of his once hit a floating cow in the surf and caved in the front end of his boat!

"Nasty business, floating cows," he said sagely.

I left the restaurant and I ran into Nigel again. He had decided to take an extra loop around Dinas Island which I had skipped. I told him the cow horror story and he kicked himself for not being there. He made me repeat it several times.

"Now, that will make a cracking story for the lads back home, what?" he quipped.

We joined up and headed the last few miles to Fishguard, our evening's overnight stop. Soon we reached a place called Castle Point, which offered a grand vista from which you can see the three local towns: Lower Town, Fishguard and Goodwick.

We arrived at the ruins of Fishguard Fort. Built in 1781 to defend the community against privateers, it commands a wonderful view of the harbor.

Due west of where we were standing, around 50 miles across St. George's Channel, was the Irish port town of Rosslare in southeast Ireland.

We entered what remained of the gates of the fort and stumbled upon a large wedding party lining up for a group photo: the bride, groom and attendants, parents and friends, etc.

They were as startled as we were when we spotted each other. Here they stood poised in their fancy tuxedos and colorful gowns while Nigel and I suddenly appeared in our muddy boots and sweaty shirts.

"We're not too late, are we?" I shouted out.

A pause and then a round of laughter followed by a response, "Not at all, come along and squeeze right in the middle." Which we did.

We all had a good visit, took some photos of our own and we continued towards town a mile or so distant. It was around 4:30, another seven hours of hard hiking.

Nigel was staying at one of those expensive harbor hotels, the Seaview. I hadn't made any prior arrangements but didn't want to spend very much so I stopped at the local Information Center for assistance. They were extremely unhelpful and it was here I learned a little about the lackluster role they play in the Welch tourist industry.

Besides not being very friendly, they were unable to come up with any lodging suggestions. I found this hard to believe but was in no position to argue. I was rather tired at this point and it was starting to get dark.

I mentioned the name of the Seaview, where Nigel was staying, and they called and reserved a room for me at the extravagant price of $70! On my way there I passed a half dozen places that were either not on their list of accommodations, or they just didn't want to make the effort.

I found out later that because of the steep service fees charged to be put on their "approved list," most B&B owners, as well as smaller hotels and inns, couldn't afford to use them and tried to attract people on their own.

As the days passed I heard this complaint over and over. I'm glad I learned this lesson early and later was able to shop around on my own and do much better.

Nigel was surprised when I showed up. We had a pint of ale together and chatted about this lodging problem. He had made all his reservations before leaving home and was surprised to learn I had made none. He agreed, however, that this late in the year, I would probably be okay. Not true as you'll see.

As picturesque as the exterior of the Seaview was, the interior "had been ridden rough and put away wet" as my father used to say. I was assigned to a rather disappointing third floor room where I showered and changed. I met Nigel for dinner downstairs and was happy to find the place at least had a decent kitchen. I had a wonderful platter of beef stroganoff, a green salad, a couple of glasses of local wine and basket of hard rolls.

Nigel was still chuckling over the cow story – and the wedding party episode, both of which he promised to embellish and share with his mates when he got home.

He told me he had four children, all married and grown. He had been a career soldier in the British Army and said he had been wounded in Belfast, Northern Ireland, in the early 1970s and showed me a wicked-looking bullet scar in his leg. He was mustered out after that, half crippled and could barely walk for a long time. Hiking turned out to be his salvation.

The next day was Sunday and I planned to attend Mass and checked to see if there was a Catholic Church in the area. I found out there was, but it was way back in Lower Town and at a late morning hour. It just wouldn't work.

By 8:30 I was back in my room, relaxing and reading. After checking over the trail map I saw it was almost 19 miles to the next town and realized there was no way I could make that. The guide recommended a shortcut bus trip that would eliminate some rather repetitive scenery and shave five miles off the distance. Made sense to me. Fourteen miles of ups and downs were still plenty.

Looking out my dormer room window over the quiet harbor, I could just make out the twinkling lights of Fishguard across the bay. Boats bobbed up and down as waves slapped their sides. It was quiet, misty and cool. I wondered if the sun would ever come out.

We stumble across more cows
at Carreg Sampson

After breakfast I walked a mile to the bus station. It was situated right in front of a great looking, rustic little inn. Out of curiosity I went in to check if they had rooms and at what price. I was irritated to find they had plenty of rooms and the charge was only $45! Thanks for nothing Information Center!

Soon the bus showed up and took me over the top of the head, or point, instead of going around, which saved me around three hours of hiking. After dropping me off close to the isolated Pwllderi hostel it was only a short walk to get back on track.

If I thought the trail would become easier, I was wrong. I still had fourteen miles of steep ups and downs! On the bright side I was finally rewarded with my first sightings of seals and their new pups. The coast in this area was particularly jagged and the seals searched for the most inaccessible sites to come in and give birth.

They were hundreds of feet down but you could clearly see them scattered around the rocky coves, looking very much like large white slugs – wiggling and squirming on the rocks. You could also see the mothers nursing them, a task that goes on for three weeks as the babies bulk up with fat before being ready to join their parents in the sea. The large males were swimming off shore keeping an eye on things.

The scenery was gorgeous despite the continuing hazy weather blowing across the sea from Ireland. Even though I kept up a steady pace all day long, early in the afternoon Nigel caught up with me. He'd left earlier than I had but taken a longer route. We stopped and took a break together and reviewed our choices of lodging. We were both staying in the village of Trevin, he at a farm a mile outside the town and I in the local hostel.

We passed through the village of Abercastle late in the afternoon and took a short detour to visit Carreg Sampson, a 5,000 year old *cromlech*, or burial chamber, which sits in the middle of a farmer's field. The capstone is over 16 feet long and 10 feet wide resting on three of six uprights. According to my guide it was probably used for at least 100 different burials by the Neolithic tribes in whose territory it lay.

The local cows did not seem particularly impressed and wandered in and around it with great abandon. We stopped to take some pictures and marched on.

The Trevin hostel was another former school – turned city hall – turned hostel. It was basically an old slate building standing in the middle of a village which, when I arrived around 5:00, looked like it had been abandoned sometime shortly after WWII.

The hostel was unstaffed, meaning there was no full time warden. I'd made my reservation over the phone the night before paying the $24 charge with my credit card. I was given a set of complicated codes to use to open the outer and inner doors. Of course they didn't work.

Luckily a hiker was just leaving when I arrived and he let me in. I was assigned to an empty six–bed dorm room. This one was quite spacious and again I had the luxury of spreading everything out to dry and repack at my leisure.

There was only one pub in town, the Ship and Anchor, but it didn't open until 6:00. I relaxed, took a long, hot shower, and wandered around the still deserted streets and waited. I was hungry, cold and sorely needed sustenance.

The wait was worth it. As the name implied, it was a venerable old pub stuffed with authentic, nautical memorabilia: nets, fishing gear, complete dories, vintage photos of boats and their crews, old ship lanterns and other miscellaneous stuff that would have kept even the most diligent eBay entrepreneur busy for years!

I ordered a pint of Guinness and, rather than an entrée, I opted for a couple of starters; a large bowl of potato and leek soup with hard rolls, and a fresh Abercastle Crab Salad. (Abercastle was the small coastal fishing village we'd passed through earlier in the day). It was just the perfect amount of food and tasted fresh and wonderful. Of course, it still cost $18.

I kept track of the cost of Guinness along the way and found it ranged from around $4.50 to $6 a pint! Very expensive I felt. Local ales, such as Worthington, could be ordered for around $3.50 a pint, perhaps as low as $3 if you kept your eyes open.

There was only one couple sitting in the pub when I left around 8:00 and walked back the wet, deserted cobblestone streets to the hostel. I wondered how much longer they could stay in business with only three people that particular evening. I don't know if it got busier later that night or not. I hoped so, but I was too bushed to wait around and see so I went back and finished reading my book, *Death In Dublin*.

I was excited about tomorrow. It was not only a relatively short day – only 12 miles – but the word at the pub was the weather was about to change for the better. Yea! I desperately needed to see the sun!

The glorious sun finally appears as we reach St. Davids

I packed up and left the hostel around 8:30 and looked for a place to eat breakfast – any place at all – but couldn't find a single shop or restaurant open. In fact, the village looked even more deserted than it did the night before if that were possible.

However the news I'd heard about the weather changing for the better was correct. The grey skies looked about ready to clear.

I walked four miles to the coastal hamlet of Porthgain where I found a wonderful little pub, the Sloop Inn. I marched in and treated myself to a glass of orange juice, a full basket of hot croissants with butter and fresh marmalade, and a mug of hot chocolate. Hot chocolate ... a real treat!

I kept up a respectable pace all day. Yes, there were still the constant ups and downs, but I think by this time I was finally getting used to them. It was still hard but they didn't seem as daunting as days prior. I suspect it was a combination of getting in shape and handling my expectations better. All I know is I no longer thought that much about them.

Just before noon the sun finally came out in earnest – and the scenery became even more spectacular. Colors suddenly became sharp and brilliant. The sea, in particular, had transformed from a drab steel gray into a sparking deep blue with bright white spray as it crashed against the stony shore. I began seeing more and more seal pups playing around in the lonely, deserted coves.

I believe the sun did more to lift my spirits than I ever would have imagined. It put a new perspective on the whole trip from that point on. I figured I'd already survived the roughest part of the trail and was looking forward to reaching St. Davids by day's end. I'd heard and read many good things about St. Davids, enough so that I was considering spending an extra day there.

I ran into Nigel sometime in the early afternoon. He was in similar high spirits and we spent most of the afternoon hiking together. With the sun out in full force, the temperature got much warmer and I soon ran out of water ... not a good thing .

By the time we reached Whitesand's Bay it was 3:30, and I was seriously parched. Luckily we found an open snack stand by the public beach. I stopped and quickly gulped down a liter of juice. Wow, I was running on empty.

Whitesand's Bay turned out to be the end of the day's hike for both of us. We still had a few miles to go but we realized there was no way we'd make it before dark. Since cliff walking in the dark is foolish we decided to catch the Celtic Coaster, a local bus service serving the tiny coastal hamlets, into St. Davids rather than hoof it in the few remaining miles. It was a wise decision.

St. Davids was a serious tourist spot and I wanted to get there early enough to find a decent place to stay.

Indeed, St. Davids turned out to be a wonderful place. The bus driver let us off on the main street, conveniently in front of the Farmer's Inn, reportedly one of the best pubs in Pembrokeshire.

We entered to a noisy crowd although it was still the middle of the day by Welsh standards. Nigel treated me to a pint of Reverend James, one of the favorite local ales. It turned out the Farmer's Inn was a favorite watering hole for tourists and locals alike.

We planned to meet there for dinner around 7:00 and I left to search for a reasonably priced room. Nigel had reserved a room in one of the hotels on the square, convenient but expensive. I finally located a comfortable little inn a few blocks away and reserved a second-story room for two nights for $90, still a little pricey but okay.

It was a homey little place with a large bed, modern shower and a back window that looked down on the spires of St. Davids Cathedral.

Although the village of St. Davids is not very large (population less than 2,000), since it has its own cathedral, it officially qualifies as a city according to some obscure British rules and is thus touted as *The smallest city in Great Britain.*

After cleaning up, I walked down to the cathedral grounds to snoop around. It really was a lovely place and the bright afternoon sun was perfect for taking pictures.

St. Davids is at the very western point of Wales, on a windswept, treeless peninsula. Founded by the Welsh patron saint in 550, the see of St. Davids had drawn pilgrims for over 1,500 years. A *see*, by the way, is the area in which a cathedral church stands, identified as the seat of authority of a bishop or archbishop. The cathedral was built beginning in the 13th century.

After a through inspection of the grounds it was time to head back to the Farmers Inn. Nigel was waiting for me and had commandeered a table in the still busy pub.

I relaxed with a lovely Jameson's Irish and ordered a beef & lamb pie baked in a large pastry served with rice. Delicious, hot and plentiful. We spent a long time relaxing and talking with another couple, Peter and Cynthia, a senior hiking couple from Cardiff. They were using St. Davids as a central point while doing various day walks from there. Not a bad way to do it, I'm thinking.

I bought Nigel a farewell drink and said good bye. He'd been a great hiking mate but he was heading home in the morning. I returned to my room around 9:00, read awhile and delighted to realize that tomorrow I could sleep in and just kick back!

I was asleep before the cathedral tower struck 10:00.

A delightful day of rest and leisure

It felt marvelous to sleep in for a change so I took full advantage and didn't get up until 9:00. Woo hoo! I cleaned up, left my pack on the floor and headed out to find a comfortable place to write some postcards. The city square seemed ideal.

It was still sunny and warm, an amazing day, and it felt positively decadent to just sit and relax for a change. I located the public library and signed onto a computer to check my email.

The evening before I hadn't spend much time at the cathedral so I decided to go back to tour the entire grounds which included the Bishop's house and museum. I'm glad I did as I learned that in the evening there would be Even' Song event with a boys' choir. I wasn't exactly sure what Even' Song was but I love boys' choirs and thought it would be interesting.

Around noon I called my wife and had a long visit. I was also able to make an advance reservation at the next village of Solva. Feeling slightly in control of things again, I took a short nap before catching The Celtic Coaster to the nearby village of St. Justinians where they boast of having one of the spiffiest life boat rescue stations on the coast.

I'd seen these life boat rescue stations at other locations around the coast but never had the opportunity to check one out. Visitors could tour this station, which I was eager to do.

It was like touring a mini maritime museum – but one that was in operation. The wooden building stood at the top and extending slightly over the cliff face. Inside there was a large trap door type of arrangement with rails running down into the water. I talked to one of the volunteers who told me they'd gone out as recently as the week prior. The huge, spotless rescue boat sat poised at the top of the rails just ready to be released.

It operated on the same principle as a volunteer fire department – only on water. When the station received a call for help from a commercial vessel or private pleasure boat, a siren would sound and local volunteers would drop whatever they were doing, rush to the station, don their gear, jump in the boat and it was released! It must be quite a sensation to go zipping down the steep ramp and hit the water running, so to speak. Like a mega-carnival ride.

Early evening found me back inside the cathedral watching a procession of fifteen or twenty young Welsh boys, dressed in colorful cassocks, file into the chapel behind similarly dressed adult men.

It was a very moving service as their well-trained soprano voices filled the inside of the ancient chapel. I'm really glad I went and afterwards, felt quite justified to return to the Farmer's Arms for a farewell pint of Reverend James!

The pub was noisy and crowded – and smoky. I wasn't used to it and found it irritating to my eyes. I finished up my pint and left to find another place to eat.

The Cross Hotel was just up the street and the menu posted out front looked rather interesting. Once inside I spied my Cardiff friends who waved me over to join them. They were anxious to tell me about their day's hike and find out how I spent my day.

I ordered fried sea bream, chips and salad – one of the most expensive items on the menu. Oddly enough it was one of the few times I ate fish on my entire walk even though I was never more than a stone's throw from the sea the whole time. I could never figure out why fish, of all things, should be so expensive.

By 10:00 I was back in my cozy little room tidying things up for my departure the next morning. I'll be sad to leave its comforts but the open road calls.

I joyfully discover another
Buckley in a hobbit village

After the standard, mega-Welsh breakfast, which I have to say, was getting darn boring by this time, I dusted off my boots and was on my way. It was shortly after 9:00.

I found a small shop open near the village green where I bought my sack lunch: an apple, a couple of hard rolls and a generous hunk of cranberry-cheddar cheese. At 10:00 I jumped on the Celtic Coaster to the oceanside village of Porth Clais, a short two or three mile ride that eliminated walking along a heavily traveled road.

Porth Clais was the original harbor for the city of St. Davids, used by saints, disciples and pilgrims since the middle ages. Not far from the village was St. Non's Bay, named after the mother of St. David.

There is also a retreat house and a holy well on the property. I stopped to have a heavenly sip and met a couple that had come from England to take home a bottle of its famous water, renowned for curing eye diseases.

All day long, according to my map, I'd been passing by Iron Age forts, but for the life of me, couldn't tell one from the other. Most of them looked to me like piles of rocks. Perhaps an over imaginative archeologist had gotten carried away.

The day was sunny and warm, but constant breezes across the sea from Ireland kept the air cool. By early afternoon I reached Upper Solva and came upon the B&B where I'd made my reservation. It was almost on the path. It had a splendid vista from the cliff overlooking the ocean, but it was quite a ways outside the main village of Solva. Since it was still early in the afternoon, I decided to pass it by and try my luck in town.

Solva was a fascinating spot, looking more like a hobbit village than something from this century. It was a wee little hamlet situated at the end of a long, narrow estuary that was filled with fishing boats of every description. Most of the houses were small and built of stone with either thatch or blue-grey slate roofs. There wasn't a straight road in the place. I half expected to see Bilbo Baggins come bouncing by at any moment.

I inquired about lodging at several B&Bs with no luck and started to panic. Would I have to walk clear back up the cliff to Upper Solva – the place I'd passed up on my way in?

I was almost ready to give up until someone directed me down a narrow lane to a delightful little cottage where I found a single room available. Very relieved, I called back to the first B&B and told them I had made other arrangements.

Mrs. Bland was my new hostess. She took me to a small, cluttered room on the second floor filled with brightly colored satin pillows, delicate little plastic stands laden with sea shells and oddball bric-a-brac. My window overlooked a tiny garden besides which ran a narrow stream. The bathroom was just across the hall.

I dropped off my pack and immediately headed back toward the estuary to the Harbour Inn for a refreshment to sip on the outside terrace as the sun went down. It was there I discovered the joys of Buckley's Best Bitters; a local ale that left me wishing I was part Welsh.

The inn was relatively vacant when I entered and approached the bar. The publican and I soon got into a long discussion of why a Yank would come all that way to do the walk and he pumped me a complimentary pint of Buckley's Best Bitters. Well, this was something new! When I pointed out to him that my last name was Buckley, he promptly unscrewed the pump handle emblazoned with *Buckley's Best Bitters* and insisted I take it home with me.

When I told him I was of Irish ancestry, he said that was close enough and pointed out that even St. Patrick, himself, was born in Wales! (At the time I thought he was just joking or mistaken, but additional research shows he was probably correct.)

Feeling quite pleased with things, I walked back to my little room to read and relax until dark when hunger drove me back to the Harbour Inn for a very disappointing seafood platter of scallops, plaice, sea bass and salmon. I hated to think it possible, but I strongly suspected it was all frozen and shipped in from somewhere else, perhaps Iowa, heavily breaded and relatively tasteless. But expensive. $18 if my memory serves me right.

After dinner, I ordered a Jameson and retreated to the lounge area. There were a half dozen locals sitting there, nursing their pints and watching a soccer match on a black and white television set about the size of a box of Kleenex.

There was an abundance of newspapers scattered around low end tables so I walked in and sat down. It was at this time I was able to learn more about the great cricket match – the Ashes. Do you remember my mentioning it earlier? The infamous cricket match held the previous weekend? England versus Australia?

By any standards, the Ashes was a mega event, the aftermath of which was a full week of over–the–top carousing by, in this case, the winning English team involving a huge fortune spent on liquor bills and destroyed hotel furniture. However, unlike the take home trophy of some of our own local sporting events, such as a bronze pig, the winning team of the Ashes gets an urn of some obscure burnt offerings (supposedly of an 1882 cricket ball) to keep.

So the ashes referred to in the *Ashes* were the burnt up remains of a cricket ball? Huh? I planned to look this up upon returning home as I never did get a satisfactory answer from anyone I asked over there. When I posed the question to the locals in the lounge it created quite a stir. The most interesting response came from one craggy, white haired fisherman who swore they were the ashes of a Welsh Saint whose name I was unable to pronounce – or even write. (I'm not making this up.) At any rate, cricket is, if possible, even more confusing to follow than hurling.

I bid farewell to the small crowd round 8:00 and walked by moonlight back down a narrow lane, across a stone bridge to my cozy little B&B to read. There was talk in the pub of nasty, wet weather coming; hopefully they're wrong.

I opened my small dormer window so I could hear the ripple of the nearby stream. As I quickly drifted into quiet sleep it dawned on me I hadn't seen a car the entire day.

Hoofing it to Broad Haven in a driving rain

Not surprising, the crusty old sea dogs in the Harbour Inn lounge were right. It started raining sometime during the night. Instead of soothing me, it was raining so hard it woke me up and prompted me to close the window. It was still raining when my alarm went off at 7:30. Drat!

Mrs. Bland seemed annoyingly cheery for some reason and fixed me a wonderful hot breakfast and shooed me off dressed in full rain attire by 9:00. I was not happy to leave.

It was a hard, wet, 12-mile, seven-hour slog most of the day, and quite dangerous I felt, scrambling up and down over slippery, sharp rocks. The path followed the estuary back out to the serious water and would have made for postcard perfect photos back toward Solva if it hadn't been for the rain.

Shortly after noon the rain had slowed to a steady drizzle. I arrived at a long, wide stretch of beach. The tide was out so I walked on the damp, hard packed sand and stopped at a stately old hotel built up on a rock face right over the beach – the Druidston. I was chilled and ready for a hot snack and a chance to pack away my rain gear. A large bowl of vegetable soup and a pot of hot tea sounded like the right thing.

While at the inn I called ahead to the Broad Haven hostel where I was planning to spend the night. It's the largest hostel in Pembrokeshire so you can imagine how shocked I was to learn it was completely filled! Apparently a school had reserved the entire place for the day. Great! Well, I was sure I'd find something so I left the security and warmth of the hotel and continued down the coast. I had no other choice.

By late afternoon – I rounded a wind-swept bend in the cliff and there it was: Broad Haven, dead ahead.

Broad Haven is located on a wide beach, a popular vacation spot since the early 1800s. The seaside village is in the middle of an area knows as the Great Pembrokeshire Coal Field and there were at least 140 abandoned mines close by. Coal was being worked in crude open pits in this area as far back as the 14th century and traces of hundreds of them were still apparent.

I walked into town and after snooping around for a half hour I was fortunate to find a place to stay. It seemed like many walkers had been turned away from the hostel and were out searching, too, but I was a single and had arrived early enough to grab one of the last rooms.

It was a lovely place, right on the water front – an older Victorian era house currently under restoration. I was shown to a large, modern room.

Himself (the man of the house) was handling the transaction. I later learned his wife was off visiting relatives in America and he was struggling to run things alone as well as take care of the kids and supervise the restoration. He was barely keeping up!

I checked in and spread out my gear to dry. It was a very attractive room with a large picture window looking out over the beach front. I was very pleased even if it did cost $50.

Still chilly from the wet day, I couldn't wait to unwind in a hot shower. Seconds after I soaped up, all the power went off. Did I mention it was one of those showers that heated water on demand – electrically?

YOW! I briskly jumped back out and dried off my shivering, soapy body and stuck my head out in the dark hall. Work men were running around trying to figure out what was going on when all of sudden, the power came back on. It must have been a blown fuse. Whew – that could have been ugly.

I jumped back in the shower, re-soaped and ZAP! – off went the electricity again. This time for good.

I gave up on the idea of a hot shower, got dressed and sat around in a dark room until I got so bored I left to get something to eat. It was then I discovered it was not a problem in the house as everyone first thought – but a district wide problem. It seemed the entire village was without power!

Great, what now? I was hungry and searched the streets for a restaurant. Nothing was open. Finally I managed to find a pub open that served hand pumped ale – but, alas, no food.

"Sorry, mate," said the publican when I inquired about a meal. "No power and the cooker's electric, you know. Plenty of ale to drink though."

There was a small group in the pub sitting around and bellyaching about the weather and about the power outage. I stuck around long enough to drink another pint of Buckley's Best

Bitters and eat a pack of peanuts hoping against hope the juice would come back on. It didn't.

After an hour I gave up and walked back to my room, ate some emergency trail mix and beef jerky in the dark and went to bed.

No lights to read by. No TV to watch. No hot water. How depressing. And quiet.

A bizarre mixup in Milford Haven

I was startled awake at 2:00 a.m. to find the electricity was back on. All the room lights were burning brightly, and the television was on (at least a snowy screen lit up). Yea!

I was tempted to get up and take a shower right then but decided to wait until morning. When I did get up at 7:00, I hurried to clean up before the power went off again. It didn't.

I went into the breakfast room and ran into Bryan, another English hiker I met the evening before in the pub. He was quite an interesting character, around 40 years of age and exhibited the typical dry humor of the English. We hit it off and decided to walk together for a while.

One of the pluses of this B&B was the availability of a computer for the use of its guests. I took advantage of it to check my email and fire off a quick progress report home before heading off.

Today's goal was the village of Dale, a 21–mile hike. Bryan and I both agreed that was way too long and decided to hop on the Celtic Coaster and ride it to St. Bride's Haven. This gave us a six–mile shortcut, still leaving 15 miles to go which was plenty. The sun was out today, but it was very, very windy.

St. Bride's Haven is the name of a lovely cove situated at one end of a broad valley with a backdrop of red cliffs, a Victorian era church and a nearby group of buildings called St. Bride's Estate.

The main building looks like an old castle and was once owned by the Barons of Kensington. It now serves as a holiday complex for vacationing families.

Bryan and I hiked together all day. By noon the wind was so ferocious we had to be very careful working our way along the cliff face. The cliffs in this area were no longer as steep as they were earlier, but still two to three hundred feet and the episode of the cow was still fresh in my mind. Several times we were rewarded by the sight of seal families in the rocky coves.

In the early afternoon we met a middle-aged couple from Chicago who were vacationing in the area – the first Americans

I'd seen. They weren't hikers, but were touring the area by car. It seemed strange to hear a midwest voice again.

Bryan, who already had a room reservation, was kind enough to use his cell phone and call his hosts to see if they had another room available for me. They didn't but said they would make some inquiries and see what they could find.

On our map, the village of Dale appeared to be a very tiny place, indeed, and it was the beginning of the weekend. Still, I wasn't worried. They'd surely find some place for me, wouldn't they? So far these things had always worked their way out. Hopefully things would work out today. They didn't!

After a late lunch we reached Marloe Sands, reportedly one of the most beautiful of all the Pembrokeshire beaches. Even at this late time of year, there were several families who'd hiked out to take advantage of the fine fall weather.

We reached the village of Dale around 4:00 in the afternoon. At the entrance of the village was the B&B where Bryan was staying. It was a lovely, sprawling, eighteenth century country home with private gardens and horse barn in which was parked a vintage Bentley. Wow! What a wonderful place. I hoped they had found an extra room for me.

Well, of course, they didn't. In fact, the host, who was a gracious and friendly, "old money" landowner, right out of a BBC Special, reported that after extensive calling around to all his friends, learned there wasn't *anything* available in the immediate area at all.

It seemed there was a wedding taking place in the village the next day and, according to him, "Every one on earth is coming."

He was right, we called several more listings on my special accommodation guide and every place was full. He was truly sorry but it appeared I had no place to stay after all! Drat! It would soon be dark.

We quickly checked the bus schedule and learned that if I hurried I could just catch the last Celtic Coaster to Milford Haven, a town around five miles distant, but still on the route.

I said goodbye to Bryan and rushed to the village center just as the bus rounded the corner and pulled up to the stop. Whew – that was close!

Milford Haven is the second largest settlement in Pembrokeshire, with a population close to 13,000. It's a port town which was founded in the late 1700s by American whalers from Nantucket. It appears to have gone downhill from then.

Here's what my guide book said about it: "Despite a magnificent site and interesting heritage, Milford Haven hasn't got much going for it. The town has seen hard times of late, with the deadbeat town centre receiving little of the development money pumped into the horribly sterile 'marina.'"

Can you guess where I ended up staying? Bingo – you got it – by the "horribly sterile 'marina'" in a very suspicious old inn.

"Oh, you'll love it," said the woman at the local Tourist Information Office. "Absolutely cracking for the adventurous traveler such as yourself! $25 with breakfast. You're quite lucky, you know. Big crowd in town all week. Here's the address. I'll just ring them up and tell them you're on your way, shall I now?"

"Okay, I guess," I said. "I'm very tired."

Gee, that seemed very reasonable. I wondered what the catch was. You'd have thought I would have learned my lesson about their local tourist offices by now.

It was late and dark by the time I found the inn, tucked away down one of the seedier side streets by the wharf. Can this be right? The whole area looked like a movie set from Dickens' *Oliver Twist.*

The Welsh version of Happy Hour was well on its way when I timidly entered its steamy, smoky interior causing all conversation to come to a screeching halt.

I looked around at the strange, foreign–looking mob and realized I had a delicate situation on hand. *Show no fear now, Yank*, I said to myself.

With all eyes following my every move I slowly took off my pack and laid it by the door and placed my walking stick on top. Then I marched directly to the bar and announced in my bravest voice, "I'd heard this place pulled the best pint of Guinness in Wales and I'd just walked 15 miles to see if it were true."

That loosened things up a bit and the bartender, who looked like he fought bears with his bare hands, smiled and said, "This Yank knows what he's up to. Give 'im a little room now, mates!"

Well, that's all it took and everything was okay. But what a mangy looking crew I was bellying up to the bar with! There was enough tattoo ink in that crowd to print a small town newspaper and not enough teeth to keep a part-time dentist busy. Unemployed dock workers, I figured.

Off in dark corners, several tables of questionable looking couples in deep, serious discussions were nursing pints of ale. A couple of nervous dogs were slinking around searching for sustenance.

We chatted for a while and questions were asked and answered (when I could understand them). The wall behind the bar was covered with currency from all over the world, stuck up willy–nilly with thumbtacks and tape.

I retrieved a Sacajawea Dollar from my backpack and offered it to the publican who had never heard or seen one before. He was delighted and promptly taped on the wall. And by the time I finished telling the crowd the "falling cow" story, it was good for a free pint of Guinness!

No farmer or cow lovers in this crowd.

When I finally asked him about my room he seemed surprised.

'You want a room?"

"I do."

"For how long?"

"How long? Well ... just one night."

"All night? Are you with someone?"

"No, just me."

"All right then. $30."

"But I thought $25 was the ..."

"$30 for all night. That's the price."

"Well ... okay."

Gosh I thought ... that was very strange. What kind of a place was this? I reminded myself to complain to Tourist Office before I left town.

My room was upstairs. To call it "badly used" would be kind. A lumpy bed and pillow, a small window looking out over a sinister alley. The W.C. (bathroom) was down the hall. But the thing that really caught my attention was several iron burns in the cheap, soiled carpet. Burns in the shape of an old iron. What in the world could have caused those, I wondered? Someone was ironing shirts on the carpet and forgot and left the iron sitting too long? That's exactly what it looked like.

The sheets looked clean enough so I took a quick shower in a room seldom visited by any cleaning crew and hurried out to find something to eat. I remembered seeing an Indian restaurant near the Tourist Office so I circled around the harbor and up the hill back towards the center of town. The Momtaj Balti was a popular place and I was led to a table in the corner.

Menu items in Indian restaurants in Britain seemed to be more authentic than they were in the USA and this one was several pages long. I liked these kind of restaurants because the food was always interesting and you were offered varying degrees of spiciness. By this time in the trip I was always on the lookout for options to the bland food I'd been eating.

I ordered a glass of wine and an unpronounceable chicken-based meal with saffron rice, expensive but I was happy with the taste.

It was almost 10:00 by the time I got back to the inn and by that time the smoke and noise levels in the pub were surely reaching illegal levels. This time no one paid me any attention. I doubt if they could focus that well.

I stepped over broken glass and passed quickly through and up a shaky staircase to my room, locked the door, went to bed and hoped for the best.

Surviving the night,
I was off to Pembroke Castle

It's a good thing I was dead tired the night before. But even then I had a very shaky night's sleep. There was non-stop goings on all night long. Sounds of raucous, bawdy laughter, slamming doors, knocks on doors (including mine, although by this time I had wedged a chair under the knob), glass breaking, maybe a fist fight or two – and not all of it coming from downstairs.

I still hadn't figured it out. I am so dumb!

Sometime during the wee morning hours I managed to get a couple hours of rest before the inn began getting creaky and noisy again so I got up at day break, quickly showered and went downstairs to eat.

I was assured there would be some kind of breakfast served in the pub. But when I entered I was told the cook had gotten " ... pee his pants drunk " the night before and wouldn't be showing up for a while, if at all.

"But I paid for breakfast with the room," I weakly protested.

I was offered a pint of ale and peanuts instead. I declined and left. Even I have standards. For breakfast, anyway.

As I exited the inn into the bright sunshiny day I noticed a very nice looking inn tucked into a little alcove down the street. Oh no, I thought to myself. Did I get the wrong address last night? I think I did. Either way, there was nothing to be done about it now. All I wanted to do was get out of town as quickly as possible.

I caught a local bus to the nearby village of Neland, a mile or two away. I stopped at a small grocer's and bought a banana, a bottle of milk and a sweet roll and walked to a nearby park to eat. It was a lovely clear day and things started to look up again. I know it sounds strange, but after several days walking in the open countryside, it felt strangely uncomfortable being in a large city. I yearned for open spaces.

Another thing about cities is it's very easy to get turned around and headed the wrong direction. Even though Neland was not what you would call a metropolis, it was big enough for me to get lost in!

After eating I tried to find the path leading to Cleddau Bridge which I had to cross to get to the village of Pembroke Dock ... and then eventually to the town of Pembroke where I was spending the night. No one I asked had ever heard of the Pembrokeshire Coastal Path. I had a devil of a time finding it, but after a frustrating hour of wrong turns, I finally did.

The path led me up a very steep embankment to one end of Cleddau Bridge which crossed the estuary to Pembroke Dock. If I had missed it, which I came very close to doing, it would have meant miles and miles out of my way.

This particular area of Wales is not very attractive; being heavily industrialized with large petroleum refineries such as ESSO and TEXACO.

I passed though Pembroke Dock, where, incidentally, I would be returning in a few days to pick up a rental car, and walked on to Pembroke, itself.

Pembroke, contrasted to the last few towns, was a marvelous place, dominated by the famous Pembroke Castle at the end of a long, attractive market street.

Woodbine House was right on the main street and I found it quickly and early in the afternoon. It was a wonderful spot, and turned out to be one of the best stays of the entire trip.

My room was huge, immaculate and filled with antiques. It also had a large, private bath. I was pleased to find no broken glass covering the parlor floor. It was a little costly but I felt it was well worth it and a giant's step up from the previous night.

I immediately changed into my one and only set of semi-clean clothes and headed back down the main street to tour the castle. Along the way I stopped in a small library and checked my email – no dire messages. Good. The day was sunny and warm and everyone I met seemed in great spirits. I know I was.

Pembroke Castle was constructed to be the strongest link in the chain of fortresses spread across south Wales, built by the Normans around 1100. The idea was to keep the rascally locals in line with English policy. It was in this castle that King Henry VII was born which marked the beginning of the Tudor Dynasty.

Considered impregnable, it was eventually subdued by the wretched Oliver Cromwell in a 48–day siege during the Second Civil War in 1648, and only then because he cut off the water supply.

Wales has many, many castles and Pembroke Castle is reportedly one of the nicest and best restored. I spent a couple of hours climbing around exploring. It really was a great spot and I had a fine time, snooping and taking pictures. But as fate would have it, it turned into an expensive venture for me.

Because it was such a warm sunny day, I decided to take my expensive, new prescription sunglasses along with me and had them hooked on my belt. Because of the past inclement weather this was the very few times I'd been able to use them. Yet when I finished touring the castle I noticed they were missing. Damn! I retraced my steps and came to believe I dropped them down into a dungeon I had been trying to peer into ... a deep, dark hole with an ancient grill letting in a little light for the poor souls kept therein.

I suspect that's where they will remain until some confused archeologist in the distant future uncovers them and has a conniption fit trying to rewrite history including the fact Henry VII was the one who discovered sunglasses, and prescription ones, to boot.

I left my name at the office just in case and told them I would check back later to see if anyone had turned them in. (It didn't happen.) Across the street was the Cromwell Tavern where I journeyed for a comforting pint of local bitters before returning to the Woodbine for a well–earned nap.

For some reason the village was almost deserted when I left my room around 7:00 and headed out to find a place to eat. Of the few restaurants I was interested in, none accepted credit cards, and those were too expensive, anyway. I'm afraid I was running low on cash and having no luck finding an ATM.

After walking up and down the main street a couple of times I finally settled in on a small, nondescript place that was empty except for one other person. I peered into the window and saw it was my friend, Bryan. Perfect. I entered and joined him.

While we were talking about our new adventures, the Danish couple I had met in the youth hostel my first night in Newport showed up and joined us. This was the first time I had seen them in all these days and I wondered what had happened to them.

Although up to this point we hadn't spoken ten words together, our common bond of hiking the path creates fast friends and we all had a great time laughing and comparing stories.

Needless to say, the "cow episode," which by this time I had shamelessly embellished, was a big hit. A casual observer would have thought we were lifelong buddies.

Visiting Saint Govan's digs

The short section of walk from Pembroke to Angle was reportedly one of the least interesting of the entire route so my Danish friends and I decided to skip it and take a bus.

As we motored out of town, we saw Bryan walking down towards the castle. He was planning to stay another day in Pembroke. We lowered the bus window and shouted out our farewells. That was the last we saw of him. We continued out to the beginning of the estuary passing ugly petroleum refineries almost all the way – a good section to skip.

By this stage of the trip, the cliff heights had leveled out quite a bit – and, of course, I was stronger – so the nine-mile walk to Bosherston did not faze me in the least. That doesn't mean there weren't plenty of ups and downs, because there were, but it was an easy day's walk, nevertheless.

The evening before, I had unsuccessfully tried to arrange a place to stay. After my earlier mishap, I was getting gun shy about not having solid plans. Bosherston was *really* tiny and offered only a handful of accommodations. The good news was the Castlemartin Artillery Range was closed so I avoided a long detour ... as well as the possibility of being blown up.

By late morning I reached the bare bones village of Castlemartin which, according to my trail guide, was known for having an inn, a substantial castle and a "magnificent cattle pound."

And what might a "cattle pound" be you're wondering? Well, I'll tell you. A cattle pound, of course, would be a medieval equivalent to today's dog pound ... only for cattle. This one was situated right in the middle of the village's cross roads.

Apparently, back in 1480, when people's cattle roamed loose and wandered into the village, they were apprehended and placed inside a large walled enclosure and kept there until the owners came and rescued them by paying a fine. The present pound was much newer than the original. This one was built in 1780, a relative youngster.

Rather common in Europe, I have since learned cattle pounds were also used in the early days in America, principally in the New England area.

While inspecting the cattle pound I spied a public phone down the lane and went to try to make some reservations. When I got there I discovered the wiring had been ripped out, I suspect by a ticked off cow.

There was a woman was watching me from a nearby house. I pointed out the damaged phone and asked if it would be possible to use her phone as I had no place to stay in Bosherston that evening.

"Come over, luv," she said waving. "We'll get ye fixed right up."

She was most accommodating and spent at least 45 minutes calling all over the area (with no luck) until she tried St. Govan's Inn. I told her I had already tried there in vain.

"Well, let's give it another shot, luv," she said. "I have some friends up that way."

Voila! It must have been the local vernacular as she smoothly made arrangements for me. Perfect! St. Govan's Inn is where I wanted to stay in the first place having heard from several walkers that it was a very pleasant place, indeed!

With spirits soaring, I thanked her profusely and headed off. For the rest of the day I had a lovely walk along interior roads, passing old farms and tons of cattle, stopping several times during the afternoon to snack or just relax. The cliff face was out of bounds in this area and apparently used for military exercises but I eventually rejoined it at a place called Stack Rocks.

Stack Rocks was a popular place for day trippers, climbers and photographers. The coast here was especially scenic, filled with challenging rock-climbing areas and an abundance of sea birds. The term "stacks" referred to tall rock pinnacles sticking out in the water, clumped in groups that have survived erosion – a favorite with repellers, several groups of which I stopped to watch.

By mid–afternoon I was close to the end of the day's walk and arrived at a place along the cliff face where there was an ancient stone chapel built down its steep face just above the rocky surf, St. Govan's Chapel. I climbed down to investigate.

My guide book had an interesting entry about it: "This tiny grey structure is at least 800 (and possibly as much as 1400 years) old. Legend has it that St. Govan chose this spot to be buried after hoodlums attacked him on the cliff top when suddenly the cliffs opened up and folded gently around him, saving him from certain death." Whatever, St. Govan was long gone by the time I arrived.

As many of you already know, he was a Catholic hermit of Irish ancestry who preached and died in this area and was a disciple of St. Ailbhe who was a native of Solva.

Solva, you may remember, was the village where the publican gave me the Buckley's Best Bitters sign and cheerfully pointed out that St. Patrick was actually Welsh! Somehow, it all seemed to slip into place.

St. Govan's feast day is either March 26th or June 20th, depending on which source you believe. I suggest you mark both dates on your calendar to be safe.

One final remark about St. Govan's Chapel. In 1902, King Edward VII and Queen Alexandra visited there and "... expressed their delight at all that they saw."

Obviously it doesn't take a lot to excite British Royalty.

Absorbing about as much as I could about the chapel, I headed directly to the nearby village of Bosherson and St. Govan's Inn.

A pint with my name on it was surely waiting my arrival.

St. Govan's Inn had a wonderful reputation as a both a place to stay and to have dinner. By the time I arrived it was just starting to fill up with locals. Warren, the publican, was justifiably proud of the fact the pub had recently been named Pembrokeshire Pub of the Year and was in tight contention for *Wales* Pub of the Year.

It was, indeed, a wonderful pub with an adjacent dining room filled with comfortable, dark leather upholstered nooks, interesting old photographs and stuffed heads of this and that. I felt immediately at home and treated myself to a pint of Guinness.

My room was up a flight of stairs and was equally comfortable with a window overlooking the garden area. Across the lane was a huge cauliflower patch. I do believe that was another first for me ... a cauliflower patch.

I cleaned up and walked down the narrow lane to a small, fascinating looking old church, St. Michael and All Angels, which was described as "... a typical Norman structure with a castellated tower, probably dating to 1250." Probably?

It was open and empty so I went in and said a few words. Since I hadn't yet been to Mass I felt that by visiting St. Govan's chapel and now the church of St. Michael and All Angels I was in good shape, spiritually speaking.

Feeling adequately purified, I headed back to the pub for dinner and another pint. Warren told me a couple had been asking for me and pointed to a table in the corner. There sat my two Danish walking mates, Bob and Jackie.

They waved me over to join them and I was delighted to do so. It was great to see friendly faces again.

I was particularly hungry that night and ordered a large meal: fish cakes of salmon and cod, baked potato, a country salad and a glass of local wine. For desert, a Lemon Lush: a towering, giant slice of yellow cake topped with a generous scoop of ice cream.

All quite decadent and expensive, but who's counting? I was able to put everything on my credit card.

On to Manorbier hostel: a strange place, indeed

I was nearing the end of my trek. Only two more days to go. It was time to make some decisions.

The official end of the walk was the hamlet of Amroth, around 30 miles distant. Why they ended it there I have no idea. Amroth was a half day's walk past Tenby and in a rather isolated area with infrequent bus service whereas Tenby was a major village. I decided to finish at Tenby. From Bosherton it was a little over 21 miles and I would do it in two easy days.

No sense pushing things at this point. I recalled the time I hurriedly finished my walk across England and was so sore I could hardly walk the next couple of days. I didn't want that to happen again.

After a wonderful night's rest, I had breakfast with Bob and Jackie and headed out. It was 11-miles to Manorbier over flatter and flatter terrain. The clouds had cleared during the night and the sun was back out in its glorious majesty. Woo hoo!

The path started with an interesting route that wound around lily ponds that spread for acres through a mixture of evergreens and hard wood trees before winding slowly back towards the ocean. It was the first time I walked through that type of terrain. I found it quite interesting.

Despite a few serious ups and downs it was a moderately easy hike. One of the highlights of the day happened when I met two lovely school teachers from Washington, D.C. heading the opposite way: Elaine and Lorie. They were the only American hikers I had run into the whole trip. We stopped and visited for a while as they asked me about the trail ahead and what to expect. They told me I was the first American they had seen in two weeks on their road trip around Wales. We exchanged addresses and took photos of each other.

As happens with many of the interesting people I met along way, we never crossed paths again but still keep in contact via Facebook and email!

I reached Manorbier in five hours; around 3:00 p.m. – my two miles per average was still holding up. As I entered the town I stopped to visit Manorbier Castle, supposedly one of Wales' best preserved castles and in as close to original condition as they come.

My guide book reported it as a typical Norman manor, complete with priory, dovecote, fishpond, water mill, orchard and deer park. Gerald of Wales was born here in 1146, but of course, you probably already knew that.

Regarding "dovecotes," my guidebook explained that a dovecote or dovecot is a structure intended to house pigeons or doves. Dovecotes may be square or circular, free-standing structures or built into the end of a house or barn and generally contain pigeonholes for the birds to nest. Pigeons and doves were historically an important food source in Western Europe and were kept for their eggs, flesh, and dung. In Scotland the tradition is continued in modern urban areas today.

It was too early to check in at the Manorbier hostel. I knew from prior experience that village hostels were normally closed until 5:00 so I was forced to stop at the Castle Inn, the village's one and only pub, to sip a Creamy Worthington Ale. Before I left the pub, I called the hostel and asked if they offered evening meals. They did, indeed, the warden informed me so I was all set for the night.

After a relaxing stop in the pub, it still took me a while to reach the hostel which sat on the edge of the cliffs a mile or so beyond the village. It was probably the strangest of all the hostels I stayed in – both architecturally and originally. This hostel was a former Welsh Ministry of Defense outpost during WWII. The main building was constructed like a bunker and boldly faced the ocean just waiting for enemy planes to come winging by.

I was assigned to a large, private stone room, so again I had the luxury of privacy with a hot shower right next door. A very unusual building, for sure – but quite comfortable.

Dinner was served at 7:00. Bob and Jackie showed up at the community dining room as did a few other couples. Dinner consisted of a huge platter of leek and pork sausages, salad, mashed potatoes and choice of drinks.

For dessert, a generous helping of treacle tart and cream. Thank heavens I neglected to ask for the recipe.

The fresh salt air, the cliff walking, the Creamy Worthington Ale and the huge meal – whatever – I was a done man and headed to my stone cell at 8:30 to read and prepare myself mentally for the big finish!

Off we go to Tenby, lads.
Step lively now – It's the grand finish!

I rose at 7:30, showered, packed and headed down to the dining room to join Bob and Jackie. After the large meal the evening before, I elected to skip the full Welsh breakfast and opted for cereal, juice, croissants and coffee instead. Smart choice. We said our farewells with hopes to someday meet again and I left.

Both tall and lanky, Bob and Jackie were much faster walkers, and I suspected I'd see them later in the day when they passed me, which is just what happened.

It seemed like a short ten miles to Tenby. I suppose that was because the steep cliffs had slowly dwindled away to an almost flat coast line. There was one area where I was stopped by a Welsh soldier and diverted around a firing range. And later, I came to an interesting ocean side retirement community and stopped for coffee. But other than that, it was a rather anti-climatic finish.

I soon reached a wide cove where the strand, or beach, stretched a couple miles to the town which you could plainly see raised up on the cliff face in the distance. I headed down to finish the walk along the water's edge.

Finally, around noon, I reached the outskirts of Tenby. A blistering two and one-half miles per hour, one of fastest paces yet. It was early in the day which was also a little different but fine by me as I needed to find a place to stay, clean up, see the sights and relax before I headed back to Pembroke the next day to pick up a rental car.

My Welsh guide book was very kind to Tenby. Here's what it said: "On a natural promontory of great strategic importance, the beguilingly old–fashioned Dinbych–y–Pysgod (Tenby) is everything a seaside resort should be. First mentioned in a ninth–century barbic poem, the town grew under the twelfth–century Normans, who erected a castle on the headland in their attempt to colonize south Pembrokeshire and create a 'Little England.'"

I have yet to learn what a *barbic poem* is. If you know, please tell me.

Tenby was, indeed, an interesting, old–fashioned, laid–back place. What I did not count on were the large numbers of people wandering around, who, according to my thinking, should have gone home by now. It was late September.

My first order of business was to find a place to stay and, once again, the local Tourist Office was completely useless. I finally set out on my own and eventually found a respectable row house that had one small, single room left.

I settled in and headed back out on the town to do some exploring. I found a quirky little internet cafe and pub combo that was advertising Worthington Cream Ale for $2.25, the cheapest I had seen yet.

By this time, as you may have already assumed, I had really taken a shine to cream ales, very smooth and ... uh ... creamy. Just the thing, I thought, for a proper celebratory drink.

As I was leaving the pub I just happened to spot an advertising circular taped on the wall touting the famous Pembroke Men's Choir. As luck would have it, they were singing at a local Tenby church that very evening. I got quite excited. Hearing a Welsh men's choir was one of the top things on my list of things to do.

The Welsh take their men's choirs very seriously. There is constant competition taking place among the different areas in Wales. Perhaps as popular and competitive as soccer. And these guys would be the cream of the Pembrokeshire crop.

Perfect! I would definitely attend.

The old, walled town of Tenby was just a few blocks from my room and was loaded with all kinds of interesting looking pubs and restaurants. That evening, to my discredit, I opted to have my meal at the Pig & Puffin, not only because of the great name, but for the cheap prices pasted on the window.

Well, I got half of what I paid for: the name. The food was absolutely the worst I had eaten yet; if I remember correctly, I had a pint of cheap ale and a doughy pasty!

The concert started at 8:00 and I arrived early to get a good seat. I had no longer sat down before I saw Bob and Jackie enter so I waved them over to join me.

Well, it definitely lived up to what I had heard about Welsh men's choirs. This group, from Pembroke, numbered around 40. They were tremendous! Two selections, in particular, had everyone there in tears; *Bring Him Home* from *Les Miserables* ... and a trilogy of U.S. Civil War songs. I don't think I'll ever forget them, they were that haunting.

For a grand and traditional finish, everyone stood and belted out the Welsh National Anthem, in Welsh, of course. It was hard to describe how delighted the audience got. After the anthem finished they became quite animated and insisted on shaking hands and clapping the backs of everyone within reach. It was quite moving to see such a sincere outpouring of national pride and it provided a memorable evening to top off my walk.

Afterwards, I said good bye to Bob and Jackie one final time and headed back to my room. Purists, they were going to trek on to Amroth in the morning to complete the whole, official walk – but I was out of time and heading back to Pembroke Dock to pick up my rental car.

Returning to the beginning
with a glimpse of the past

Well, the walk was over and I'd survived quite nicely, thank you. I'll admit now there was a moment or two, especially during the few first days, when I didn't think I would. I didn't do the entire 185 miles but I still managed around 160 in a respectable 11 days instead of the prescribed 12. I was satisfied.

I still had two days before my flight home from London's Heathrow Airport. I would head back slowly. I decided early on I would rent a car for those two days for a couple of reasons; first, I wanted to unwind a little before having to rush back. Secondly another benefit I received from British Airways was a short term, dirt cheap, car rental offer, cheaper than mass transportation.

I caught a late morning bus from Tenby back to Pembroke Dock. It was a bit shocking to find myself, in less than an hour, transported back to a spot that had taken me several days to cover on foot. When I arrived at the car rental agency, I was pleased to see I was upgraded to a Vauxhall instead of the Ford Ka I was told I would get.

I took a few hours to slowly work my way cross country to *The Well of the Cuckoo Bird,* dear Mrs. Cave's B&B, where I stayed the night before the walk started.

For one thing I had to get used to driving on the opposite side of the road.

She had been expecting me and made me come in for a cheery tea and biscuit session. She wanted to know all about my adventures so I spent an hour or so hitting the high points. She was greatly amused to hear of the cow disaster.

But I was anxious to be on my way so I quickly packed my nasty trail clothes and changed into my wrinkled but clean travel clothes and bid her farewell.

My rather loose plan was to drive up the coast to the seaside resort of Aberystwyth and spend the night.

I had no sooner left the house and driven down her lane when I spied Bob and Jackie hiking up the road to the hotel they stayed in their first night. I pulled over and we had a good laugh; it seemed we just couldn't lose each other. One more absolutely final goodbye and I drove off.

By late afternoon I arrived at Aberystwyth, a name, by the way, I never did learn how to pronounce. It was a delightful, old-fashioned, Victorian era seaside resort that time seemed to have forgotten somewhere around 1925.

I found a comfortable room in the Marine Hotel, directly across the promenade from the ocean. My room was a small but spotless third floor garret and I just loved it. The best thing about it was the crashing sounds of the nearby surf.

For dinner that evening I walked around the village and found a restaurant called Little Italy, which was an enchanting looking place complete with leaded glass windows, small tables with red and white checkered table cloths and lighted candles. And it smelled great. I was really looking forward to a good old fashioned Italian meal and finally I must say, things clicked and I had a delicious, garlicky, winey meal.

Afterwards I slowly strolled a couple of blocks down to the water front and headed back toward my hotel along a mostly deserted promenade. I had been within constant sight of the ocean for almost two weeks. It was going to be sad to leave it behind.

Soon, off in the distance, I heard muted sounds of voices and music coming out of a large wooden building that was placed right out over the water. As I got closer, I noticed a wooden bridge so I crossed over and entered to see what was going on.

I had stumbled upon a WWII stage show just ready to begin. I was waved to a seat.

Talk about your basic *time warp*, this was it! On an old wooden stage stood a lineup of a dozen local theatre people, all dressed in WWII era British military uniforms performing their version of a vintage British USO Club.

It was an old fashioned musical revue or perhaps, more accurately, a cabaret show complete with jokes, stories and many songs of the early 1940s. The crowd, mostly seniors, were loving it and I suspect there were many there with teary eyes who clearly remembered those dire times.

It was a very heartwarming event and you could have sworn you'd walked into a BBC set portraying life in London, or Glasgow, or Dublin – or even Aberystwyth during the Great War.

All too soon it was over. I walked back over the bridge and slowly headed to the hotel. Before I entered I stopped in front and stared long and hard out to sea. So much water. Tomorrow I'd return the car to London and find a cheap room near Heathrow.

Back in my cozy garret I fell asleep to the soothing sounds of waves rolling in over the gravel beach. As I fell off I could swear I could hear the distant, melancholy strains of the famous old WWII song, *The White Cliffs of Dover*, echoing down from 1942.

Great Britain. They don't call it "Great" for nothing.

Epilogue

It's been a few years since that last long distance walk – and I still think about it – as well as all the others – often. I still have my backpack, the same old Vasque boots, my Leki staff – and lots and lots of fond memories.

I often get asked to give talks about the walks, particularly to grade school kids who cling on every word and have an insatiable taste for adventure. I love their innocent approach to every thing that happened and I always remember to bring my hiking gear along with me to show them.

I particularly appreciate their innocent and honest questions, usually about things no one else has thought about (or were too timid to ask).

"Mr. Buckley," one curious third grader asked me one morning, "When you were out all day walking with girls around, how did you go to the bathroom?"

I also talk to many adult groups at libraries, churches and retirement homes. I encourage them to keep active as long as they can and to not give in just because they're older and witnessing growing aches and pains.

If I'd had listened to everyone who told me I was foolish to go on one of my walks because it was not the thing one did at my age, I would surely have missed out on a lot.

I've been asked numerous times which one of the walks was my favorite. I never know what to say about that. It's like being asked which one of your children do you love the most. I think the best answer is you love each one of them equally, but for different reasons.

I loved walking the Appalachian Trail because it was a brand new adventure for me. I'd never attempted a long walk before and even though I made tons of silly mistakes – it taught me a lot about myself and what I could do if I set my mind to it. Best of all, it gave me confidence to try doing it again – which, as you now know, I did.

I loved the English Coast-To-Coast walk because it was my first walk in the British Isles and a major commitment of time and effort. It was my first exposure to forgotten landscapes, ancient civilizations and quaint little hamlets which haven't changed much in centuries. And it was the first walk where I had a chance to meet some great fellow walkers, many of whom, although it's been many years ago, I still correspond.

I loved the Irish Head-To-Head walk because I made it *my* walk, having designed the entire route myself from the very beginning. Ireland will always be a magical place for me – I suppose because I'm 100% Irish, and the last of my line. There was definitely something very special about getting close and personal with the land from which all your ancestors came.

I loved the West Highland Way in Scotland because, in my opinion, it had the most beautiful scenery of all the walks – and that's going some to say that. The stark, haunting beauty of the misty highlands alone is hard to describe and impossible to forget. It was also the only walk on which I went with someone, my friend, Jim Giesen. That also made it very special for me.

And finally, I loved the Pembrokeshire Coastal Path in Wales because I was able to finish it. For me it was the most difficult walk of all. Of course, I was older at the time and it was the one walk I really didn't do much training for. I was under the mistaken impression it would be an easy, flat walk along a cliff edge. (I should have read the fine print.) And perhaps among all the walks and memorable events that occurred, I definitely think the "falling Welsh cow" story will endure forever.

About The Author

Robert Buckley was born and raised in New York. A graduate of Iowa State University with majors in Psychology and American Literature, he spent his career in the advertising agency business, as copywriter, creative director and manager of Young & Rubicam affiliated agencies.

Two Miles An Hour is available in both printed and ebook format from Amazon.com. Autographed copies are available directly from the author at: repb35@gmail.com.

Buckley lives with his wife, Lois, in Marion, Iowa. They are the parents of three grown sons and have seven grandchildren.

Printed in Great Britain
by Amazon